PRAISE FOR

Animal, Vegetable, Junk

"The climate crisis, COVID-19, and the recent reckoning with systemic and institutional racism have all revealed the many cracks in our global food system. In this thorough and revealing book, Mark Bittman discusses how we got to this point when reform is so essential, and presents the solutions to improve how we grow, distribute, and consume our food. A must-read for policymakers, activists, and concerned citizens looking to better understand our food system, and how we can fix it."

—Vice President Al Gore

"Compelling and ambitious, Bittman's *Animal, Vegetable, Junk* is the authoritative text on the 1.8-million-year history of the food system. We begin our journey with the first taming of fire to hunt and cook, witness the use of fire in Indigenous swidden agriculture to prepare the ground, and finally arrive at the fanning of revolutionary fire of peasant farmers organizing against multinational agribusiness. Bittman leaves no stone unturned in the quest to understand how Big Food expropriated our land, water, and sustenance. Everyone who eats needs to read this book. The future of our species and our planet depends on it."

—Leah Penniman, founding codirector of
Soul Fire Farm and author of *Farming While Black*

"Eating well, as Mark Bittman has taught so many of us over the years, is as much about collective health as it is about elegant recipes. In this, his most radical and profound book to date, Bittman brings his trademark wit, precision, and user-friendliness to a sweeping history of sustenance. The result is a joyful and transformational read."

—Naomi Klein, author of *This Changes Everything*

"Food is critically important to everyone, and Bittman's analysis is succinct and incisive: To fix food, you have to address everything."
— Tunde Wey, chef and writer

"If you, like me, think and worry about what you eat and also about the planet that is actually providing sustenance to you — and the other seven billion of us — you need to read this amazing book. You also, as Mr. Bittman suggests, need to become an eater *and* an advocate, and push for the policy change needed to give everyone access to the nutritious food necessary to survive and thrive."
— Ted Danson, actor and activist

"This is the perfect book for this moment in time, and Mark is the perfect person to write it."
— Alice Waters, chef, activist, and author

"There is a saying: 'Humans are what they eat.' Yes, what isn't our food connected to? Food is crucial for our survival, our health, our welfare, our land, our laws, our energy supplies, our water, and almost everything else. Mark Bittman's thought-provoking, wide-ranging new book will open your eyes to the crisis facing our food system, and to the world impact of every bite you eat."
— Jared Diamond, author of *Guns, Germs, and Steel* and *Collapse*

"Unraveling the mess that is our food system is critical to improving our health and the health of the planet. Mark Bittman is just the person to break this down for all of us."
— Laurie David, producer, author, environmentalist

"The irrepressibly curious Mark Bittman has opened a new window to our understanding of this perilous moment. By expanding the concept of 'junk food,' he takes us on a fascinating tour of modernity, with some powerful suggestions for change."
— Bill McKibben, author of *Falter*

"It's easy to be jealous of Mark Bittman. He knows how to cook everything and writes so clearly that you'll feel you can too. Now, he brings his prodigious talents to a history of how we eat. Once again, he has trimmed the fat and delivered it all. From the origins of the human diet to the World Trade Organization, you'll find out how they're all connected in a broken food system. And his analysis is so compelling, you'll not only understand what's wrong, but also how to start to make it better."

—Raj Patel, author of *Stuffed and Starved*

"A brilliant and insightful explanation of the food system. Bittman's writing is succinct and entertaining, and his recommendations are spot on."

—David A. Kessler, MD,
former FDA commissioner and author of
The End of Overeating and *Fast Carbs, Slow Carbs*

"In *Animal, Vegetable, Junk*, Mark Bittman takes us on a journey to show how the mechanistic, reductionist, industrial paradigm got to this nightmarish place in agriculture and food. Food has become the biggest threat to the health of the planet—and our health. But we can, and must, change the food system. Mark also offers a wonderful guide to beginning to find our way toward a food system that works for the earth and its people."

—Dr. Vandana Shiva,
founder of Navdanya and author of
Who Really Feeds the World?

"Bittman was born to write this book. He's spent most of his life learning about the food system, and he has brilliantly distilled that knowledge into an accessible book that will educate, activate, and inspire you. Read it to save your soul and—while you're at it—the planet."

—Ricardo Salvador,
director and senior scientist,
Food & Environment, Union of Concerned Scientists

"To change the current food system, we need to know how we got here. Mark Bittman's *Animal, Vegetable, Junk* provides a roadmap to a more healthy and equitable future for all."
— Tom Colicchio, chef and owner of Crafted Hospitality

"This is a book of yesterday, of today, of tomorrow. Bittman has done something amazing here, tracing the long path from farming to fast food to explain the ills of our modern diet — all while helping us look beyond, to solutions for a healthier, more sustainable future."
— José Andrés, chef and owner of ThinkFoodGroup

"*Animal, Vegetable, Junk* is a landmark project, and its publishing couldn't be more timely. Bittman's history of the world as told through the seeds we've sown reminds us that our food system has been hijacked by a handful of multinational corporations (with the support of public policies), and that this new industrialized system has led to food apartheid, climate chaos, and an exponential rise in preventable diet-related illness. I'm sure you'll feel an urgency to fight like hell for a more healthy, just, and sustainable food system after reading this important book."
— Bryant Terry,
James Beard award–winning author of
Vegetable Kingdom and chef-in-residence of MoAD

Animal, Vegetable, Junk

A History of Food,
from Sustainable to Suicidal

Mark Bittman

MARINER BOOKS

Boston   New York

For Kathleen

HarperCollins books may be purchased for educational, business,
or sales promotional use. For information, please email the
Special Markets Department at SPsales@harpercollins.com.

A hardcover edition of this book was published
in 2021 by Houghton Mifflin Harcourt

FIRST MARINER BOOKS PAPERBACK PUBLISHED 2022

Designed by Kelly Dubeau Smydra

Library of Congress Cataloging-in-
Publication Data has been applied for.

ISBN 978-0-358-64552-8

22 23 24 25   LSC   10 9 8 7 6 5 4 3 2 1

Contents

Our economic system and our planetary system are now at war. . . . Only one of these sets of rules can be changed, and it's not the laws of nature.

— NAOMI KLEIN

When we try to pick out anything by itself, we find it hitched to everything else in the universe.

— JOHN MUIR

This is a book about man's war against nature, and because man is part of nature it is also inevitably a book about man's war against himself.

— RACHEL CARSON

Land is the basis of all independence. Land is the basis of freedom, justice, and equality.

— MALCOLM X

Introduction

FOOD AFFECTS EVERYTHING. Not only is it crucial to existence, but its quality can change us for better or worse. Yet over the course of modern history the nature of growing and producing our most important substance has been changed in ways that made increasing numbers of humans begin to eat manufactured creations that had little in common with the food from which they were made, while the land used for their production has been degraded and humans ruthlessly exploited. These were mistakes, and there were—and still are—many others.

Long before there were *Homo sapiens*, food drove evolutionary changes. Until about 540 million years ago, animals blindly (literally) grazed on vegetal matter or dead animals, often without even moving. (Think of the way an oyster filters nutrients out of water that passes around and through it.) That era saw the first appearance of animals we'd recognize today, like worms, fish, and crabs. After the development of limbs, fins, and eyes, animals began to interact with one another.

Most notably, they improved their abilities to kill and eat one another, and to defend themselves against getting killed and eaten. From that time until recently, getting food or avoiding *being* food became every animal's number-one job.

Not everyone realizes it, but plants create biomass, and animals, for the most part, consume it. Plants turn sunlight, air, water, and soil into stuff, including food. Dependent and even parasitic, animals do none of that: We can create biomass only by helping and encouraging—or at least not hindering or destroying—the work of plants. Yet, pathetic as we are in that regard, we've become the most powerful creatures in history. We could destroy much of the world.

That ability began to develop around ten thousand years ago, when humans started to intentionally grow plants and raise animals. With the development of agriculture—a mashup of two Latin words meaning "field" and "growing"—came the birth of societies and the invention of knives, axes, canoes, wheels, and more, each with profound effects on history. Humans built entire industries—entire civilizations—around their ability to bend the land and its fruits to their will. Land became the foundation of wealth.

But agriculture has had a dark side: It's sparked disputes over landownership, water use, and the extraction of resources. It's driven exploitation and injustice, slavery and war. It's even, paradoxically enough, created disease and famine.

Simply put: Agriculture has, over the course of human history, gotten away with murder. With each passing century, it's gotten better at it, until it became a justification for imperialism and genocide.

Until recently, almost all humans were engaged in growing food. It's likely that you, dear reader, have no daily relationship to soil—that you take food for granted. It just shows up in your store or restaurant, often ready to eat. Few of us actually witness the steps required to produce, process, move, and prepare that food.

These events require land, water, energy, a variety of resources, and lots of labor. The net result, we're told, is "feeding the seven billion." Yet the stranglehold Big Agriculture maintains over food production in much of the world fails to provide even the minimal necessary calories for many, and its most recent products sicken billions of people.

A dictionary definition of "food" reads something like "a substance that provides nourishment." And until a century ago, we had two types of food: plants and animals. But as agriculture and food processing became industries, they developed a third type of

"food," more akin to poison—"a substance that is capable of causing illness or death." These engineered edible substances, barely
recognizable as products of the earth, are commonly called "junk."

Junk has hijacked our diets and created a public health crisis
that diminishes the lives of perhaps half of all humans. And junk
is more than a dietary issue: The industrialized agriculture that
has spawned junk—an agriculture that, along with its related industries, concentrates on maximizing the yield of the most profitable crops—has done more damage to the earth than strip mining, urbanization, even fossil fuel extraction. Yet it remains not
only underregulated but subsidized by the governments of most
countries.

For decades, Americans believed that we had the world's
healthiest and safest diet. We didn't worry about its effects on our
health, on the environment, on resources, or on the lives of the animals or even the workers it relies upon. Nor did we worry about
its ability to endure—that is, its sustainability. We have been encouraged, even forced, to remain ignorant of both the costs of industrial agriculture and the non-environment-wrecking, healthier alternatives.

Yet if terrorists stole or poisoned a large share of our land, water, and other natural resources, underfed as much as a quarter
of the population and seeded disease among half, threatened our
ability to feed ourselves in the future, deceived, lied to, and poisoned our children, tortured our animals, and ruthlessly exploited
many of our citizens—we'd consider that a threat to national security and respond accordingly.

Contemporary agriculture, food production, and marketing
have done all of that, with government support and without pen-
alty.

That must end. To meet the human and environmental crises
head-on, we must ask ourselves: What would a just food system
look like?

I believe we can answer that question (and I try to), and although getting to that place won't be easy, it's crucial—because
nothing is more important than food. You can't talk about reforming a toxic diet without talking about reforming the land and

labor laws that determine that diet. You can't talk about agriculture without talking about the environment, about clean sources of energy, and about the water supply. You can't talk about animal welfare without talking about the welfare of food workers, and you can't talk about food workers without talking about income inequality, racism, and immigration.

In fact, you can't have a serious conversation about food without talking about human rights, climate change, and justice. Food not only affects everything, it represents everything.

My goals are to show how we got here, to describe the existential threats presented by the state of food and agriculture, and —perhaps most important—to describe the beginnings of a way forward. It's a given that Big Food, like Big Oil, is unsustainable, if for no other reason than that energy and matter are finite, and the extraction of limited resources is precarious. As with the climate crisis—to which food production is a major contributor— there's still time to come to our senses and change things for the better. It isn't a sure bet, but it's possible.

The conversation starts with an understanding of the origins, evolution, and influence of food. *Animal, Vegetable, Junk* attempts to provide that understanding, and to imagine a better future. It's a chronological telling that blends scientific, historical, and societal analyses. (It also occasionally reflects my personal experience.)

Many people reading this book know me only as a cookbook author, and as someone who's produced thirty-odd cookbooks, I understand that. But I've also been a journalist-of-many-trades for forty years, and for ten years routinely wrote non–cooking pieces for the *New York Times* and others, including a stint as a weekly opinion columnist for that paper. *Animal, Vegetable, Junk* is my most serious book, and I believe I'm uniquely qualified to have written it. Although it's ambitious, it's also crucially important, and a book I had to write. I hope it changes the way you think about food, and everything it touches.

Mark Bittman
Philipstown, New York, September 2020

PART I

The Birth of Growing

1

The Food-Brain Feedback Loop

YOU GOTTA EAT. Since survival is *the* most basic impera- tive of all living things, it's no surprise that obtaining food has driven human history from the start. Our brains' abil- ity to learn and change, with intent, has made that easier for us over time.

Most animals have fixed diets, eating pretty much the same things all their lives, for infinite generations. Not us, or our kind. Four million years ago, our ancestors evolved to be distinct from chimps and other apes. Their descendants — the first hominins — began to walk upright. That enabled them to cover more ground, scan the land better, and become skilled hunters.

Their diets became flexible and opportunistic, and they ate what nature gave them based on climate, season, and geography. That flexible diet provided more and better nutrition than the relatively fixed diets of tree-dwelling apes, so early humans had more nutrients available to them. As a result, their already siz- able brains grew even bigger. The cerebral cortex, the part of the brain responsible for "higher" thought, was disproportionately large.

Those big brains were energy hogs, hardworking electrical systems that needed frequent refueling in order to fire constantly. They made up only about two percent of the body's weight, but they consumed up to a quarter of its energy. And since fuel went to the brain at the expense of feeding muscle, those brains had to figure out how to compensate for decreasing strength. Hence, small-brained apes are much stronger than we humans.

In time, we developed more flexible thumbs (all primates have opposable thumbs, but our models are newer and better), which gave us a different kind of grip, one more suited to the development and use of tools. They also enabled us to find and eat previously unavailable foods.

In search of not only new foods but new ways to find, catch, gather, and prepare them, the early humans became more clever. Their new-model brains enabled them to get more and better food, which further grew their brains. And that food-brain feedback loop, which continued over a few million years, created *Homo sapiens.*

Many other changes—some subtle, some dramatic, all gradual—took place over those intervening millions of years, affecting bone length and positioning, joint development, gestation and birthing, and, probably to accommodate a different jaw shape, the emergence of a chin.

For example, we *sapiens* have markedly different facial structures than our ancient, now extinct relatives, who needed huge molars and jaw muscles to chew tough, woody plants. An animal that eats raw leaves must chew them a long time to make them digestible: Think of a cow and its cud. Even then, that animal needs a long digestive canal to extract nutrients (cows have four stomachs), especially if that greenery is its major or only source of protein. Our molars, jaws, and digestive canals are all comparatively smaller, adaptations that are compatible with a diet that includes meat.

Our ancestors—like *Homo erectus,* who preceded Neanderthal and *sapiens*—always had supremely omnivorous diets, eating whatever they could forage or catch: a variety of fruits, leaves, nuts, and animals, including insects, birds, mollusks, crustaceans, turtles, snails, small mammals like rabbits, and fish. Most of that food was eaten raw, although some was cooked by fires, probably sparked by lightning strikes.

They also scavenged. A lion or other predator would make a

kill and, after the scary animal ate itself full, humans would pick apart the remains.

Our ancestors themselves were decidedly unscary, though, and they weren't even close to the top of the food chain. The open grasslands of Africa brought new risks as well as new foods, because *Homo erectus* were vulnerable while they were eating, not nearly as quick as that crow that flies away from the dead squirrel just before your car gets there, and certainly no match for big, meat-eating cats.

But because they didn't cultivate food, they had little choice but to hunt, gather, and scavenge—to compete with other species. At some point they began to protect and encourage the growth of tubers like yams and potatoes, but mostly they found food or they didn't, whatever the risks.

These feast-or-famine conditions meant that when they came across a fruit-laden bush or the remains of an animal, and as long as they weren't threatened, they tucked in big-time. They ate as much as they could, whenever they could.

Gradually, early humans evolved to track faster prey, run them down over long distances, and kill them by stampeding them over cliffs or chasing them to exhaustion and clubbing them. With little ability to preserve the bounty of a big kill, our ancestors stuffed themselves on the spot, took what they could carry, and ate that until it was finished.

This is an important factor in explaining contemporary overeating: We're hardwired to eat what we can, when we can; we have little or no built-in counterweight to overindulgence. Overeating wasn't much of a problem when lifestyles were active and there was no such thing as junk food, and we might yet evolve to sense when enough is enough. But to our collective and often individual misfortune, that hasn't yet happened.

Smarter and more efficient food gathering and hunting are best performed in groups, so humans' dietary needs brought about more social behavior and more sophisticated communication. Warmer climates made a wide range of land more hospitable, so our ancestors roamed farther afield, even out of Africa.

Eventually, the quest for food led to toolmaking. While other animals *use* tools—apes, birds, crustaceans, even insects—only primates learned to make them. And only humans "mastered" toolmaking. Beginning with a rock for bone-cracking, they spent literally a million years, maybe more, developing tools, and by 400,000 years ago that skill had become sophisticated. Our ancestors began making spears, followed by arrows and darts, cutting and scraping tools to process hides, wood, and bone, and eventually needles.

Tools were one thing, technology something else. One form of technology, which far predates *Homo sapiens* and their tools, would shape human civilization more than any other. That was cooking.

Many animals take advantage of food cooked by fire. Fire makes otherwise indigestible food edible, and many animals eat food cooked by accidental fires, such as those started by lightning strikes. Some animals, including Australian firehawks, even "forage" for fire and move it, carrying flaming sticks from one place to another to flush out prey.

But only humans tamed fire. We learned to create and control it, which allowed us to cook at will, a discovery that Darwin ranked as our second most important development after language.

It's impossible to overstate the importance of cooking. Cooking made available countless new foods that can't be eaten raw, and with them more nutrients. From roots and tubers to a variety of cuts of meat—much uncooked meat does not readily yield its nutrients, and requires a *lot* of chewing to break it down—to most legumes and grains, cooking enabled the introduction of several foods that have become essential to human life.

In addition to reducing the time humans spent chewing, cooking reduced the time they spent foraging. Soon after humans began cooking, they entered a period of greater longevity and general health than in almost any other time before or since. While the life expectancies of these human populations seem low because of high infant and maternal mortality rates, those figures belie the evidence of robust and well-aged foragers. This period of health—after our kind learned to cook but before they became sedentary farmers—lasted around a million years. That's about two hundred times as long as recorded history.

Exactly when cooking began is the subject of a lively debate. The biological anthropologist Richard Wrangham argued in his 2009 book *Catching Fire* that our ancestors began to control fire and cook purposefully around 1.8 million years ago, a *million* or so years earlier than most of his colleagues reckon. Wrangham maintains that it was cooking that made us human, that cooking in effect drove the evolutionary emergence of *Homo sapiens*.

Whenever it happened, cooking opened up a world of ingredients that wasn't previously available. We continued to eat no fixed diet (no, not even what's now called "Paleo"), but rather what was available wherever we lived. Some humans had diets high in fat and protein, and some had diets in which carbohydrates dominated.

For hundreds of thousands of years, we survived on almost every imaginable combination of meat, fish, vegetables, grains, fruit, nuts, and seeds. Often we thrived. And as humans' diets evolved, so did our social structures.

Controlling fire greatly increased our options, both for where we lived and what we ate. Dry spells could be handled better, for example, because humans could turn to hunting and cooking animals when plant food was scarce, and because our expanded diets gave us the energy needed to search farther afield for different food sources, and to become even more clever in doing so.

And cooking helped build community. Most of those primates that hunt and gather do so in groups. But cooking allowed humans to collaborate in novel ways, from dividing labor to sharing resources and forming cooperative groups.

It's important to acknowledge that "facts" about our early human ancestors are mostly deductions and interpretations based on indirect evidence and influenced by current prejudices. For a long time, we "knew" that male hunters provided most of the food humans ate while women tended fires and babies. And we were inclined to find evidence supporting those beliefs. This despite the incongruities, which would have us believe that men were protecting the home and hearth at the same time that they were out hunting.

As scholarship has become less patriarchal, however, the notion that men hunted while women gathered has been challenged. Research now shows that not only did women have more varied roles than the old literature described, but it's likely that every able-bodied person took part in gathering, and that specialization was complementary, designed to enable a small, egalitarian society in which everyone's contribution was critical. People worked cooperatively, forming groups of individuals who specialized in different tasks. Roles based on gender were less fixed than we've been led to believe until recently. From a 2018 article by Colin Scanes: "The assumption of defined gender roles is challenged by the Agta, a hunter-gatherer people of the Philippines where women are responsible for about half the game killed."

And it may well be that women provided *more* calories than men, even if men tended to hunt larger animals. It's mostly speculative, but, as Linda Owen writes in *Distorting the Past*, "if Ice Age females collected plants, bird eggs, shellfish, and edible insects; and if they hunted or trapped small game and participated in the hunting of large game" — as northern women did — "they most likely contributed seventy percent of the consumed calories." Owen argues that we previously saw what we believed to be men's work as more important because we were looking at the past through the lens of male-dominated postwar America, rather than seeing gender roles for what they actually were then.

Among women's specialties was basketmaking. Baskets were needed to carry foraged bounty. The skills involved in making baskets led to the making of nets, and nets led to more sophisticated fishing and hunting of small game. This was significant, because even if it takes two hundred rabbits to equal one bison in net calories (a rough calculation shows that there are 7,000 calories in a rabbit and 1,400,000 calories in a bison), if you catch two hundred and one rabbits for every bison, you're better off hunting rabbits.

There will never be consensus on this, but many if not most anthropologists now believe that cooperation and equality were norms among individuals, family groups, clans, and bands. They believe these norms were enforced, and the system was successful. There were certainly times of scarcity and regions that went barren, but a varied, ever-expanding diet coupled with hunter-gatherers' ability to move in search of food meant that malnutrition was the exception for early humans.

In this pre-agriculture period, groups roamed into new territory, uncertain of finding sustenance and of what they might encounter. They were isolated and undoubtedly frightened, and had almost no choice but to stick together. There was no ownership, least of all of land, since settlements changed all the time. Influence was probably gained through generosity, negotiation, and strength.

In short, everyone needed food — again, it was the primary motivator — and it was in everyone's best interest to share it.

Equality, cooperation, and even generosity were more advantageous than conflict, as they advanced social networks and spurred creativity. Even the rare "surplus" was likely just a small hoard, since movement made storage methods like long-term burial, for example, inconvenient at best. That hoard may have been considered selfish, and selfishness was often treated with ridicule and sometimes even expulsion. This isn't to say people didn't grab or fight, or that there weren't hierarchies or "big men." But for the most part, there weren't permanently dominant categories of people. Power was largely earned through leadership or respect, not inherited.

By definition, hunter-gatherers ate what their surroundings gave them, so long as it didn't poison them. They operated according to principles sometimes described as the optimal foraging theory (OFT), a complicated (and disputed) formula that dictates, logically, that you eat those foods that provide the maximum calories for the least energy expenditure, shifting locations and seasons as needed.

The more omnivorous an animal is, the more likely it is to thrive while foraging in a variety of conditions. And few mammals have ever been as omnivorous as humans.

Armed with this superior level of dietary flexibility, modern humans—meaning *Homo sapiens*—spread through Asia and then Europe beginning about seventy thousand years ago, and coexisted there with Neanderthals. By thirty thousand years ago, humans were nearly everywhere on those continents, as well as Africa, of course.

We roamed, always in pursuit of food, and for the most part found it, including "new" foods, like seal, wheat, rice, and bison. Our storage capabilities improved: Some people froze meat, and some buried tubers, nuts, and bulbs to eat off-season. In the just-before-agriculture period that came at the end of the last ice age —which lasted from about 100,000 BCE to just over 10,000 BCE— some of our ancestors made bread from ground-foraged wheat. Others ate rice. Some hunted mammals, from rabbits to mammoths, and dried, smoked, or froze foods. Fishing villages began to appear at least twenty thousand and perhaps even fifty thousand years ago.

Measured by population growth and territorial spread, success followed. So did increased cooperation, both within and even between groups. Meanwhile, competition between humans and other primates decreased, due to a combination of our own dominance and their extinctions. In that sense, human dominance is nothing new: We've always competed with other species for limited resources, and we've hunted those species into extinction, too.

It was a good time for humans, who were on the verge of making the biggest and, some would say, most disastrous change in the history of the species, a change that would eventually affect not only every living human, then or afterwards, but the planet itself.

It didn't take a genius to notice that some plants produce seeds, that those seeds drop, and that they sometimes create new plants of the same type. Nor did it take any particular brilliance or courage to move some of those seeds to a more convenient place. And it didn't take much experience or skill to figure out how to tend those seedlings, at least minimally.

Making plants grow where you wanted them to—and encouraging, coercing, or forcing animals to stick around so you could fatten and even breed or milk them — must have seemed like easier, more reliable alternatives than running around looking for food all the time. And even though planting seeds and domesticating animals required a great deal of trial and error — these experiments likely took place over hundreds and thousands of years — foraging was always there as a backup.

Thus was agriculture invented, though by no means suddenly or in one place by one person or group. It developed gradually and spontaneously; simultaneously and sequentially; independently and eventually cooperatively. It happened all over the world and over many generations of humans, who lived to be seventy years old only in the best circumstances, and who learned slowly and forgot easily.

By human standards, it was a long process. No one group of people plopped down, formed a village, and started planning for the planting of next autumn's harvest, or for the impregnation of animals for next spring's birthing. Early agriculture varied from place to place, and it occurred over a span of millennia.

A thousand years is an easy enough concept to imagine, but it's harder to imagine forty generations of humans when most of us can trace back only three or four in our own families. We barely know what gradual change means. So perhaps it's quibbling, but calling the beginning of agriculture a "revolution" seems inaccurate. It implies a single moment of invention, and there doesn't appear to have been one. It's better to think of humankind's development of agriculture as an evolution.

Whatever you call it, the beginnings of agriculture were not marked simply by techniques like planting and storing seeds, or taming and breeding animals, activities that in and of themselves didn't change daily life and may have existed in some places for millennia. The human innovation called "agriculture" is also marked by the beginning of societies in which people cooperated to plan for the future, planting and storing seeds, taming and breeding animals for milk or meat or eggs, and *protecting their ability to do so*.

Saving seeds and planting them wasn't that complicated, but

conflicts arose because the crops resulting from those activities belonged to the agriculturalists: the farmers. They owned the crops their labor produced, and those plants were not to be foraged by anyone else. It was the same with animals: Once they were domesticated (this could have been as simple as managing a herd in a secluded and semi-closed valley), they were no longer fair game for hunting. Planning and doing the work meant owning the results.

From all this planning came rules about property, and breaking these rules had consequences—at least as long as your group could enforce them. And if it couldn't enforce them, well, your group might not survive.

When rules are consistently enforced, they become laws. As agriculture developed and grew, so did these laws; it was a period of profound change.

In his 1936 book *Man Makes Himself*, V. Gordon Childe argued that both the Agricultural Revolution and the resulting urban revolution (by which he meant the development of classes and governments) "affected all departments of human life."

Historians have advanced and refined these concepts since Childe's time, but the basic notions stand: Between the moment we came down from the trees and the eras of exploration, colonization, science, and capitalism, no collection of events had a greater impact on early human civilization than the development of agriculture.

Archaeologists have determined with near certainty that the first area to practice organized planting and adhere to its rules was the Fertile Crescent—the "cradle of civilization," which stretched from the Nile River in the west to the Tigris and Euphrates rivers in the east, all the way to the Persian Gulf. The area is sometimes called the Eastern Mediterranean, other times Southwest Asia (even though Egypt is in Africa), or the Middle or Near East.

In the Fertile Crescent, wheat (or, more accurately, its ancestor, einkorn, and a number of its varieties) grew naturally and readily. Where the soil was disturbed, churned, and fertilized by fire or animals, the wheat grew even better—well enough to attract settlers.

It was there that wheat was probably first cultivated in an organized, "This is *our* wheat" fashion, more than ten thousand years ago. By 7000 BCE—which allowed plenty of time to learn through trial and error—wheat was joined by barley and other grains, along with legumes like lentils and chickpeas.

People began to propagate fruit, including olives, and to more systematically care for and breed animals. There were cattle, pigs, sheep, goats, and dogs. And as the years and centuries passed, more and more of these people found it beneficial to attend to these tasks and spend less time foraging for food.

We don't know the sequencing here: Did bigger brains, more mobility, better tools, and more successful foraging and hunting lead to population growth, which essentially compelled our ancestors to settle down and start growing wheat and rice, because they needed more calories than foraging could provide? Or were people lured into permanent settlements by the belief in an easier life, the assessment that they could control their food supply by planting, taming, harvesting, dairying, and slaughtering?

There's no written history and therefore no clear answers. It was likely a combination and, again, inconceivably gradual. The Ice Age ended around 10,000 BCE, and the ensuing hospitable change in climate (from which we still benefit) set people free to roam a far greater area of the earth. The planet could support more people, and it became easier to grow food, especially life-sustaining grain.

Agriculture expanded, often at the expense of land used by foragers. Hunters and gatherers remained—especially throughout the Americas, where they predominated until the Europeans came—and nomadic herding continued to rule in semi-arid areas of Asia and Africa where farming was difficult or impossible.

Similar events were happening in the Indus River valley of India and the Yellow River valley of China. By about 5000 BCE there was agriculture in Britain, Central America, the Andes, and elsewhere. By 2000 BCE agriculture was widespread and quite sophisticated, and by the Common Era it was the global norm.

Eventually sedentary agricultural people took over almost everywhere, and ideas and techniques began to spread and be shared. People still hunted, from necessity or for recreation. But domestication became the standard, and its appeal was evident. Again, imagine the convenience of producing your own dairy, eggs, and meat and, in theory at least, controlling when you eat what.

It's likely that most of the earliest agriculture took one of two forms. There was nomadic herding, in which groups roamed with herds of their animals (camels, sheep, goats, reindeer, horses) in search of pasture and variety of diet. And there was shifting horticulture, where forests and grassland were cleared by fire and then planted. Before the invention of the plow, this was the easiest way to create new farmland. It also created grassland for animals and more sun for a greater variety of edible plants. People still do both today. Isolated and small populations practice traditional methods, while livestock producers set afire huge tracts of the Amazon to grow feed.

Animals became increasingly important, and Eurasia had a natural advantage over other areas, because nearly all of the world's large animals capable of being domesticated — those that could be put to work as well as eaten — were indigenous. Beginning with dogs, domesticated from wolves perhaps as long as thirty thousand years ago, and continuing with sheep, goats, pigs, and, later, cattle, animals became a part of most settlements, providing dairy, manure, hides (valuable for clothing, boats, containers, and tools), and, increasingly, transportation and labor.

Domesticated animals were often too valuable to be eaten. Indeed, the amount of meat consumed per person may well have gone down with the advent of farming as wild animals became scarce, at least near villages. (In fact, it's safe to say that meat consumption has fluctuated greatly throughout history and throughout the world, and that, with very few exceptions, until recently it was mostly eaten occasionally.)

Another consequence of the transition from foraging to farming was that families grew larger. Hunter-gatherers had to carry their children until they could walk, an inconvenience when foraging. Farmers, on the other hand, welcomed more children, who became laborers with value greater than the cost of feeding them.

As a result, population increased something like tenfold, and pretty quickly. At the end of the last ice age, global population was, according to most estimates, at around five million. It's impossible to know the exact number, but no expert believes it was less than one million or more than ten. Within five thousand years, with the establishment of farms and villages on most continents, it's estimated that there were at least fifty million people on the planet, but possibly even more than a hundred million.

With those people came an alteration of both landscape and ecosystem, as we systematically created and devoured biomass in a new, sweeping way, generating new versions of plants and animals that suited our needs while causing thousands of others to become extinct.

From the beginning, there were different approaches to farming, largely based on the type and availability of land. Did you graze animals or herd them? Did you use them for dairy or meat? What kinds of crops did you grow? The approaches also differed based on the availability of water (Was there enough? Did you have to bring it in from somewhere else? Could you use it for power?), of sun (Not enough or too much?), of labor (Were you the beast of burden, or did you have an ox?), and of technology (How did you break the soil? How did you replenish it?).

With time, people came to understand how to maintain soil, how to manage livestock, and how to use manure as fertilizer to grow crops that, with luck, would feed both people and their livestock. They learned how to select seeds, move and store water, develop fields, cope with weeds, and store grain and preserve other foods. All of this, as well as basic foods and tools, developed at different paces in different places.

If seed could be fruitfully planted, it was. If not, the land was grazed. Before the plow, there was only the digging stick—exactly what you imagine it to be—so in many areas the fastest way to clear land was to burn it. What was grown was largely determined by what *could* be grown, meaning what was right for the region.

By 2000 BCE we'd figured out how to bend wood and develop the wheel, and to build fires hot enough to shape metal. Then we created plows, canals, bricks, better boats, clothing made from fabrics like wool and flax, and heat-resistant pottery, which immeasurably increased our cooking skills.

In addition to the dominant grains —wheat, barley, corn, rice, millet, amaranth, and sorghum— this explosive period saw the development of beer and wine; tortillas and yeasted breads; honey from bees; milk, butter, yogurt, and cheese from cows, sheep, and goats; beasts of labor such as oxen (usually castrated bulls), horses, donkeys, and mules; and many other domesticated animals, including dogs, rabbits and other rodents, llamas, horses, camels, deer, and poultry.

Cultivated vegetables and fruits included greens; alliums like onions, garlic, and so on; squash; legumes, including peanuts; sesame, sunflower, and other seeds; grapes, melons, bananas, sugarcane, dates, figs, tomatoes, avocados, peppers, papaya, watermelon, citrus, bulbs from lilies and irises, yams and other roots, and probably much more that we don't know about.

The Chinese ate noodles two thousand years before Christ was born; the Aztecs were drinking cocoa before the Common Era, too. The Incas thrived on potatoes. Olives and especially olive oil were prized on and near the Mediterranean, and people in other places made oil from safflower, sunflower, sesame, coconut, avocado, and castor. Many foods from this time remain popular: tamales, pickled roots, sweetened yogurt, salted and smoked meat, and probably fried chicken, or at least fried rabbit.

Some things haven't changed much. Rice, corn, and wheat were staples, and they still provide about two-thirds of human calories. All of these grains were grown in their native regions, and to a large extent they determined the future of those regions and their people.

But even as agriculture was creating civilizations, giving shape to and reason for societies, it was also setting us on an irreversible course of change.

————

By five thousand years ago, civilization—government, cities, record-keeping, writing, culture—was on every habitable continent, and the increase in production thanks to improvements in soil maintenance, fertilization, and irrigation, along with better storage and more sophisticated animal breeding, had led to the largest human population ever.

Although this development was gradual, in the grand scheme of things it had happened quickly. After 200,000 years of hunting and gathering, most people settled down within a few thousand years. It also happened relatively recently. Humans have been farming for less than five percent of our existence.

As more land was cultivated, more food was grown. As more food was grown, more people could be supported. And, as populations grew, more land was needed to sustain them. If at first the idea of agriculture was to make life easier, the practice quickly morphed into a race to produce *enough* food to live.

Life turned out not to be easier. Farming is hard, and there are no guarantees. There were also unforeseen consequences. Lots of them.

That the Neolithic/Agricultural Revolution was of inestimable importance in our history is inarguable. But whether that change was for better or worse—that's way less certain. Some—most famously Jared Diamond, the author of *Guns, Germs and Steel*—argue that it was "the worst mistake in the history of the human race."

His 1987 essay of that title begins, "The adoption of agriculture, supposedly our most decisive step toward a better life, was in many ways a catastrophe from which we have never recovered." Similarly, Yuval Noah Harari, the author of *Sapiens*, calls the Agricultural Revolution "history's biggest fraud." This kind of thinking is now quite common, if not the norm.

It's true that agriculture made life possible for billions of humans, and for some of those, life has been pleasant. But agriculture also led to a new kind of society that bred injustice, poverty, disease, slavery, and war.

Was it worth it? You tell me. What can't be questioned is that

the development of agriculture led to consequences whose importance is impossible to overstate.

For one, diets became monotonous. The diets of pre-agricultural
people may have been unpredictable, even unreliable, but they
were often *supremely* varied. Farmers, by contrast, focused on just
a few crops, usually grains, and were often dependent on *very* few
—sometimes just one. As a result, people starved when there
were crop failures, and crop failures were common. They were
also routinely malnourished, which is what happens when you eat
rice or corn or millet at every meal, or *for* every meal, without
augmenting it with different foods containing other nutrients.

That malnourishment left them vulnerable to disease, which
became more common as settlements grew more densely popu-
lated and (in some areas, especially Europe) people began living
with their animals.

There's evidence that a precursor to plumbing with running
water existed in Mesopotamia as early as 4000 BCE. Much more
common, however, were omnipresent garbage, human waste, and
roaming animals, like rats, all of which spread disease. Furthermore, more children meant less breast milk given to each one,
which probably meant weaker immune systems.

Life became not only nasty and brutish, but short. There's evidence that the average life span *decreased* by about seven years after the development of agriculture, as did height, by as much as
six inches in men, from five foot nine to five-three. Tooth decay
increased as well. These trends continued, and the average Roman lived ten years less than the average Mesopotamian.

Farmers also had to work harder than hunter-gatherers. If they
expected payoffs of guaranteed food, lots of time off, and a better life, that certainly wasn't the way it worked out. Rather, they
were trapped in a nonstop scramble to break soil, plant, irrigate,
weed, harvest, thresh, store, tend animals, and more—the generally backbreaking labor that constituted the daily lives of almost
all humans until the eighteenth century.

Civilization also brought inequality, and class distinction became a defining feature. There were certainly bossy people before
agriculture (every family has them), and even positions of power,

usually held by men. But there were no societies in which some people lived largely off the labor of others. After the establishment of agriculture, there was surplus, inequality, and elites. Archeological evidence even points to the new nobility being taller and healthier than the hoi polloi. At the same time, stricter gender roles took hold, leading to the oppression of women.

In fact, agriculture hasn't been kind to most people. For the past ten thousand years, the vast majority of humankind has toiled as farmers and laborers who—in clearing the land, growing the crops, carrying the water, and, later, digging the mines and staffing the factories and firing the guns—make history happen. Few of them have had easy lives.

But the consequences of what must have seemed like simple changes couldn't be foreseen. Our ancestors could no more predict the development of infectious disease or armies than they could have predicted global warming, another unintended consequence stemming, in large part, from agriculture. No doubt, everyone was just trying to do what made the most sense, and it's improbable that those first few decisions, made over the course of hundreds and even thousands of years, over dozens of generations, could have been made much differently. Seed saving and animal breeding appeared to promise more security and a better life. We are hardwired to feed ourselves reliably, to try to make life work. Like all things that don't turn out as we would have wished, it seemed a good idea at the time.

And even if early farmers did spot these problems, within a few generations it was too late to turn back. Hunting and gathering skills were lost, the landscape had been permanently changed, and, most important, the population had boomed. From then on, only agriculture could produce enough food to sustain humankind. If hunger, malnutrition, a ruling class, inequality, political systems, poverty, war, disease, environmental destruction, and so on were the results, they were necessary evils. We're only now beginning to see the consequences and to grapple with them.

2

Soil and Civilization

AGRICULTURE IS AN eternal experiment. Performed annually or seasonally, it's always being improved in the eyes of its practitioners or those who govern them. Its key components are sun, water, soil, and labor. Sun, one of the few resources we can truly consider infinite, is not even marginally under humans' control. Water and soil, however, are precious and finite resources that must be manipulated and stewarded responsibly. That work is the farmer's labor. The choices humankind has made about soil and water management, and the manner in which that management was executed—who's worked the land, how, and for whom—have largely determined the fate of civilized society. Naturally, some choices were better than others.

Civilization sprouted from agriculture, and there has never been a successful agricultural practice without adequate water. If you have a reliable water source, and you don't pollute or deplete it at a quicker rate than nature can replenish it, it's likely to remain reliable. As such, two questions become important: Who has access to this water? And how can we best channel and use this water? Wars are fought over the first question, and the success or failure of agriculture depends on the second.

Soil is more complicated. Take some pounded, ground, eroded, washed, tumbled, and wind-blown clay, sand, and gravel and combine it with organic matter: the waste and carcasses of microbes, mammoths, and all living animals in between; rotted leaves and woody material from trees, shrubs, and other plants; air- and wa-

terborne detritus of all kinds; and the excrement of living creatures. That makes soil. The minerals in soil change with the addition of water, creating other chemical compounds. Additionally,
soil is aerated by plants, animals, fungi, bacteria, and weather, a
necessary process for the survival of those life forms that live in it
—around a billion creatures in every teaspoon. The synergy between these components gives soil a specific character. Healthy
soil in one part of the world looks different from healthy soil
somewhere else.

In fact, soil is a living thing that changes and grows. It gives to
us, and in return it needs care. Without care, using soil will kill it.
The health of society also depends on that care, which ultimately
is the job of the farmer, the land's steward. The conservation-
ist Walter Clay Lowdermilk, writing in 1938, put it well: "[The]
partnership of land and farmer is the rock foundation of our complex social structure." Between a good farmer and good soil, there
must be a good relationship. This is an understatement: Soil and
the people who work it are the foundation of a thriving society.
Wealth has its source in nature, and that wealth must be protected
as well as spent.

Healthy soil serves as a living pantry for plants, which draw
on the nutrients contained in it. Those nutrients must be replenished, or each successive crop will be smaller than its predeces-
sors. Just as there are empty pantries and full pantries, there are
also "poor" and "rich" soils.

Soil replenishment can be simple, even automatic. In dying, all
plants and animals (and living creatures like bacteria) leave whatever nutrients and organic matter they've absorbed or created
through their growth. Some plants even replenish nutrients while
still alive. But if soil is exposed to erosion and deprived of organic
matter, it will produce less with each passing year.

Some agricultural systems are better at maintaining healthy
soil than others. Recognizing this, many early farmers established
protective measures to prevent erosion, like terracing slopes with
rock walls and planting deep-rooted perennials. They quickly figured out ways to replenish their soil, or allow it to replenish itself.

Others remained ignorant and quickly saw diminished harvests, failed crops, hunger, forced migration, and even the failure of entire societies. Lowdermilk called this "suicidal agriculture," an accurate if harsh term. Soil degradation may not have directly destroyed those early civilizations, writes David Montgomery in *Dirt: The Erosion of Civilizations,* "but time and again it left societies increasingly vulnerable to hostile neighbors, internal sociopolitical disruption, and harsh winters or droughts."

It sounds dramatic, given how far removed we are from our food sources, but civilizations live or die by the strength and resilience of their food systems. And these depend on healthy soil.

There are four major ways in which a field can be planted repeatedly and still have its nutrients replenished: fallowing, planting cover crops, rotating crops, and fertilizing. All of these have been used, alone or together and at times unwittingly, since agriculture began.

Like everything else that lives, soil needs nitrogen. It's one of three essential plant nutrients, along with phosphorus and potassium. But although the earth's air is rich with nitrogen — there's more of it than of any other gas — atmospheric nitrogen is nearly inert, which means it can't be absorbed by plants.

For soil to use nitrogen, the gas must be converted into another compound, like ammonia, which is a combination of nitrogen and hydrogen. When plants and animals die and their mass lies in or on the soil, bacteria convert the nitrogen in their cells to ammonia. In addition, there are some organisms that can "fix" atmospheric nitrogen, making it useful for plants. (Lightning also creates a usable form of nitrogen, which falls into the soil with rain, but it's a less significant source.)

Almost all agriculture removes nitrogen far more quickly than it can be replenished, though, and successive crops yield less if nitrogen isn't somehow added. To revisit the pantry analogy, it's like cooking every day and never going shopping.

If you don't use soil, in time it replenishes itself. That's called "fallowing": After a harvest, a farmer can simply plant nothing. In the absence of a crop to nourish, the nitrogen levels in the soil are restored by organic matter, and after a year—but preferably several—the area usually can be planted again with good results. The biblical notion that you plant for six years and rest for one (a kind of Sabbath pattern for planting) is not a good system. In reality, for fallowing to be most effective, land should lie dormant for longer than it's actively planted.

Fallowing may be simple, but it's not always easy. It has a built-in challenge that's both major and obvious: It takes land out of production. If you can find new land to take its place or if your needs aren't great, this isn't anything to worry about. You can either work the new land or just take a few years off. Two thousand years ago, farmers had plenty of new land to claim. Now, not so much. And, sadly, a years-long vacation has been impractical for almost every farmer who's ever lived.

The best approach was a combination of the two. Farmers who had enough land could simply plant one field while one or more others lay fallow in turn. This is still a fine option, when it's available.

There are alternatives to fallowing. Some plants host microbes that actually *add* usable nitrogen to the soil. Almost all of these are legumes, like beans and lentils (but also alfalfa, clover, and some others), and are sometimes called "green manure." Their roots host microbes like cyanobacteria (and others), which grab nitrogen from the air and fix it in the soil, making it useful for plants.

When these plants are not intended for harvest, they're usually called cover crops, as they provide cover for the soil and prevent erosion. Cover crops can be grown alongside a main crop, or alone when the land would otherwise be fallow.

When nitrogen-fixing crops are planted *instead* of a main or normal crop, that's a form of crop rotation. You can rotate any combination of crops, of course, but only by using a nitrogen-fixing crop in rotation can you put nitrogen back in the soil. The practice of alternating corn and soybeans, a fine nitrogen-fixing crop, is a common form of crop rotation.

Crop rotation and cover cropping should not be seen as

sacrifices. Neither should fallowing, really. Building the soil up is as important as producing the next crop, though it's sometimes difficult to see it that way, since, in the short term, a fallow field can yield no crop. You can grow a nitrogen-fixing crop that you have no intention of eating, selling, or even feeding to animals, turning this green manure back into the soil. Or you can grow a nitrogen-fixing crop for harvest and sale—not quite as effective for the soil as the first option, but way better than nothing.

Another soil replenishment strategy is growing a crop that animals like to eat (even better if it's nitrogen-fixing) and turning your ruminants—cud chewers, like cattle and sheep—loose in that field, where they can eat nonstop. When those animals pee and poop, they add nitrogen, phosphorus, potassium, and more to the soil, fertilizing it for future plantings.

The first fertilizing methods were unintentional: Animals or humans "added" their waste to the soil simply because it was convenient. Along with that waste came nitrogen and a host of other nutrients and organic matter. Farmers soon discovered that if they mixed and maintained compost—the intentionally rotted mix of animal and plant waste, living creatures like bacteria and earthworms, and almost anything else that decomposes quickly —they could add that to the soil as a cocktail even more potent than straight manure.

With the addition of adequate organic matter from any source —green manure, composted material, or the replenishment that comes with fallowing—agriculture could in theory thrive indefinitely.

But as populations grew, there was pressure for soil to be more productive and increase its yield. Fallowing became more difficult, and crop rotation was too often sacrificed to "efficiency." And with more land to fertilize, animal waste or other organic matter became harder to come by.

Thus the paradox: As agriculture succeeded and populations grew, more was demanded of soil. As more was demanded, soil health was sacrificed and productivity declined. Until the twentieth century, the only possible resolutions were rediscovering sustainable agriculture, settling for the "suicidal agriculture" to which Lowdermilk referred, or finding new land. Ideally, this new land would have been unsettled, but increasingly that wasn't the case.

> When you have to work the field with the seeder-plough, keep your eye on the man who drops the seed. The grain should fall two fingers deep. You should put one *gij* of seed per *ninda*. If the barley seed is not being inserted into the hollow of the furrow, change the wedge of your plough share.

Those words are from a thousand-word Sumerian document written on a clay tablet around 1500 BCE, and, opaque as they might be, you get the idea. "The Farmer's Instructions" is a letter, a father's advice to his son, discussing a variety of tools, animal-handling and harnessing equipment, levees and canals, repairs, plowing, planting, winnowing techniques, and more. It's the earliest example of recorded history that showcases the importance of agriculture.

Sumer, in southern Mesopotamia (roughly present-day southern Iraq), is generally accepted to have been among the first advanced civilizations, along with those in India, Egypt, and China. First settled around 5000 BCE, by 3000 BCE Sumer boasted cities, and in the thousand years that followed, Sumerians developed systems of timekeeping and writing. The latter provides us with the first sophisticated and contemporary accounts of daily life.

Thanks to those accounts, we know a lot about Sumerian food and agriculture. People ate a variety of grains, many in the form of barley cakes (barley is not as nutritious as wheat, but it's easier to grow), fruit, and vegetables (records mention more than a hundred kinds). They made beer and wine, bread, oils, yogurt and cheese, and more. They raised animals and understood all aspects of husbandry, including how to use everything an animal gives, including fertilizer.

The natural soil quality in Mesopotamia was enviable. But for agriculture to thrive in such an arid climate, the marshes in the plains surrounding the Tigris and Euphrates rivers had to be adapted to irrigation. These challenges required organization and cooperation among major settlements, and jobs were eventually organized by the state, which employed and enslaved many thousands of people to build and maintain an impressive system of reservoirs and canals. These were by far the biggest public works projects to date, guaranteeing water during the dry season even for villages far from the rivers.

Few of the laborers working on these projects grew their own food, which meant that in order for the society as a whole to thrive, farmers needed to produce surplus. For the most part, that surplus was "contributed" to — or more likely seized by — the state.

These kinds of divisions made social classes inevitable.

Experts say that size alone leads to stratification, and that egalitarianism in social groups starts to break down when the number of people reaches about five hundred. At that point, leaders and a ruling elite emerge. And as villages became towns and towns became cities, universal personal contact — the feeling that everyone knew everyone else — was lost. Intervillage contact also became common, as did cooperation and conflict.

Whether elitism is forever inevitable is arguable, but historically it's long been present, and leadership was essential. *Someone* had to take responsibility for organizing solutions to municipal issues like irrigation, waste disposal, fence building, and the need for communal ovens and temples, and *someone* had to orchestrate intervillage relationships and broker trade and grazing rights. It was impossible to do these things individually, or by mutual and universal consent. The projects were too big, and there were simply too many people.

The result was the establishment of private property, government, laws and regulations . . . and inequality. Cities grew up around irrigation projects and ports, and they began to dominate the surrounding countryside and, to some extent, its populace. Surplus meant that former and non-farmers could find ways to make a living, as tradesmen, administrators, religious leaders, or what we'd now call professionals: scribes, accountants, traders, doctors, lawyers, and so on. The less lucky majority, of course, were laborers or slaves.

It's worth noting that slavery became profitable only once humans had settled into sedentary societies. It made little sense to send other humans out into the wild to gather food for you. Such people would first have to feed themselves, and once they were out in the wild, they were under little obligation to come back.

But with the arrival of agriculture, sedentariness, and non-communal work, it became desirable to have others work for you. If you were rich and/or powerful enough, you could simply persuade or force others into servitude, with little consequence. Initially, slaves were captives from conquered lands or armies. But once a society established a slave population, slaves were bought, sold, and born; any child of a slave was a slave as well. With each passing century, slavery became more common, until, in some places, it was the dominant form of labor.

Sumer, a full-fledged class-based society with slaves—most often prisoners of war, debt, or crime—as well as priest-kings (religion was core) and dynasties, was one such place. For a thousand years at least, it was successful, and its size was unprecedented. It reached the point where several cities had populations of up to fifty thousand people.

But wars with neighboring territories interrupted important public works projects, including maintenance. The floodplains were fully irrigated, but in order to avoid salt buildup in the soil from the groundwater, the land needed time to rest. As populations boomed, that rest became impossible, and salinization forced Sumer to abandon wheat, until then its most reliably nutritious food source. Over a thousand years, canals filled up with silt, crops withered, food became scarce, and populations shrank. When the land could no longer support the former population, the cities simply stopped working. Just as Sumer became famous as one of the first advanced civilizations, it's known as the first example of a failed society.

Egypt was more successful in the long term. By 3000 BCE several cities containing many thousands of people had been built along the Nile, and they united for their mutual benefit. The river provided a reliable water supply and, through its annual flooding, enriched the soil. Once irrigation and drainage were mastered, a surplus of food was virtually assured in every growing season, something that can't be said of many places.

It took a thousand years or more to develop an Egyptian state strong enough to control enough surplus to fund massive public works projects. But once it consolidated, Egypt became a nation of unparalleled stability when measured against the standards of any era you choose. Though most people were farmers, few controlled their production, which went directly to the land's owners or the state.

Excess production, along with taxes, first supported Egypt's canal projects and massive armies, as well as its pyramids, among the world's first large-scale and grandest (and most impractical) public works projects, serving little purpose other than to glorify the ruling class.

Other cultures used their agricultural surplus in different ways. The first public water tank and citywide sanitation systems were built in the cities of Mohenjo-Daro and Harappa, on the Indus River in present-day Pakistan. The Hongshan culture in China was building underground temples and crafting with jade. Later, the Mesoamericans built pyramids and other structures almost as impressive as those of Egypt, and the Chinese built their famous wall.

As in Egypt, the agriculturally advanced regions of China produced surplus: Farmers were developing row crops, the seed drill (which came far later), and the plow, which was probably invented independently at about the same time in Egypt. These, along with water control, allowed the Chinese to build and preserve huge swaths of first-rate farmland. They even developed the first symbiotic cultivation of rice, fish, and ducks, in which the animals fertilize the paddies and eat pests while nibbling at plant matter.

Rice itself was a game changer, producing many more calories per given land area than wheat and most other grains. Since rice and other plants fed most of the population, animals were largely reserved for labor and sometimes dairy.

This plant-dependent system was more stable than growing food for animals and then relying on meat to feed people. And that turned out to be a determinant of much that happened in the coming millennia, as rice-growing people, who tended toward vegetarianism or near-vegetarianism, grew larger and more stable populations than wheat-growing people, who mostly bred animals for meat.

Generally, as Franklin Hiram King describes in *Farmers of Forty Centuries*, Asia developed "permanent agriculture" that was "strong, patient, persevering, thoughtful." These seeds of sustainable agriculture were planted in Asia well over three thousand years ago and were maintained until recently.

This kind of agriculture also became more sophisticated and usually more successful with each passing century, thanks to better irrigation, terracing, and other techniques, as well as wider distribution of (originally Vietnamese) rice varieties that were drought-tolerant and quick to mature, allowing for two or even three harvests a year in some areas, which means two or three times as much food produced each year. (Parts of China and India also relied on millet, which is equally productive, sustainable, and sustaining.)

Advanced irrigation, ongoing improvements in already high-yielding crops, innovations in tools (some of which involved early bronze-making and even high-heat iron-making), and water-powered grain mills made Asia the world's most productive agricultural region until well into the Common Era—in fact, until the Europeans arrived.

Although it came a little later, advanced and sustainable agriculture would eventually develop in the Americas as well, and we can still see its legacy.

Some regions of the Americas, most notably the Pacific Northwest, had such natural abundance that complex societies developed entirely without agriculture. People remained hunter-gatherers, and population densities still reached such high numbers that social stratification developed.

But in the most populous part of the hemisphere, Mesoamerica —which includes present-day southern Mexico, Central America, and northern South America—a new style of farming was developing. Mesoamerica was not as fertile as the Nile Valley and some other early centers of civilization, flat grasslands that naturally produced grains like wheat and developed a kind of near monoculture.

In the Americas, people found that the rainforest presented another kind of structure, with a variety of plants occupying different niches in the canopy. Farmers imitated that structure, clearing sections of the forest and planting edibles. Some called their farms "milpa" — which in the Aztec language means "field" — and relied on slash-and-burn agriculture, sustainably planting for four or five years, then fallowing for fifteen years or more as the soil replenished.

Like other areas of the world, the Americas were blessed with dozens of important endemic plants we now take for granted. Two of them changed history. While the people of the Andes were developing thousands of kinds of potatoes, around 5000 BCE the Maya began selective breeding of a pathetic little spindle called teosinte, converting it to a plant that was easy to grow, easy to harvest, and highly nutritious.

That plant was corn (usually called maize outside the United States), and with further breeding it became supremely productive. Eventually, in favorable conditions, corn could even be grown twice a year on the same land.

It's a near-ideal crop, but it's not a near-ideal food, because corn must undergo a special process to maximize its nutritional potential. That process was developed sometime between 2000 and 1000 BCE, when corn began to be treated with ash or slaked lime (a solution of quicklime and water, which produces calcium hydroxide, also called cal). Much later, analysis showed that nixtamal, or cal-soaked corn, has more bioavailable niacin and a better mix of amino acids, the building blocks of protein.

You've eaten this form of corn in tortillas and tamales (note the similarity between "tamale" and "nixtamal"), and you may have wondered why they taste so much brighter and even better than products made with plain cornmeal. That's the result of nixtamalization.

But even nixtamalized corn doesn't provide enough protein on its own. So the milpa famously became a place to grow squash and beans along with corn, a system known as the "Three Sisters" that works so well it migrated both north and south and it remains a crucial practice today.

To those who associated agriculture with fields of golden grain, the milpa doesn't look like much. In fact, the first time I saw one, I was wondering where the farm was, because I was standing in the middle of what felt like a forest. But all around me were productive plants. And that's something common among many of the agricultural methods that have continued to support most of the world's people: They aren't as impressive-looking as industrial agriculture, but they're less disruptive and destructive and are built to last.

In the milpa, corn is planted first, followed by beans and squash. The corn allows for free growth of "pole beans," but without the poles—the cornstalks provide support. The microorganisms living on the beans' roots fix nitrogen, which restores some of the soil's nutrients. And the large leaves of the squash, whose seeds are a major protein source, provide shade, moderating soil temperature and helping to retain moisture.

The technique is simple, but calling it "primitive" is akin to calling the use of a cow for milk, meat, and hide "primitive." It's an ancient practice, but it still works, so "venerable" is the more accurate word. With proper rest for soil replenishment, it's a perfectly sustainable system, in harmony internally (the Three Sisters live well together) and externally, providing nourishment for their cultivators and coexisting with the surrounding forest.

The milpa supported great civilizations for thousands of years, during which time Mesoamerica was as populous and sophisticated as Eurasia, in agriculture as well as architecture, mathematics, and astronomy. In fact, it's one of only four early civilizations, along with Egypt, China, and Sumer, to have developed writing. Mesoamericans also thrived enough to produce Egypt-scale public works, including pyramids, many of which are still standing.

But for the Maya and other Mesoamerican societies, as population increased, thin tropical soils gave way. Without domesticated animals for manure, farmers had to push onto more erodible lands. And, according to David Montgomery, "soil erosion peaked shortly before Mayan civilization unraveled about AD 900 when the food surpluses that sustained the social hierarchy disappeared." Fossil records show a dip in population owing to higher infant and childhood mortality, thought to be the result of food scarcity and thus declining nutrition. (Much of the historical record, of course, was destroyed in the Spanish invasion and subsequent genocide.)

In collapsing, Mayan civilization followed the pattern set by the Sumerians and later agricultural societies. Around the world, through the ages, larger populations demanded that land become more productive. When that wasn't possible, as was often the case, more land had to be found. This usually meant mobilizing armies, which in turn needed feeding. And the pattern continued, with humans innovating tools, techniques, and the skills to conquer others faster than they could develop shared values.

Beginning around 4000 BCE, tin and copper were extracted from their ore and combined to produce bronze, a malleable material that made better tools, weapons, ornaments, lamps, and cooking utensils. Along with metals that were developed later, like iron and steel, bronze gradually changed agriculture, war, cooking, and more.

Because some of these metals were not easy to come by—tin, for example, is especially hard to find—trade increased. And that trade, which involved not just metals but salt, wood, precious stones, pitch (or tar, used for torches and for waterproofing both seagoing and liquid-holding vessels), and, later, wine, spices, and textiles, encouraged the development of roads, wheels, harnessed animals, and sail- or oar-powered boats.

The exploitation of the earth—extracting, mining, clearing, digging, planting, harvesting, and so on—became more efficient. Population growth, still slow by today's standards—it took around a thousand years for the planet's population to double from 50 million to 100 million, and probably a thousand more to grow to almost 300 million by the time of Christ—meant that there was always a need for more food. New land was brought into production whenever possible, either through settling new territories or clearing forests. "Erosion," writes Montgomery, "increased tenfold."

Among the most important inventions during this age was the plow. Its precise origins are unclear, but it certainly existed long before the Common Era, perhaps first in China but eventually in Sumer and Egypt, too. With its ability to make long, straight rows, the plow encouraged monoculture, the planting of one crop over large areas. So important was its development that the great historian Fernand Braudel asked, "Should one call the arrival of the plough a revolution?"

His thinking, and that of others, goes something like this: Until this point, gathering women had a closer relationship to the bounty of the soil and the sea than did hunting men. They probably provided more calories, too, because it's a safe bet that women were the first primary seed gatherers and the first planters. They were likely also the primary hunters of small game and, if not the first animal breeders, then important players in domestication. They may have developed the first agricultural tools and planting techniques, too, and there's evidence that in some areas, especially the Americas, women initially controlled the use of the land.

There were certainly divisions of labor between men and women, but until the development of the plow, these divisions were not defined by dominance and subservience. According to a number of academics writing over the past fifty years or so, it seems likely that roles shifted toward patriarchy as the plow and other heavier equipment that required significant brawn were introduced to farming.

Operating a plow means wrangling a blade through soil. That's tough work, even with the aid of a draft animal. And research done by economist Ester Boserup (among the first to argue that agricultural innovation stemmed largely from population growth) in the 1960s and '70s showed that the upper-body strength of most men gave them the sheer power needed to control a plow, which became a real advantage. Plowing also made planting easier and

reduced weeding, jobs that until then had been primarily wom-
en's. Gradually, men spent more time outside and women more
time inside.

As men took over, ideologies changed, too. "The Neolithic revolution put societies on a path on which patriarchal norms and beliefs are adopted," write Casper Worm Hansen et al. in "Modern
Gender Roles and Agricultural History," one of the more recent
works on the topic.

These new norms of inequality accompanied an increasingly
codified construct of gender, one traditionally and even still often
thought of as "part of human nature," "predetermined," or "God-
given." Of course it's none of these, but rather the result of a widespread change that transcended politics, philosophy, and religion,
and it became pretty much ubiquitous in a world where supply
and demand ruled.

Nothing about this can be truly conclusive, but it's compelling.
Whatever the case, in all of the cultures where physical strength
became paramount in agriculture, the familiar division of labor
arose: Men worked the fields while women tended to remain inside. In turn, men's work became disproportionately paramount
economically; we're still seeing the effects of that today.

We think of the south-facing coast of the Mediterranean, especially in France, Italy, and Greece, as idyllic: craggy mountains,
boulder-strewn beaches with crashing waves, abundant sun, and
simple, herb-and-olive-oil-laced food with wine sturdy enough to
complement those bold flavors. It's one of the birthplaces of great
eating, and, as Homer's contemporary Hesiod made clear in about
700 BCE, it has been for three thousand years:

> Let me have a shady rock and wine of Biblis, a clot of curds and
> milk of drained goats with the flesh of a heifer fed in the woods, that
> has never calved, and of firstling kids; then also let me drink bright
> wine, sitting in the shade . . .

Yet some parts of "the Mediterranean" required more bounty
than the homeland could produce to flourish. If you're like Egypt

and blessed with the Nile, a place of fertility and abundance, you can be more or less self-reliant.

But Greece and Italy have never been easy to farm. Their mountains plunge right down to the coast, often making transportation by boat almost essential, even though the rocky coast is tricky to navigate. The slopes leave little flat ground on which to farm, and what's there is often flooded, its topsoil washed away by water pouring out of the mountains during spring rains and snowmelt. Those torrents often do little good from an irrigation perspective, because spring plants are fragile. And the next rainy season, usually in mid-autumn, may be too late, the crop already harvested or parched—and doomed. In between the rains comes a hot, dry season, and that's when farmers are in the fields. Hesiod, the earliest reliable chronicler of Greek agriculture, recommended that farmers work naked: "strip to sow and strip to plough and strip to reap."

Good years could bring farmers surplus, but no one could expect only good years. And bad years, which came often, brought disappointing crops, reduced income, and sometimes famine. While there were times of adequate barley and even harder-to-grow wheat, there were other times when flour was ground from acorns.

The land was simply not productive enough to feed growing and increasingly urban populations. At the risk of being overly simplistic, this pressure to fulfill a growing food demand is arguably the foundation of imperialism and colonization. To build surplus and wealth in this region took an empire, one that extended to neighboring lands where farming was more reliable and productive.

And so, around 600 BCE, the Greeks first colonized nearby and then more remote areas, as far away as the Black Sea in the east, Egypt in the south, and Catalonia, two thousand miles to the west, places where barley, wheat, olives, and grapes grew more reliably and sheep and goats could graze greener pastures. As a result, there were more cash crops and therefore more surplus as seagoing boats brought cheap grain, grapes, olives, and wine to market.

With the near-holy trinity of wheat, olives, and grapes established throughout the Mediterranean and Western Europe, the Romans, too, claimed crops from an area measured in millions of square miles. They also imported—and planted widely—once exotic fruits and vegetables from the Near and Far East: apricots, cherries, peaches, quince, almonds, walnuts, chestnuts, and much more.

Roman productivity also benefited from the existence of a special "property": slaves. They served under insufferable, deadly conditions, forced to work in chain gangs and perform as gladiators. It's possible that no group of slaves in pre-Columbian history was treated worse than those in Rome, and it's not a coincidence that Rome was among the richest civilizations in history. "Free" labor will do that for you.

As elsewhere, the majority of people under Roman rule were farmers, and many of the rest were involved in moving, trading, buying, and selling food. As long as the empire lasted, almost everyone ate bread every day, often made from wheat imported from North Africa. But that rich land, too, was subject to Lowdermilk's prediction, and the soil was exploited to the point of agricultural failure. Deforestation, overgrazing, and failure to fallow eventually led to decreased production and even desertification. You need look no further than the Egyptian desert for evidence of this.

The fall of the Roman Empire is usually portrayed as a military failure, of drawn-out civil wars and vicious barbarian raids. Less recognized, though, is the role that food played. Rome's collapse was in part a result of food shortages, as the soil of distant lands devoted to "permanent" monoculture of wheat was exhausted, while interior soils prioritized export products like olives and grapes. Until the downfall, Roman agricultural technology rivaled that of China. But it would take a thousand years for any part of Europe to reclaim that level of productivity.

3

Agriculture Goes Global

T HE MIDDLE AGES —from roughly 500 CE to 1500 CE—are often called the Dark Ages. It's a misleading term, as civilization was still flourishing in the East. But for disease-prone Europe, the name was not entirely inaccurate: The reading and writing of Greek and Latin had all but disappeared, and the science those civilizations developed had been forgotten.

By 1300, nearly half of the world's population lived in China and India, and most of the lasting post-Greco-Roman innovations— agricultural, scientific, mathematical, and industrial—had been developed in Asia. The Chinese had invented paper, gunpowder, and the compass. Their ships had sailed to southern Africa (a far longer voyage than the Spanish would undertake to reach the Caribbean), and China had been exporting spices and silk to Europe for centuries. Meanwhile, to the west, the Islamic world was advancing farming so quickly that some historians refer to the period as the Muslim (or Arab) Agricultural Revolution.

Through experimentation, record-keeping, study, and innovation, Asia had steadily advanced agriculture. A variety of crops were raised far from their origins: Sugar had come from India and citrus from China. Millet and rice were planted widely, and farmers developed new breeds of crops and livestock, many of which were more productive and drought-, disease-, or pest-resistant. Accurate calendars allowed for better planning, crop rotation was improved, and the mechanics of irrigation were advanced, or at least rediscovered.

   The degree to which Muslims elevated agriculture is still the subject of debate among historians: Some call it revolutionary, and others just restorative, arguing that Muslim nations simply rediscovered techniques mastered by the Romans and lost after their downfall. It's true that Muslims began this period of development by repairing Roman water systems that had lain in disrepair for hundreds of years, then improved upon them. What seems inarguable is that these advances, which included a host of new crops, moved to Europe through the Muslim conquest of Iberia, and later through the Crusades.

   Trade between China, India, and western Asia had become common, and the Mediterranean–East Asian trade routes meant an exchange of goods, of cultures, and, increasingly, of scientific discoveries, which had barely advanced in Europe since Aristotle and Ptolemy.

   Nor were things standing entirely still in the rest of the world. In the Western Hemisphere, too, dams, reservoirs, aqueducts, and canals (some of which still exist today) were constructed, and landholding, toolmaking, record-keeping, organized experimentation, ongoing soil maintenance, and cross-breeding of both crops and animals were widespread.

   There was less progress in Europe, where feudalism prioritized the needs and desires of lords over the survival of serfs and peasants, creating a stark disparity in food and agriculture. With population growing, more primitive farming made hunger inevitable, and starvation was common. Fernand Braudel, in his readable and academically respected (a combination you don't find too often) *The Structures of Everyday Life*, estimates that France, "a privileged country . . . experienced 10 general famines during the tenth century; 26 in the eleventh." That's one every four years.

   "Any national calculation shows a sad story," he writes. Hunger, starvation, and outright famine "recurred so insistently for centuries on end that it became incorporated into man's biological regime and built into his daily life." At all too frighteningly short intervals, whole populations would suffer vitamin deficiencies, disease, and death.

   Chronicles of suffering from the late Middle Ages describe diets that included everything from wild plants to mud, bark, grass, and occasionally other people. In *Before the Industrial Revolution*, author Carlo M. Cipolla writes that most European townspeople spent nearly their entire budgets on food alone. Even "the purchase of a garment or of the cloth for a garment," he writes, "remained a luxury the common people could only afford a few times in their lives."

Many of these problems stemmed from stunted social and agricultural systems. As Raj Patel and Jason W. Moore write in *A History of the World in Seven Cheap Things*, "a transition [from feudalism] to different ways of working land, with more peasant autonomy and power over what and how to grow, would have allowed medieval Europe to feed up to three times as many people."

That transition didn't happen. And yet, despite rampant food shortages and their dire consequences, Western Europe would soon emerge as a global superpower. Its ascent to world dominance would forever shape human existence and its relationship with food.

Europe's population, which had declined to a low of around thirty million people, had, by the eleventh century, climbed back to about sixty million, which is almost what it had been at the height of Rome.

Change was in the air. The climate had warmed, contact among urban centers was becoming more common, money was increasingly replacing goods as a means of exchange, and traders sought new markets. Europe was emerging as a major world power.

The Crusades of the twelfth and thirteenth centuries were a turning point, and although they're rarely discussed in terms of their effect on food, we can't ignore the relationship. Crusaders were raiders, religious fanatics, spiritualists, idealists, romantics, and sinners seeking redemption. They were unemployed itinerants and aristocrats, failed farmers and militarists, thrill seekers and disinherited second sons, imperialists and power-grabbers, rapists and murderers, pillagers and plunderers, anti-Semites and anti-Islamists.

The common thread was opportunism. For many Crusaders,

the "reward" for their service was death and (in theory) salvation. But others became traders in spices, sugar, and "new" foods like rice, coffee, a variety of fruits, and more, as well as fabrics, tools, and crafted items. These new commodities were the foundation for the world of exploration, trade, colonization, and exploitation that was about to explode.

But the spread of wealth was delayed by the plague, which arrived in Sicily in 1347 on ships coming from the East—a direct result of increased international trade in the wake of the Crusades. The Black Death killed at least twenty million people, ruptured European society, and paved a path for change.

After Europe's population was reduced by around a third (some scholars say half), food was relatively plentiful. But the surviving nobility, dependent on a massive peasant population for income (and, of course, labor), was suddenly squeezed for cash.

With fewer peasants paying rent and taxes, landlords pivoted to trade as their primary revenue source. This created a heightened pressure to maximize the land's potential to yield goods for exchange. If it were ever a priority to nurture the people who worked that land, that priority was all but extinguished, and the ruling class accelerated the process of enclosure, making communal lands private.

Enclosure ruptured traditional feudal arrangements, under which peasants had been guaranteed that they could remain on their land regardless of its output, and almost always had at least a little acreage they could work for themselves. With the closure of the commons, their livelihoods became dependent on the profit generated by their crop or, increasingly, their flock or herd. In any case, the value of whatever they produced was often determined by a distant market and ever-changing conditions. Landowners may have been thriving, but the new cash economy didn't help most farmers or eaters, and those who couldn't produce food for themselves were always at risk of starving.

Animals, which provided meat, wool, dairy, fur, tallow, labor, manure, and more, became an important source of wealth. (There's a reason farm animals are called "stock," like shares in a company.) Thus, pasture became a more reliable investment than arable land. In England, writes the mid-twentieth-century Dutch historian Slicher van Bath, "whole villages were wiped out to make room for grassland where the flocks could graze."

But animals were cultivated to feed the wealthy, not the peasants who reared them, and the peasants were increasingly limited in their ability to grow food for themselves. This would have disastrous consequences extending across centuries.

As more land became pasture, that which was used for crops became not only less abundant but also more stressed and less fertile. Ongoing monoculture, especially of wheat, says Braudel, "devours the soil and forces it to rest regularly." Yet it wasn't being fallowed or otherwise replenished, which virtually guaranteed that each year's crop would be worse than the last.

Peasants were losing land to animals that they couldn't eat and working soil that was decreasingly productive. Yet their numbers were growing. How, exactly, was that supposed to work?

With no solutions in sight, Europe began to look beyond its borders.

By the fourteenth and especially the fifteenth century, wealth and capital were emerging in a more modern sense, ratcheting up the pressure to grow and borrow that capital to pay debts and stirring up a furious storm of competition to monopolize trade routes. War and conquest became common as monarchs were compelled to look far afield for new sources of cash flow, at first in the form of gold, jewels, textiles (especially silk), and porcelain. But of all these luxuries, the most influential turned out to be something we've come to take for granted: spices.

Wealthy Europeans were obsessed with spices. Pepper, nutmeg, cinnamon, cloves, and sugar—originally considered a spice of sorts and even considered a medicine—made food taste different, sometimes wonderfully so. Spices were also used in scented medicines and many perfumes, important in masking the unpleasant and omnipresent odors of waste and death.

Most of these goods came to Europe via the Silk Road, which

stretched as far as China, Southeast Asia, and even Indonesia. Though it was called a road, much of the route was by sea, and its far end was unknown to almost everyone in Europe, since trade was the domain of middlemen from North Africa and the Middle East. That was frustrating to European businessmen, and it kept goods costly.

In 1453, when Constantinople fell to the Ottomans, who closed all the trade routes except Alexandria-to-Venice, items from the East became so expensive that not even the aristocracy could afford them. If they wanted exotica from Asia, they had to create new ways to trade.

This was an opportunity, and it spoke to monarchs like Ferdinand and Isabella, whose marriage created a unified Spain powerful enough to expel the Moors from southern Iberia in 1492, and for whom wealth and glory were top priorities. Eager to find their own route to the spice trade—and ostensibly interested in spreading Christianity, though this was little more than a rationale for opportunism—Ferdinand and Isabella were primed to back exploration.

And exploration was exactly what the Genoan Cristòffa Cónbo (better known as Christopher Columbus) pitched to the monarchs, convincing them to finance his trip, whose goal was (ostensibly) India, but whose end point would soon be called the Americas. If he hadn't "discovered" America, another European would have done so before long. The name would've been different, but it's unlikely that much else would have changed.

A few years later, the Portuguese Vasco da Gama, via the Cape of Good Hope, succeeded where Columbus had failed, making the first known direct sea voyage from Europe to India. His men, landing in Calicut (Kerala), shouted, "For Christ and spices." Colonialism, imperialism, capitalism, and all that went with them had arrived.

While Columbus may have come up short on his promises, his successors delivered by exploiting the land and its people. As a result, two intertwined "products"—sugar and slaves—rose above all others in the quest to satisfy Europe's demand for wealth.

The first evidence of sugarcane's existence was found in New Guinea, and dates to about ten thousand years ago. Cane made its way to Asia a couple of thousand years later, and the process of refining it into sugar is believed to have originated in India sometime before the time of Christ. Europeans found sugar production in the Middle East and North Africa during the Crusades.

Sugar and slavery may have been linked as early as the fourteenth century, according to J. H. Galloway, who writes in *The Sugar Cane Industry: An Historical Geography from Its Origins to 1914* that labor on Crete and Cyprus, two early European sugar-producing islands, "became scarce because of the ravages of war and plague; in response to this shortage slave labor was increasingly used."

Cane must be cut when it's ripe and processed immediately, or else it will spoil, so processing was always local. It's complicated, laborious, and by all reports torturous work, beginning with harvest and milling and continuing with a series of evaporation and crystallization techniques.

You need a lot of well-orchestrated labor (and a lot of water — about three hundred gallons per pound) to make sugar, which has led some scholars to refer to the sugar-making process as the beginning of industrialization.

And because sugarcane quickly depletes soil, new land was a constant requirement. As a result, sugar production steadily moved west from the Mediterranean, first to Spain and then to the Portuguese island of Madeira, in the Atlantic.

Madeira is often thought of as the first casualty of the so-called Age of Discovery, because it was deforested for its wood (*madeira* means "wood" in Portuguese), then planted with wheat before becoming, in the fifteenth century, the world's leading sugar producer. The Canary Islands and São Tomé, a tiny, previously uninhabited island just off the west coast of Africa, followed soon after.

When, in Columbus's wake, the Spanish and the Portuguese stumbled upon and conquered the islands of the Caribbean, they brought sugar production and slavery with them. And when the Europeans brought sugar across the Atlantic, they also better organized the slave trade. Indigenous workers were dying of disease and maltreatment, and the Europeans themselves refused to fill the labor void. Instead, by the sixteenth century, they were kidnapping people from West Africa to do the work for them.

Thus began the notorious triangles of trade that treated humans as agricultural machinery: Tools and supplies from the homeland—mostly Britain, which by then had semi-colonized Portugal—were sent to both Africa and the colonies. Humans were bought, traded for, or outright kidnapped in Africa and then transported to the ever-expanding colonies across the Atlantic. Sugar and molasses, a by-product of sugar production used to make rum, were shipped from the Americas back to Europe. And the cycle continued.

While it's a stretch to say that sugar was the sole reason for slavery's existence—the primary factor was the money behind the sugar, of course—there's no other food product whose growth was as dynamic or universal, which spawned so much trade, including the horrifying trade in humans, and whose demand matched its supply so closely. No matter how much sugar was produced, it was always readily shipped and sold.

Neither coffee nor tea nor tobacco—all popular luxury goods —saw the same kind of growth that sugar has seen over centuries. In 1700, England's annual per capita consumption was about five pounds. By 1800, that had risen close to twenty pounds, and in 1900 it was nearly a hundred. It topped out there globally over the centuries, though per capita annual consumption in some countries (including the United States) is more than one hundred pounds even now—close to ten tablespoons per day.

Those other luxury products, discovered by the Europeans at roughly the same time, were all turned into objects of marketing and trade, and they all gave further impetus to imperialism and colonialism. As the late legendary sugar scholar Sidney Mintz says, the English quickly understood that "the whole process—from the establishment of colonies, the seizure of slaves, the amassing of capital, the protection of shipping, and all else to actual consumption—took shape under the wing of the state."

Thus, the world's most far-reaching and powerful empire was borne on the backs of Brown and Black humans and the sale of sugar, cotton, and a handful of luxury commodities that quickly became "necessities" for Europeans, whose wealth was increasing as the empire grew.

Slavery's impact can hardly be overstated. What began as a brutal way to produce food for the rich helped establish a pattern of global food production that became the norm. Food was no longer something you cultivated outside your door to feed your community. It was produced far afield, by exploited labor overseen by strangers, then shipped in previously unimaginable quantities to supply huge markets. It didn't take long for the Americas to become the center of this kind of food production. And the costs to nature and humans were even more staggering than the profits.

An exchange is defined as a trade for something of equal or near-equal value. In what's usually referred to as "the Columbian Exchange"—one of history's great misnomers, given the genocide that followed—Europe took so much of value from the Indigenous people of what became known as North and South America that it was able to rule most of the world until the mid-twentieth century. The riches Europeans reaped included the land of two entire continents and all that was found there, including literal boatloads of silver and other raw materials of immeasurable worth.

Also inestimably valuable were America's native foods: corn (now, according to the UN's Food and Agriculture Organization, the world's second most important crop by weight), potatoes (the fifth most important), sweet potatoes (sixteenth), cassava (usually in the top ten), and a host of other foods, from avocados to quinoa and a wide variety of legumes, including peanuts.

Famously, there were also chiles—erroneously called peppers by Columbus, who, in his refusal to see reality, regarded Native Americans as the "Indians" that he was searching for and sought to sell their crops as exotic spices. Chiles became as popular globally as they had been in Mesoamerica, although not in palate-challenged Northern Europe.

These foods were global game changers, radically altering the cuisines, agricultural priorities, and nutritional profiles of the rest of the world, as many of the "new" crops grew well on previously unproductive land.

And what did the Europeans bring to this "exchange"? In addition to outright murder, smallpox, measles, flu, dysentery, tuberculosis, anthrax, trichinosis, and other diseases, as well as slavery, oppression, land theft, an historically violent religion, and cultural destruction—just about everything terrible that can happen to a civilization.

Until then, the people of what are now the Americas were mostly fortunate. Endemic staples like those mentioned above— corn, potatoes, cassava, sweet potatoes, and legumes—were more productive than wheat, barley, oats, and millet, and as productive as rice. And there was more: tomatoes, pineapples, strawberries, and blueberries, a wide variety of squashes, melons, and other cucurbits, several kinds of tree nuts, chocolate (to some, the world's most important crop), and tobacco.

These foods, along with abundant, fertile land, more-than-adequate water in most places, generally favorable climates, and mostly sustainable agriculture, had largely protected original inhabitants from want and starvation. They'd also helped build great cultures. Hundreds of tribes (and thousands of "tribelets") established full-fledged societies and cities, formed alliances, and advanced science, agriculture, record-keeping, art and architecture, and more, from Tierra del Fuego to the Arctic.

None of this could protect them from the conquistadors. Within fifty years, Spain controlled more than half of the New World, trade of goods across both great oceans was common, and the most horrendous genocide in the world's history was well underway. As many as one hundred million Indigenous people died— representing ninety percent of the Indigenous population and about twenty percent of the earth's total population at the time —which was far more than were killed by the plague in Europe and at least the equal of the great wars of the twentieth century.

The environmental consequences were equally dramatic, if perhaps a little slower to develop. Shortly after they began to arrive in numbers, the Europeans embarked on a campaign to establish their own foods in these new lands, shunning the existing tortillas or potatoes or turkey or guinea pigs or beans: They wanted their pork and bread. When Hernando de Soto, in 1539, brought thirteen pigs to what is now Florida, they began to breed. And because a sow can give birth to twenty piglets a year, there was soon enough pork to satisfy the invaders.

Just as Indigenous people had no resistance to either the bacteria or the viruses brought by the Europeans, there were no natural predators of these new four-legged animals, which proceeded to multiply without restraint. By the mid-1600s the Europeans were bringing cattle as well as pigs, and meat, hides, tallow (for candles), and dairy all became less expensive and more common throughout the Western Hemisphere than they had been in Europe.

At first these newly arrived animals were entirely free-range. In Europe, farmers needed fences to keep their animals in or out, or to prevent poaching, but neither was much of an issue for farmers in pre-Columbian America, where the concept of land "ownership"—as in deeds, transference, inheritance—didn't exist. When land was farmed by one person or group, the borders were simply known and respected by others. When land was fallow, it was open for foraging or hunting by anyone.

Much of this land was already in cultivation by the Indigenous people, often governed by intertribal agreement. But in no case did food production require fences. Whether the Europeans deluded themselves into believing that the land wasn't in use is not the point: They wouldn't have cared even if they'd known otherwise. What mattered is that there were practically no limits to what they could take for themselves, and they proceeded to steal the most productive land and turn it into plantations, haciendas, farms, or pasture for their invading animal species.

Eventually the Europeans fenced in much of the land that could be owned, bought, and sold at a profit. They established monoculture and used the surplus for global trade, and their property laws reshaped the landscape to suit the occupiers' traditions of ownership and agriculture. Those Indigenous people who survived, many of whom had lived in agricultural communities for centuries, resorted to nomadic hunting.

It's impossible to imagine the tumult that had come to the earth in such a short time. A century before, almost every human spent their entire life within a few miles of where they were born. Most were only rarely affected by human-caused external events. Of course, there were wars, invaders, and crusaders, and these occasionally affected the general population, but, generation upon generation, the daily lives of all but a small percentage of living people were isolated and, even if poor, fairly stable.

The riches coming out of the Western Hemisphere quickly changed life for millions, and eventually for almost everyone on earth. While the Indigenous population of the Americas was all but wiped out, the plundered bounty of their land brought unprecedented population growth to the rest of the world.

The cost of bread and even the cost of living in much of Europe tripled, leading to what historians refer to as the "price revolution" and the general crisis of the seventeenth century: food riots, famine, poverty, and malnutrition, which led to the revolutions and wars of the next two hundred years and then some. All of these were growing pains of building a new system of production and trade.

The French, Dutch, Spanish, Portuguese, and British had taken over most of the world, with riches an obvious driver. But it's easy to forget that the land itself, and its potential to provide desperately needed food, was an important motive. And over the next couple of centuries, European powers enslaved Indigenous people, forcing them to farm their newly conquered land for luxury goods like tea, coffee, and sugar, stunting economic growth by establishing cash-crop monoculture as the primary (and often only) industry, mostly for the benefit of Europeans. They first worked Indigenous people literally to death, and then turned elsewhere for free labor, kidnapping and enslaving millions of Africans and establishing a global economy in which humans became the commodity, the engine that kept an entire continent fed. And they used the profits from the whole operation to build and buttress their industrial and financial sectors at home and the presence of their military and political machines abroad, ultimately depriving the conquered and coerced territories of natural development, or indeed of any of the fruits of their forced labor.

It's not likely that the colonizers felt remorse over the damage, because their methods were justified by the kind of thinking popularized by René Descartes, who in the seventeenth century unveiled a proto-scientific understanding of the world that divided the earth into two kinds of matter. There was sentient, alive, and intelligent matter—almost exclusively the minds of educated white men—and then there was the rest of existence, called "extended." This simplistic view of nature is known as mind-body (or Cartesian) dualism, and its impact on even today's thinking can't be overstated.

Descartes's second category, the extended sector, included almost everything in nature: animals, forests, and rocks, as well as emotions and whatever is seen as "irrational." It also included most humans, who were seen as bodies, lifeless containers for brains that were more "wild" than they were "thinking." Women, uneducated men, and "savages"—all of these were "extended," another way of saying inferior.

Thus, *all* women and people of color were lumped in with animals (whom Descartes saw as noisemaking machines), minerals, mountains, soil, you name it—and all of this was placed under the domain of white men. Positioned as a form of scientific thinking, Cartesian dualism was really no more than an extension of the religious rationalization of white male supremacy.

This way of thinking bonded racism, sexism, the destruction of the earth, and the enslavement of its people. As Naomi Klein wrote in *This Changes Everything*, "patriarchy's dual war against women's bodies and against the body of the earth were connected to that essential, corrosive separation between mind and body—and between body and earth—from which both the Scientific Revolution and Industrial Revolution sprang."

If you wanted a global, industrial economy, as the nascent ruling classes did, peasant agriculture and its accompanying way of life had to die, regardless of the consequences. And that's exactly what happened. By the seventeenth century, after ten thousand years during which almost everyone farmed or at least depended on local farming, everything changed. The old ways had been sacrificed to give birth to a new god—what's euphemistically called the market economy, or what we know as unrestrained capitalism.

It would take Western science centuries to develop a truly rational branch of thinking, one that recognizes that everything is connected—the body, the natural and spiritual worlds, the wondrous and the inexplicable and the irrational. That branch of thought, the opposite of Cartesian dualism, is called ecology. Before that way of thinking could emerge, however, the world would first need to suffer the consequences of capitalism's reckless relationship with food firsthand.

4

Creating Famine

EVERYBODY'S EATING HISTORY is a unique story, one that in part defines us. I grew up in New York, a city of immigrants, the son of first-generation Jewish Americans whose parents came from Poland, Romania, and Czechoslovakia, though three out of my grandparents' four villages are in different countries now than when they left. I never felt like anything other than an "American," but I was repeatedly made aware of our relative newness. The Irish Americans, whose ancestors had arrived fifty years before mine and matched us in numbers in our Manhattan neighborhood, were way better established.

I knew next to nothing about my Irish neighbors, except that they went to Roman Catholic churches and schools (I remember this being confusing, the Irish/Rome thing) and were rumored to drink too much and eat potatoes.

That last part wasn't unfamiliar: We were potato eaters, too. Whenever my younger sister and I didn't appreciate the food our mother had cooked, my father was quick to remind us that he'd grown up eating boiled potatoes, "with sour cream when we were lucky." My Sicilian friends were reminded that in their old country, bread was often wiped on a single anchovy that hung from the door. Some of the Irish grandparents talked about dinners of "potatoes and point"—you'd point to where the ham would have been hung, if there were one, and went about eating your potatoes. My family wasn't entirely humorless, but no one even talked about the old country.

Our potatoes were usually mashed, sometimes with sour cream, and we had come a long way from the Depression years of my parents' childhoods: They were a side dish. We ate meat almost every night—usually beef, but sometimes lamb or chicken, and occasionally pork. My mother stopped keeping kosher when I was two.

This being the fifties and barely post-Holocaust, most of what was known about our family's past was tragic. Cut off at the roots, we had lost all history beyond a couple of generations. By all accounts, my great-grandfathers were tailors and bakers. I knew my maternal grandparents once owned a restaurant, in which my grandmother cooked. My grandfather was a waiter. Like many Jews of my generation, I had an indeterminable number of relatives who died in the Holocaust, and those who did make it to America fled from difficult-at-best lives racked by hunger, poverty, and persecution. My grandparents' stories about the old countries involved mostly random anti-Semitic acts of violence or vandalism, which became bad enough for them to embark on the adventure of emigration that was then becoming more common.

The Irish had a different story. Fifty years before my grandparents were born, for a brief period beginning in 1845, something like a quarter of the population of that country either emigrated or died of starvation. This was the Irish Potato Famine, the worst demographic tragedy in Europe since the plague.

It wasn't the fault of the potato—no real food is "bad"—but of people's dependence on it. That dependence was just one result of the Columbian Exchange, and the outpouring of riches from the Americas that followed. At or near the top of the list of these prized foods was the potato.

There are hundreds of varieties of wild potatoes endemic to the Andes region and thousands of cultivars bred from them. Potatoes grow well in an incomparable range of conditions. They require little tending, as their flesh is underground and therefore less vulnerable to rain, wind, heat, and so on. And they are tremendously productive, producing more calories per acre than even corn. They can also be made to last almost indefinitely. In the Andes, Quechua and Aymara people developed chuño, a freeze-dried potato that is lightweight and can be stored for years.

When the Spanish brought the potato to Europe in the mid-sixteenth century, most people were too blinded by arrogance and tradition to recognize its value, and many considered it poisonous. But root vegetables were nothing new, and soon enough the potato was being grown for animal fodder. By the end of the eighteenth century it had become a widespread staple, credited not only with ending famine but with boosting population in just about every country where it became popular.

Nowhere was this more prevalent than in Ireland. In a pattern set by post-feudal landowners and repeated throughout the colonial era all across the world, the best land in Ireland had been enclosed and was used either for grazing cattle or for growing corn and other crops; most of this was tended by impoverished Irish sharecroppers before being shipped across the Irish Sea.

What was left for the native population was small plots of land perfect for the potato, and so by 1800 Ireland had become a country of smallholders, most with "farms" under an acre in size, who ate potatoes several times a day. Some estimates put daily per capita potato consumption at twelve pounds, and nearly half the population ate almost nothing but.

Despite what you might have been led to believe, the Irish thrived on the potato diet. Because contrary to reigning current opinion, if there were such a thing as a superfood (there really isn't), potatoes would be on the list, ahead of berries, avocados, green tea, and many other heralded foods. Especially when eaten skin-on, potatoes contain most of the important vitamins, including vitamin C (they effectively ended scurvy in many countries), minerals, fiber, and protein. Add a little milk and you have a nearly complete, if unexciting, diet.

Eating potatoes, then, can be a good thing. And in Ireland, between 1780 and 1840, infectious diseases and infant mortality decreased, life spans increased, and the population *doubled* to eight million, mostly thanks to the potato.

But the potato crop was vulnerable. As I said, the Irish famine of the 1840s wasn't the fault of the potato. The blame falls on *Phytophthora infestans*, the microorganism that began the blight. It falls on the British for their exploitative extraction of cash crops overseas, which the starving Irish poor couldn't afford to buy and the British wouldn't give. And it falls on the dominance of monoculture, which saw entire plots of land devoted to a single crop. Not only were many of the Irish growing only potatoes; they were growing only one *type* of potato.

Potatoes do produce seeds under some conditions, but those seeds don't often "breed true," or produce plants with the same characteristics as their parents. So most potatoes are grown from chunks of potatoes (the "eye" is the sprout) and have identical characteristics—they are, in fact, clones. And although Andean farmers had developed more than four thousand varieties of potato, bred to thrive in different soils, seasons, locales, climates, and elevations, most of the Irish had only one clone. As it happened, that clone was susceptible to the blight, and when the blight attacked, it was all over.

No one knows exactly how many Irish went blind (a symptom of smallpox, one consequence of the famine), led otherwise diminished lives, died, or simply left, most to America.

The Irish Potato Famine is famous, but it's hardly unique. Famines have been a part of human history from the beginning. The horrible irony, however, is that once agriculture had advanced enough to nourish all the world's people, famines only became even more common and horrific, a direct result of imperialism and colonialism, which demanded of agriculture not food for people, but goods for market.

To paraphrase Frantz Fanon, colonialism meant that the riches of the rest of the world were stolen to create a powerful, beautiful, and cultured Europe. And by the eighteenth century, not only luxuries, like spices, tea, and sugar, but real food, like grain and meat, was being shipped around the world, often grown in one place for consumption in another. Under colonial regimes, cash crops and monoculture were fast becoming the norm, and maximum productivity for maximum immediate profit was the goal.

Soil health was often ignored until crop size diminished, and the "cure" for dwindling crops was less fallowing, crop rotation, and cover-crop use, and more fertilizing. The problem was that fertilizer was in limited supply.

Humankind's inability to maintain soil health while pushing productivity to the maximum was making it apparent that agriculture would eventually fail to keep up with population growth, leading to a new and horrific era of famine. Representing this pessimistic view was the Englishman Thomas Robert Malthus.

In 1798, Malthus published *An Essay on the Principle of Population*, predicting that the numbers of humans would soon be doubling every twenty-five years but that agricultural production could increase only incrementally. Therefore, he reasoned, food security was unachievable without drastic solutions — whether "positive," by which he meant more deaths, or "preventive," by which he meant birth control, later marriages, abstinence, and abortion.

A careful reading of Malthus shows that he was not necessarily a doomsayer: His essay was a cogent and insightful analysis of the reality of the late-eighteenth-century agricultural economy. In fact, agricultural production *couldn't* keep up with population growth at that point, at least not with the techniques available then. And, in fact, global starvation has been stabilizing, in large part thanks to birth control.

But to this day, Malthusian rhetoric is contorted into a lame device for those who argue that only input-intensive agriculture can prevent starvation. Whenever you hear someone wail, "How are we going to feed the ten billion?" you are hearing the legacy of Malthus.

That question *sounds* reasonable, but the answer is far more complex than simply boosting production. Food security isn't just an agricultural issue; it's a political issue. Hunger is not a symptom of underproduction but of inequality, of abusive power and wealth. Even in Malthus's time, this was fast becoming evident.

The truth is there could be enough food for everyone if farming were to prioritize human and soil health. Instead, the past couple hundred years have seen once-resilient and thriving societies decimated by famine. Unlike most precolonial famines, which were the result of agricultural underproduction or environmental disaster, these more frequent famines were the result of hostility, abuse, racism, greed, and neglect by the state.

And—no surprise—the United Kingdom, which in the early twentieth century controlled a quarter of the world, was most often culpable, although other governments, especially those of Stalin and Mao, would cause fewer but even more catastrophic famines. The first modern, environmentally triggered, and politically exacerbated famine was in Ireland. But it was far from an isolated incident.

At the time of the Potato Famine, Ireland was part of the UK, so not technically a colony. But its Catholic people farmed land that they couldn't own, raising crops and livestock to pay rent to English landlords. They had more in common with the people of the colonies than with the colonizers.

They also had no cash and no crop reserve, so although the catalyst for the famine may have been the potato blight, the real killer was the trade-based economy, which shipped the bulk of food grown in Ireland elsewhere, with most of the profits going to absentee landowners.

Losing a crop is never a good thing, but it becomes deadly when the system has been so perverted that there are no communal resources held in reserve, and people can no longer care for one another. When no help comes from outside, a lost crop becomes a famine.

The British response to the crisis in Ireland was informed by the ideologies of Malthus and Adam Smith, the latter among the founders of modern political economy, famous for coining the term "invisible hand" to describe the miracle of the market. His writings on famine insisted that government interference, either by lowering the prices of goods to help struggling communities or directly providing aid—cash or food, or both—would only worsen matters by draining supply. What he hadn't anticipated was the total crop failure experienced in Ireland, because the potato wasn't integrated into European society at the time, and a complete grain failure is far more rare. This may be why his assertions sound so cruel in light of the Irish catastrophe, but they were nonetheless divorced from their context and invoked by British officials who opposed sending aid to the Irish.

An especially cynical reading of Malthus and Smith's theories insinuates that the people who "deserved" to live would find a way to survive, and that death by famine was either "God" or "natural laws" telling us that the world could not support its current population.

This way of thinking was used as a justification for greed and cruelty. English Poor Laws, adapted for the "lazy" Irish, held that those who worked more than a quarter of an acre of land were too comfortable to qualify for assistance. And yet those farmers could barely pay their rent, and their land was only becoming less productive. Hundreds of thousands of Irish eventually fled their farms to join public works programs.

These programs were Dickensian levels of horrible. As the British pressured local Irish municipalities to finance them, towns were plunged deeper into debt, and cost cutting became a top priority. The result was that no one in these state-sponsored programs was paid enough to feed their families. By Smith's standards, even these programs constituted too much interference and would keep the free market from working its magic. If this sounds familiar, it's because little about ruling economic theory has changed in the time since.

Workers who'd originally been paid by the day were soon paid for piecework. In other words, starving people were being forced to produce more just to earn enough to eat. This is not unlike the employment requirements for food stamps that opponents of a social safety net have long advocated for.

Had the Irish been allowed to grow crops for their own families on the land they worked, other crops could have filled in for the potato crop lost to the blight. Instead, their land, labor, and livestock were all feeding the English, while the Irish were written off as justifiable victims of natural law. And this was explicit, according to historian James Vernon: "Charles Trevelyan, knighted for his handling of the famine when he was an assistant secretary at the Treasury, reflected that the potato blight was 'a direct

stroke of an all wise and all-merciful Providence,' which had provided overpopulated Ireland with 'the sharp but effectual remedy
by which the cure is likely to be effected.'"

And so the starving Irish left their farms to work on road and
bridge construction in near-slave-labor conditions that encouraged dysentery and typhus (known as "famine poison"), the most
common causes of death at the time.

Eventually, in 1847, with the public works programs overwhelmed by starving Irish, the British established soup kitchens
to feed people directly and free of charge. After all the suffering,
it turned out that free aid was an effective way to alleviate death
and disease. Imagine that!

But the damage had been done. About a million people had
died, and a million more had emigrated. What's more, the British didn't seem to learn from the experience. Rather, they used
this tragedy as the rubric for how to handle crop failures in other
countries under their control.

In fact, this pattern would play out globally. Death counts increase while the myth of the free market justifies mass casualties
by painting the poor as unmotivated, complaining, lazy, stupid,
or all of the above, while ignoring the circumstances colonialists
created.

Like many or even most white middle-class children of the fifties
and sixties, I was told to finish my dinner because "children are
starving in India" (or China). No doubt some were, just as some
were within miles or blocks of our apartment.

But as we've already seen, famine was hardly unique to Asia.
Nor, historically, was wealth confined to the West. In 1700, China
and India each had just over twenty percent of the global GDP
(gross domestic product, or the measure of all goods and services
produced in a given period). That was the equivalent of the entire
continent of Europe.

By 1890, however, Europe's GDP had doubled. Those of China
and India had halved.

Before the establishment of the Raj, many regions of India had
complex and effective systems for regulating their food supply,

along with legal systems that adapted to local farming styles. Some areas were more productive than others, of course, but there was a track record of caring for peasant populations. One Bengali norm that survives today is to give food to those in need "ungrudgingly."

Until the British East India Company (called, by the historian William Dalrymple in his book *The Anarchy* "the first great multinational corporation, and the first to run amok") took over in the late seventeenth century, the Mughal Empire was a paradigm of wealth. Not only was its GDP among the world's highest, it also controlled a quarter of the global manufacturing market, mostly through clothing shipped to Europe. Its workforce largely comprised artisan weavers, who had more economic power and enjoyed higher standards of living than European peasants and industrial factory workers.

But Britain was more interested in nonindustrial colonies that would simply supply raw material for the motherland's own factories, so it forced India to deindustrialize, levying crushing taxes on India's manufactured products to protect Lancashire's growing textile industry. As a result, India's share of the global manufacturing market fell to less than three percent by 1880, a theft of value that in today's currency would be worth trillions of dollars.

This isn't just a numbers game: In the two millennia preceding English colonization, only seventeen famines were recorded in India. During the hundred or so years of English rule, there were thirty-one. Put another way, India went from averaging less than one famine per century to averaging thirty per century, or one every three years. The half century of 1850 to 1900 saw more famines in India than in any fifty-year period in its history, and the famines were twice as deadly as anything that came before.

The catastrophe stemmed from a performance not unlike Britain's in Ireland. After establishing the Raj, the British swiftly and brutally restructured the peasant countryside, naming the government de facto landlord and forcing farmers to grow only cotton. The rational response from those farmers was to produce as much cotton as possible, even though cotton prices were low and unpredictable.

Production soared, increasing almost fourfold between 1791 and 1860. Per D. B. Grigg's *Agricultural Systems of the World*, the country became the world's second-largest producer of raw cotton, growing three times more than any area besides the United States.

This offered farmers no guarantee of income, however. The British wanted a steady cotton supply *available* in India, but they bought and traded in it only when it benefited them. For example, prices boomed in the lead-up to the American Civil War, when Britain feared disruption of American supply, but when the war ended, in 1865, Britain resumed purchasing its cheap cotton from the American South. Prices all across the globe crashed, and millions in India went hungry.

All of this coincided with an occurrence of the El Niño Southern Oscillation, a phenomenon that, every five to seven years, causes a large swath of the Pacific to become warmer than usual, disturbing the global climate and bringing either prolonged wetness or dryness throughout the Pacific Rim, southeastern Africa, parts of America, and most of southern Asia, including the Indian subcontinent.

El Niño is the kind of cyclical, less-than-predictable but always vaguely expected weather pattern that traditional Indian norms and political structures were designed to protect against. It was worse than usual when it arrived in the 1870s, causing mostly drought, but its impact should not have been apocalyptic.

However, in the face of agricultural catastrophe, the British punished their Indian subjects for their poverty the same way they had the Irish: by making them work for food. A result, in the three-year period beginning in 1876, famine killed more than five million people in India, and perhaps as many as ten million.

Rulers and subjects alike in India knew that the state's role in times of disaster should be to help the struggling. In China, that tradition began with the imperial dynasties in 221 BCE. The Confucian philosopher Mèngzǐ wrote that blaming starvation on a bad harvest was like "killing a man by running him through, while saying all the time, 'It is none of my doing. It is the fault of the weapon.'"

The Qing dynasty, which ruled China from 1644 to 1912, saw peasant prosperity as central to the stability of the empire. Generally, landownership was high and inequality low; the state trained farmers in irrigation and soil maintenance, and it regulated the price of wheat to guarantee that the market wouldn't be flooded. It also purchased surplus, storing grain for distribution during shortages and giving it to people for free—far more effective than waiting for invisible hands to do their work.

That system was all but destroyed by the new globalized economy engineered by the United Kingdom. The British demand for Chinese tea was obsessive. (Caffeine, as you probably know from experience, is addictive.) More than a luxury, tea was considered by the colonialists to be an engine for productivity: It kept the new industrial workforce caffeinated and was an excellent vehicle for the consumption of sugar. Perhaps just as important, ten percent of the British government's budget came from import taxes on tea.

But the imbalance of trade was out of hand. The British paid for tea with silver, and they were quickly running out of it. Silver is, after all, a precious metal and not easy to come by.

Something had to be done, and the solution was as cunning as it was evil. The British essentially became drug dealers with superpowers, ramping up opium manufacturing in India and then cultivating demand and addiction in China. They then substituted opium for silver as currency for tea and other goods.

When, in the 1840s, Qing officials demanded that the British respect their trade laws and cease or at least restrict opium imports, the British responded with overpowering force, bombarding cities, attacking with infantry, and extracting concessions from China on trade sovereignty and government power. These were the famous Opium Wars, designed to muscle China into "free" trade economies that would benefit the British Empire.

In the words of historian David Arnold, these blows sent the Qing dynasty down a "slippery slope of imperial decline, into poverty, decay and addiction on a scale almost incomprehensible today."

Within decades, Chinese grain reserves were at twenty percent of what they had been before British intervention, and half that again in some regions. Communities in northern China that had been among the most robust in the world fell victim to the El Niño events of the 1870s and '90s, and in the droughts of those two decades, more than thirty million Chinese people starved to death. The British once again chalked these deaths up to natural causes, and even claimed that the famines would have a positive impact if they convinced rulers to double their efforts to adapt to free market principles and further "modernize."

The British argument was that if the Chinese had only built railroads deeper into the countryside, they could have moved grain inland in time for these starving people to eat. But railroads are not built quickly, and, as Mike Davis says in *Late Victorian Holocausts*—the best analysis of famines driven by the combination of ecology and politics, and an important source here—while "in the eighteenth century [the government] had both the technology and political will to shift grain massively between regions and thus relieve hunger on a larger scale than any previous polity in world history," in the nineteenth, China's depleted government "was reduced to desultory cash relief augmented by private donations and humiliating foreign charity."

Millions starved while the British drank sugared tea, pushed opium, fixed their trade deficit, and financed colonial wars in South Africa, Afghanistan, and Egypt. And this famine destabilized the Chinese government for decades. Compounded by Japanese Western-style imperialism, it made China susceptible to the rule of Mao, whose own politically induced famine was even worse.

It should come as no surprise that colonization decimated social structures and orchestrated famines on the African continent as well. Before Europeans arrived in West Africa, farmers grew a dozen different life-sustaining grains, among them millet, teff, sorghum, and fonio, as well as yams and a wide variety of leafy greens. These plants were indigenous, hardy, and tolerant of temperature change, drought, and even infertile soil.

For example, an agricultural region surrounding Kumasi, Ghana's second largest city, did well even during a drought that began in the fifteenth century and lasted almost two hundred years. Archaeologists have determined that there was no shortage of food or shift in diet during that period. The combination of indigenous crops and a strong regional economy of craftspeople trading iron, pottery, and cloth had created a robust society with comfortable food security that continued to thrive despite generations of challenging weather.

But Europeans, beginning with the Portuguese in the mid-fifteenth century, destroyed those regional networks in favor of global trade. The imperialists brought heavy taxes and a preference for mining, urban development, and monoculture, in this case of cocoa and coffee. As in China and India, these luxury goods began to supplant the indigenous, life-sustaining crops, which the invaders categorized as "cattle feed."

This took a heavy toll on human health. Diets worsened, and it became increasingly difficult to put food aside for emergencies. The environment suffered, too. Farmland began to shrink, and the desert grew. The result was a society that went from being healthier and less famine-prone than its European contemporaries in pre-invasion days to experiencing chronic hunger.

Nor was this the only example: The French forced the planting of peanuts in Senegal, making farmers increasingly dependent on imports of rice, their traditional staple. Often, this rice came from French Indochina, a convenient and profitable arrangement for France. As rice prices increased, the Senegalese were compelled to plant more and more peanuts, sacrificing soil quality in the process.

The French were also responsible for famine in Niger in 1931 and in Gabon from 1924 to 1926. As usual, they blamed the crisis on those who were starving. David Arnold recounts that "French officials characteristically blamed African 'idleness,' 'apathy' and 'fatalism.'"

Colonizers and invaders fostered ideas of the African continent

as an unexplored, wild land filled with starving, uncivilized people, just as they fostered ideas of Indigenous Americans as wild
hunters and nomads. Globally, as Evaggelos Vallianatos writes,
"the violence of the old colonial system keeps resurfacing in the
bleak faces of malnutrition and hunger."

The British exploited the American colonies as well, which of
course was the main reason for the Revolutionary War. But unlike
India, North America was wide open for a kind of internal colonization. In the wake of the genocide of its Indigenous people, there
was virtually unlimited land, and a burgeoning market. From colonial days until well after the Civil War, there were several ways
in which native-born and immigrant Americans could readily ac-
quire land—as long as they were white and male.

One was to establish a charter company, such as the Plymouth
Company or the Virginia Company. That was unusual, but if you
were an early stockholder in one of those, you would be given
land to own or sell.

Then there was the headright system, originally established in
Virginia and later adopted by a few other colonies and mostly
limited to the seventeenth century. Under this system, you were
given fifty acres of land, and sometimes more, for every person
whose voyage to America you paid for—including yourself, your
family members, your indentured servants, and even your enslaved workers. So, for example, if you could afford to import sixty
slaves, servants, relatives, or any combination of the three, your
property would increase by at least three thousand acres.

You could also be given a direct grant of land by the king, or by
the village or the church. Later on, it was more common to buy
land for cheap, or you could simply move onto "unoccupied" land
and claim it for yourself.

The point, really, is that once the state claimed ownership of a
portion of land, regardless of whether it was still inhabited by Na-
tives, white males—the only citizens recognized by government
—could settle it and gain both title and the protection of the government.

Indigenous Americans did not think of land as alienable, sellable property. And yet, suddenly, those who fallowed and moved to new land every year or two could no longer farm. Other Indigenous farmers saw their land "legally" stolen and treated as a commodity, whose primary existence was not to grow a variety of foods to support its dwellers but rather to yield specific crops or raise one or two kinds of animals for trade.

Looked at one way, a group of people who understood nature and its workings was disposed of by another, one that believed that both nature and the people living in it were beneath consideration. (As for animals: There were originally thirty million bison on the Great Plains; by 1889 there were just over a thousand. Similarly, there were literally billions of passenger pigeons shot, netted, and even gassed without limit and packed into barrels until, by 1914, not a single one was left.)

In the eighteenth century, Europeans considered anything west of the Appalachians to be the "frontier," which came to mean "the furthest west place that white people didn't yet control." Even before the Constitution was finalized, Congress was taking land by fiat, beginning with the Northwest Ordinance. As the country's "first guarantee of freedom of contract," the Ordinance determined that all previously unowned land (Indigenous people "owned" nothing, by the invaders' definition) was now controlled by the federal government, and that land could be freely bought and sold.

The new arrivals had become federally mandated land grabbers, and all the while, the available land seemed to do nothing but grow. It's difficult to wrap your head around the rate at which, whether sold, given, or stolen, land was accumulated and transformed.

The phenomenon was enabled by a number of international events. In 1789, people of color in the French colony of Saint-Domingue (now Haiti) began a struggle against colonial rule and slavery. This was the year of the French Revolution, and following the successful American Revolution, more than a decade earlier, human rights were being discussed everywhere and actively fought for in many places.

Despite the efforts of Napoleon and others, Haiti became the first Caribbean nation to outlaw slavery and, by 1804, the second independent republic in the New World. This might have been reason to celebrate, yet better-established governments—including that of the United States—treated Haiti pretty much the way they would treat the Soviet Union more than a century later: with outright hostility.

Disheartened over the loss of Haiti, and fearful of the same fate befalling their North American colonies, the French agreed to sell those remaining colonies to the neighboring United States. This territory became known as the Louisiana Purchase. At a cost of fifteen million dollars, it doubled the size of the United States.

Because settlers in North America were driven mainly by land and greed, and because they were able to gain land mostly free of charge, they soon set their sights on the richer, more fertile, less rock-strewn soil that we now call the Midwest and the heartland. At first, these western regions were explored and exploited by hunters, trappers, traders, and isolated homesteaders, all willing to venture past the frontier to seek their fortune.

To these newcomers and those who followed, the incomprehensibly vast expanses of fertile, sunny, well-watered land were an irresistible draw. And, most incredibly, the government wanted them to have it.

Whether these pilgrims were fleeing religious persecution or only claiming to do so, the land grants they received from the Crown (and later the republic) were never meant to guarantee freedom or a good life in earnest. They were meant to allow white colonizers to claim and develop land as their own private property. As an exercise in wealth building for the privileged, it was brilliant.

So, long before *New York Tribune* editor Horace Greeley (or one of many others, as the quote predates Greeley's use) said, "Go west, young man," Europeans—northerners at first, primarily from Scotland, Ireland, Germany, and Scandinavia, but later southerners as well—began to settle the Midwest. It was the largest voluntary movement of humans from one continent to another.

Anything that got in the way of newcomers filling the conti-

nent was considered a nuisance, and often the most expedient solution was violence. Indigenous people were murdered or chased
or coerced or tricked off their land, for the most part legally. The
most egregious example was President Andrew Jackson's Indian
Removal Act, which resulted in the 1838 death march along the
Trail of Tears by the Cherokee people (along with those from the
Seminole, Choctaw, and other nations), exiled from their territory east of the Mississippi River to what is now Oklahoma. Some
Cherokee descendants still won't carry twenty-dollar bills, which
bear Jackson's face.

In many western areas, mining accompanied farming as the
first major industry. In some states, like coal-rich Pennsylvania,
West Virginia, and Kentucky and gold-encrusted California, mining even preceded farming and dominated the landscape for a few
decades.

But except in the most inhospitable or mineral-rich regions,
farming soon dominated the country as forests were cleared, rivers tamed, and hills leveled. The environment was transformed
entirely, with activity now centered around housing people and
producing food and other goods, mostly for trade.

The Louisiana Purchase enhanced the growing sense of "manifest destiny," that occupying the continent from the Atlantic to the
Pacific was the young nation's God-given right, with its northern
and southern borders also pushed to the extremes. Manifest destiny—a real estate marketing term, essentially—was a pseudo-
religious excuse to overrun, buy, and sell land. Credit for the term
is usually given to John O'Sullivan, a journalist and big influencer
of Presidents Jackson and Polk, both of whom can be thought of
as legal land grabbers.

In the 1840s, the United States instigated a war with Mexico,
and the resulting Treaty of Guadalupe Hidalgo forced our neighbor to cede, at a cost of less than twenty million dollars, the territories roughly equivalent to California and most of the five other
states of the Southwest—an area about equal to that of the Louisiana Purchase. In that same decade, the American government
annexed present-day Texas along with the eastern half of New
Mexico and a part of central Colorado, and the Americans and the

British negotiated a deal called the Oregon Treaty that effectively gave the United States the modern-day Pacific Northwest, Idaho, and parts of Montana and Wyoming.

With the addition of the Gadsden Purchase of 1853, the European Americans now claimed ownership of everything north of Mexico and south of Canada, an area of three million square miles, just a bit smaller than all of Europe. Although they were no longer technically in control of it—their brothers, or at least their descendants, were—the Europeans had taken over. All that remained was to fill this unimaginably broad expanse with white people.

To do that required improvements in transportation and communication. These improvements happened quickly, in the form of canals, roads, railroads, and the telegraph. It's difficult to pick a starting moment for this transformation, but the 1825 opening of the Erie Canal, which connected New York and other cities of the Northeast to the midwestern frontier, is a fine example of how things got going. The canal opened what was then "the West"—Ohio and beyond—in a new way, making it possible for people with no particular physical prowess or stamina, or even a pair of boots, to leave New York City and arrive in Ohio without breaking a sweat.

The pace of change was almost unimaginable, but the appeal of better, cheaper, and more abundant farmland drove both longtime residents and newly arrived immigrants to uproot everything, settle new land, and farm it in whatever ways were most profitable and, in the short term at least, efficient. Globally, land under cultivation nearly doubled in the nineteenth century, but that was nothing compared with the United States, where it quadrupled in the second half of the century.

Until the canal's opening, settlers either hiked or rode in carts or on horseback, and they got by for the first few months or longer either by hunting—though many of them initially had no clue how to do so—or on the food they brought with them: bags of cornmeal and dried beans, a barrel of salted pork, bottles or kegs of whiskey. Those who stayed in one place planted corn, raised pigs, made cornbread, salted pork, and distilled whiskey, as well as applejack, peach brandy, and any other alcoholic beverage that could be coaxed from whatever they grew or found.

It didn't take long before the United States ceased to be a few coastal urban centers backed by an inhospitable and forbidding interior. When California became a state, in 1850, it was just over sixty years after the passage of the Northwest Ordinance. Over those sixty years, the country had expanded from the Appalachians till it touched both the Atlantic and Pacific coasts, and all of the land in between.

And one could live quite nicely in places like Ohio, with regular shipments of manufactured goods from the East Coast. The appeal was so great that the new territories became a siren song for Europeans. Before the Erie Canal was completed, the number of immigrants per decade was about sixty thousand. Thirty years later it was close to two million. Nearly thirty million followed in the next seventy-five years.

Those immigrants were the tool by which an environment that had been sustainable for thousands of years was converted into an engine for tradable commodities. In the one hundred years that followed, agriculture would become an industrial behemoth that threatened air, water, the general public health, and the land itself.

5

The American Way of Farming

FOOD DRIVES HISTORY, and soil drives food. As industrial agriculture developed, it demanded more and more of the soil. That meant that fertilizer—until the twentieth century almost always in the form of human or animal waste—was in higher demand than ever. For trade and for the increasingly cash-based economy, agricultural success is rarely measured by the quality of one's crop, and almost never by the quality of one's soil; yield and volume are far more important than sustainability and long-term planning. The trick is to increase yield on any given amount of land, even if it's detrimental to that land in the long run.

By the nineteenth century, despite the emigration and urbanization of tens of millions of people, farmland had become overused and exhausted in Europe. The population continued to grow while some agricultural techniques had actually regressed. The kind of planning that allowed for soil replenishment was nearly abandoned, and the use of green manure and crop rotation (the eighteenth-century British agriculturalist Jethro Tull declared the latter unnecessary) were declining.

This is largely because "science" had emerged not so much as a tool for understanding how to farm, but as a framework for contorting nature into shapes that squeezed out the most profit. Per Descartes, Western logic often divided things understood by other cultures to be connected: people and the earth, men and women, the head and the heart.

This instinct to subdivide complex systems dominated scientific inquiry, and it advanced a framework that attempted to reorganize nature into deceptively simple components. This was the logic of reductionism, a way of thinking that can be traced at least as far back as Aristotle. Reductionism analyzes complicated things (bicycles, cities, humans) by breaking them into distinct parts (wheels and gears, streets and people, organs and cells). In theory, everything is the sum of its parts. So if you understand those parts, you understand the whole.

This black-and-white logic can sometimes work even for complex systems. But it ignores the complicated ways in which parts interact with one another. Reductionism may serve to explain how a bird flies, but not how a flock of birds move in unison. It may describe internal combustion, but not traffic patterns. It may describe electric patterns in the brain, but not consciousness, and it's unlikely that anyone or anything—not even the world's most powerful computers—will ever fully analyze the interactions that make for healthy soil.

But reductionist thought rendered those inexplicable wonders irrelevant. Likewise, in the world of agriculture, if there were elements of soil health or plant growth that could not be readily explained with a formula, they were simply ignored.

By the late nineteenth century, almost no European farmer could afford intentional fallowing. This was true in North America, too, which was by now a major player in the international economy. Why would a farmer take land out of production when the only way to create surplus—to have more goods to trade or sell—is to force the land to yield more? And even if crop rotation seemed feasible for a farmer, common sense demanded that the land be used to grow the crop that brought the most profit.

These relentless annual demands led to a crisis of soil depletion and even exhaustion. Eventually, it created a full-scale agricultural depression, especially in Western Europe, where the amount of manure generated by farm animals and humans was insufficient and, with time, was becoming more so. The fix, almost everyone believed, was more powerful fertilizers.

Plants need nitrogen, which as discussed can come from a variety of sources, including manure. But they also need potassium and phosphorus. Farmers everywhere knew that, at a minimum, they could get the former from potash (from the Dutch *potaschen*, literally "pot ashes") and the latter from bonemeal.

There was a long and lively trade in both: A form of potash had been mined in Ethiopia since the fourteenth century, and bonemeal was in such high demand that the remains of soldiers at Waterloo and other major battles were sold, ground, and resold, mostly to England. In America, frontier farmers used the ground bones of bison, which were in the process of being all but exterminated. Both potash and bonemeal—from animals, not soldiers—are still used as organic fertilizers today.

Even still, there never was enough manure. By 1840, the German scientist Justus von Liebig had determined that it was nitrogen that made manure so valuable. With Europeans desperate for that essential element, a temporary solution turned out to be another of those miracle cures resulting from the colonization of the Americas. Around 1800, the German naturalist Alexander von Humboldt embarked on a five-year expedition to the Caribbean, Mexico, and the northern parts of South America. There, off the coast of Peru, he observed—and smelled, "a quarter of a mile away"—ships traveling to and from the nearby islands.

These ships were carrying guano, which in Quechua, the Andean language spoken in the highlands by Indigenous people of the same name, means any kind of fertilizer from animal waste. In the rest of the world, the word was to become synonymous with the droppings of the local bats and seabirds, manure that is so high in nitrogen that direct application can burn plants' roots.

The locals knew that guano made an especially fine fertilizer, and they had developed methods for harvesting, transporting, and even distributing the stuff fairly and sustainably. Each household was assigned a share of the guano on a given island, and those who disobeyed the system were penalized. Like so many systems of Indigenous people, however, this one was destroyed a few decades after Humboldt's guano samples were analyzed back in Europe and discovered to outperform everything previously used to add nitrogen to the soil.

To the fertilizer-starved Europeans, guano was a godsend. Not only was it higher in nitrogen than other manures, but it had high levels of potassium and phosphorus as well. And better still, there was an unimaginably large store of it, a world's history's worth, all in one place.

Like the remnants of plants and animals that had turned into drillable petroleum, that guano was the accumulation of millennia. And, also like oil, it was ripe for the taking, as long as you were arrogant enough to discount the rights of local people. The Europeans found the piles of guano, and all they knew or cared about was that it solved a crying need and that it would make them ultra-wealthy. So they took it.

Had guano not made an appearance, it's conceivable that the pressure to research new crop rotation and green manure methods might have led farming in an entirely different direction, equally productive but healthier from every perspective.

But unfortunately, that's not how it went down. Wherever guano was sold, it reinforced the style of agriculture that ignored a holistic view of soil health and simply added nutrients as needed, and then some. Demand soared, and in the 1840s British imports of guano multiplied one hundredfold.

To be clear, as a superior composted manure, guano is a terrific soil builder. The problem was that it was a traditional product of a traditional society, and, like so many other treasures of the Western Hemisphere, that product was simply stolen and shipped to Europe. What's more, guano is a limited and nonrenewable resource.

The key to healthy agriculture is something approaching a closed system, in which soil's nutrients and even its non-nutritive physical components are, to whatever extent possible, locally recycled. In what would become one of reductionism's finest moments, guano-mania helped pave the way to two centuries of increasingly extractive and soil-depleting agriculture.

Methods of treating the soil became predictably and tragically

oversimplified, as it was incorrectly determined that plants didn't
need healthy soil and all that it contained—literally hundreds of
elements and compounds and trillions of microbes. According to
reductionist analysis, soil and plants quite simply needed nitrogen, potassium, and phosphorus.

Thousands upon millions of years of fertilizer was being carted
across the globe, only to be exhausted in decades. Europeans
would realize the folly of this approach over the following half
century—and especially after the development of chemical fertilizer—as it became clear that flouting the natural laws that prevent infinite growth was not a system built to last.

This shouldn't have been news to the Europeans. Newton had
discussed the finite nature of matter, and the ancient Greek Epicurus said, "The totality of things was always such as it is now,
and always will be." Even the arch-reductionist Liebig pointed
out the "folly" of operating as if "the Earth is inexhaustible in
its gifts." Similarly, Karl Marx critiqued the new style of farming as one of "robbing" the soil, and he lamented the end of "self-
sustaining agriculture" as early as 1861. A few years later, he described a "system of exhaustion in North America" where "it was
cheaper and more profitable to clear and crop new land than to
renovate the old." Needless to say, that cheaper, more profitable
style of agriculture became dominant.

British Parliament had struggled for decades to keep domestic
farming relevant and alive. It did so formally with the 1815 Corn
Laws, protecting its landowning class with steep tariffs on imports of corn, rye, barley, wheat, and many other foods. These
kept domestic food prices high and farm country happy. But as
crops became more abundant on the global market, it became
easier and cheaper to grow food abroad and import it. In 1846,
the Corn Laws were repealed, and tariffs were lifted on corn and
other grains and a few other food products.

Guano kept British agriculture going for a while, but with land
and labor at a premium, British agricultural self-sufficiency was
fast becoming as impractical as farming was for individual land-

owners. And with the rise of industry, more farmers were becoming factory workers, rural migrants competing in cities for cash wages, which plummeted. Still, food had to be affordable enough for this new class of wage laborers, who, to produce efficiently and remain peaceful, had to be kept at least minimally nourished. Since women cooked, tended children, and kept house without compensation, wages needed to cover food costs, rent, and little else.

These were historic developments: The UK's reliance on cheap imported food, combined with urbanization, meant that its agriculture would collapse. Indeed, the 1870s saw the "great depression of agriculture," which lasted until after World War II.

More than ever, agricultural products became global commodities, a phenomenon we now take as a given. With money, we can put bananas on the table every day and buy blueberries, tomatoes, mangoes, fresh tuna, and coffee anywhere at any time. Big farms and a global system provide many of us with almost all of the world's food at once.

But there were consequences to this availability. The first was more politically enhanced famines as free trade policies shifted food production overseas and eroded traditional agricultural communities' ability to farm for themselves. Former farmers fueled the Industrial Revolution, and new urbanites became "consumers," a class of people who earned money but produced almost nothing that they needed to survive.

Some parts of the world proved better at raising cheap food than others, and from the late nineteenth through most of the twentieth century, no country was better at doing so than the United States.

No farmland is perfect, but what came to be called America's heartland is among the most fertile, flat, and well watered on earth. At first, there wasn't even a need for fallowing or crop rotation. Much of the land was virgin, or had been well maintained for centuries by the sound agriculture performed by Indigenous people.

So it didn't take long for the spreading mass of newcomers to realize that the land's most profitable use lay in producing two major commodities — wheat and meat.

These drivers of westward migration shaped the land itself, water and energy use, patterns of settlement, and, ultimately, American diets. A century later, they shaped these same aspects of much of the rest of the world. And with the rise of industrial agriculture practices, wheat and meat production — wheat gradually being replaced by the more productive corn and soybeans — became the envy of the rest of the world.

Wheat, corn, and meat grew together, and because nineteenth-century Ohio, for example, could grow *way* more grain than even its burgeoning population could consume, much of it was shipped back east and even abroad. This was critical, as the young country relied immensely on its trade with Britain.

But shipping grain, even after the midcentury completion of rail lines, was burdensome, risky, and not always profitable. What were eastern city dwellers going to do with all that corn?

Like the reliance on imported fertilizer, the reliance on meat production may have ultimately been another bargain with the devil, but at the time the decision was easy. Animals, especially pigs, were a great way to convert grain into profit.

Simply put, if you feed six pounds of grain to a pig, it converts (roughly) to a pound of meat. That conversion varies from one animal to another — it takes more grain to get a pound of beef than a pound of pork, and less to get a pound of chicken. But that conversion, which can also be thought of as a concentration of nutrients, is a good thing if you're looking for a product that's easier to ship and more marketable than corn.

The pattern of using farmland primarily to grow food for trade became even more focused as grain was fed increasingly to animals instead of people and as those animals were sold for a profit.

A similar pattern would arise for distilling alcohol, which was considerably easier than animal husbandry. But daily drunkenness was eventually frowned upon, and alcohol consumption gradually decreased. Meat, however, became more and more popular.

Meat was always more valuable than plant crops, in part because of its concentrated nature but also because it was always in high demand and, until the nineteenth century, hard to come by. Especially once refrigeration became common, meat was also easier to process and ship than grain. Animals walk to processing plants under their own power, for starters. And, once slaughtered, they yield a product that is compact and relatively easy to handle. Grain was subject to rot, to attack by vermin, and simply to spilling off carts, wagons, and barges.

Before the advent of railroads, most meat and grain were shipped by water. By the 1820s the Erie Canal, the Mississippi River, and the port of New Orleans—obtained in the Louisiana Purchase—were all instrumental in the meat trade.

The powerful Ohio River, which flows into the Mississippi, also became more navigable in 1825, when a canal was built to bypass its falls in Louisville. This encouraged the growth of Cincinnati, which by 1850 was the biggest city in the West and produced more pork than any other place in the country, so much so that it became known as Porkopolis.

Pigs were the business of Cincinnati, a place where the animals roamed the streets so freely and in such numbers that they eliminated the need for garbage collection. Slaughterhouses and meatpacking plants cropped up all over town, and pork was cured (there was abundant salt from nearby Kentucky), packed into barrels, and shipped east for consumption or trade on the international market. Lard was rendered for soap and candles. Every other part of the animal was turned into something, from buttons to brushes.

Cincinnati's reign was short-lived, though. With the Mississippi largely closed to Northern trade during the Civil War —and with the northern spur of the up-and-coming rail system connecting New York to Chicago via Albany, Buffalo, and Cleveland—"Mud City," as Chicago was then known (it was built on a mudflat), seized its opportunity. While packing pork for Union troops during the Civil War, the city designated hundreds of acres to develop stockyards, which became the ultimate destination for the animals raised in the most productive cattle-grazing region the world had ever seen, the land west of the Mississippi.

The exploitation of that seemingly infinite landscape helped turn the United States into a powerful economic engine, and by 1870 Chicago was processing three million hogs and cattle a year, a number that was previously unimaginable. (New York's population of one million people consumed around that same number of animals each year.) The city became, in the words of Carl Sandburg, "Hog Butcher for the World," and by 1890 it was the second-biggest city in the country. The owners of its great packinghouses, with still-recognizable names like Armour and Swift, set up plants in a dozen fast-growing western cities and before long would pioneer the use of refrigerated shipping.

Meanwhile, the Great Plains — 500,000 square miles, representing about one-sixth of the area of the Lower 48 — were transformed into the world's greatest experiment in cattle breeding and raising. Cattle were taking over from pork, thanks to this unprecedently broad catch basin in which seemingly infinite numbers could graze, its proximity to Chicago, and, beginning in the 1830s, the thousands of miles of new rail that were laid each year. This ever-expanding system meant that the animals could be moved farther and farther west, just as their yield was carried east to feed the country. Colorado and Wyoming would soon become cattle-based states.

All of those cattle were what we'd now call "grass-fed." As cattle were meant to do, they grazed. And, like the bison preceding them, the cattle roamed the Plains without human intervention.

That all changed once farmers began to herd their cattle, driving them for hundreds of miles, crowded together and subjected to treatment that bred disease, exhaustion, and emaciation. Many cattle arrived in Chicago underweight and in otherwise poor condition. Some of these were slaughtered and packed, but others were fattened on grain. The feedlot system had begun.

As the cattle industry swept across the Great Plains, changing its flora and fauna forever as it went, and as the Northeast industrialized, the American South remained a stronghold for a singu-

lar, increasingly productive form of old-fashioned agriculture—
and its most shameful tradition.

The differences between pre–Civil War North and South were
stark. The South thrived as an agricultural subnation on the backs
of its enslaved people and in an ongoing dependent relationship
with Great Britain, while the North was fast becoming a modern
industrial state. But the two halves of the United States had this
in common: Enslaved Africans were the foundation of prosperity.
(*The Half Has Never Been Told*, by Edward Baptist, is a compelling
read on this subject.)

American slavery, the cruelest and most nakedly evil economic
system ever created, was a profitable and growing business. Mississippi was the richest state in the country at the beginning of the
Civil War, and, as Matthew Desmond writes in the *New York Times
Magazine*'s 1619 Project, "The combined value of enslaved people
exceeded that of all the railroads and factories in the nation."

The North may have abolished slavery, but it continued to grow
fabulously rich off the institution's value, industrializing early to
make textiles out of cotton grown by enslaved people while building wealth in finance, insurance, transportation, government, and
real estate.

Southern planters, meanwhile, were heavily indebted and re-
liant on an anachronistic way of life. When recession hit, as it
routinely did, other businesses could liquidate their holdings
and move out of sensitive markets. But the Cotton Kingdom was
trapped. "Their capital would not simply rust or lie fallow," wrote
historian Walter Johnson of the enslavers. "It would starve. It
would steal. It would revolt." To generate cash, plantation owners needed more cotton, and more cotton required more land and
more labor. In Johnson's words, "In order to survive, slaveholders
had to expand."

The protracted, violent removal of Native Americans from Ten-
nessee, Florida, Georgia, Alabama, and elsewhere satisfied plantation owners for a few decades. But enslavers and their politicians
dreamed of an American empire that included the Caribbean and

even extended down to Brazil. For years they pursued Cuba. In 1823, Secretary of State John Quincy Adams wrote that the "laws of nature" determined that the United States would eventually govern Cuba, and his sentiment had persisted.

American rule was attractive to the (white) Cuban-born sugar plantation owners who suffered when Spain outlawed slavery in 1845. In 1848 American president James Polk offered one hundred million dollars to buy Cuba from the Spaniards, and in 1854 government officials were arguing to take it by force. (That happened, though too late for slaveholders, in 1898, when the United States provoked a war with Spain and gained control of Cuba, Puerto Rico, Guam, and the Philippines.)

As manifest destiny became a popular slogan, the fracture grew between those who wanted more slaveholding states and colonies —Texas, Missouri, Kansas, Cuba, and Nicaragua were all prospects—and those who wanted to see white-owned land worked by white people moving west. The latter argued that freedom (for white men, of course) was, for the overall economy, preferable to slavery. And when it suited their needs, they argued that it was morally preferable, too. The Civil War was the result of this dispute.

The South's secession gave Northern legislators an unstoppable majority in Congress, and even before the war ended, Abraham Lincoln and his new Republican Party hustled to implement their interpretation of manifest destiny, to, in the words of John O'Sullivan, "overspread the continent allotted by Providence for the free development of our yearly multiplying millions." This overspreading was performed with the stated intent of removing and even killing Indigenous people while giving land to white men who were deemed worthy.

That process accelerated in 1862, when Lincoln and Congress joined to pass the first of several Homestead Acts, giving settlers 160 acres of land for a small filing fee if they kept a residence for five years, or for outright purchase at $1.25 per acre. This was the greatest land giveaway in history, and it was, of course, for white men only. Formerly enslaved people weren't eligible for this deal, nor were independent women, Indigenous people, or the Chinese, who made up the largest non-European immigrant group.

In all, about 270 million acres of "public" land, one-seventh of the landmass of the contiguous United States, was given away to homesteaders. In addition, the railroads were (ultimately) given upwards of 180 million acres, and, in short order, more than 80 million acres were sold to the highest bidder, usually for $1.25 per acre. Because land was so quickly turned into a financial asset, and owned by bankers, financiers, and speculators, it's easy to see how debt has figured so prominently in the plight of American farmers.

In all, more than a quarter of *all* of the nation's land was given away or sold for cheap, and since much of that total (two billion acres) is unfarmable mountains or desert, that quarter represents the majority of arable land. If you are looking for the roots of today's income inequality, you might start here, with a federal donation of land—the foundation of most wealth—to an exclusive club of white men.

Things could've developed differently. On the evening of January 12, 1865, twenty African American preachers sat with Union general William T. Sherman at his temporary headquarters in Savannah. Speaking for the group was Garrison Frazier, a sixty-seven-year-old Baptist minister who'd been enslaved for the first fifty-nine years of his life, until buying his and his wife's freedom for one thousand dollars in gold and silver.

Sherman asked the group to "state in what manner you think you can take care of yourselves, and how can you best assist the Government in maintaining your freedom."

It did not appear to fluster Frazier that the descendants of kidnapped and enslaved Africans were being asked what they could give to the federal government. He replied, "The way we can best take care of ourselves is to have land, and turn it and till it by our labor."

Sherman listened. A few days later, he issued Special Field Order No. 15, which promised that a stretch of coastline running thirty miles inland and stretching 250 miles from Jacksonville to Charleston would be designated for resettlement by African Americans. When asked whether they would like to live among white people, Frazier said, "I would prefer to live by ourselves, for there is a prejudice against us in the South that will take years to get over."

Forty acres of "tillable ground" would be allotted per family, provided the head of household enlisted with the Union "to contribute their share towards maintaining their own freedom, and securing their rights as citizens of the United States." Upon enlisting to fight with the Union, formerly enslaved people could put their pay toward "procuring agricultural implements, seed, tools, boots, clothing, and other articles necessary for their livelihood."

To work one's own land and reap the benefits can be seen as a fundamental element of freedom, and the one time the United States asked what former slaves wanted, this was their request. The 1862 Homestead Act had guaranteed that every "person who is the head of a family"—which excluded most women in letter, and all in spirit—and who is a citizen, which in 1862 excluded African Americans, was given the opportunity to fulfill this basic wish.

In disqualifying noncitizens, the act robbed enslaved people of land. But it also excluded those who had "borne arms against the United States Government." Yet even after African Americans became citizens, they were almost entirely excluded from the bonanza of the Homestead Act, whereas former Confederate soldiers—traitors—were welcome participants. Whether things would have been different if Lincoln had lived is moot, but after he was shot, President Andrew Johnson promptly overturned Sherman's Field Orders.

In a meager attempt to compensate for the Homestead Act's exclusion of Black people, the Freedmen's Bureau allowed former slaves to lease and eventually own land confiscated from enslavers. And, for a short time, the military enforced these regulations.

But that wouldn't last. And even though the forty acres Sherman promised to freedmen were just a quarter of the homestead normally granted to whites, it was more than the federal government delivered. Northern industry was more interested in workers than in subsistence farmers, and the notion that African Americans were going to get any reparations in the form of land grants faded almost as quickly as it started.

Furthermore, those former slaves who legally settled land they'd been forced to work before the war saw that land given back to their former captors by 1877. The returning landowners quickly set up a system of wage and tenant farming, along with a social system that included imprisonment, near slavery, Jim Crow laws, and lynching, devised to make sure Black people remained, for all practical purposes, perennially subjugated.

This trend blossomed. Since the Thirteenth Amendment outlawed outright slavery but allowed for penal servitude, an arrest was almost all that was needed to force former slaves and their descendants to perform free labor as prisoners. Although African Americans could no longer be bought and sold, they could (and their descendants can) still be separated from their families and lose their freedom.

Even before Reconstruction officially ended, many former slaves and their relatives gave up hope of a good life in the South and began the Great Exodus. The self-named Exodusters, comparing themselves to the biblical Israelites who fled slavery in search of a promised land, headed west, primarily to Kansas (a pre-war free state, and proud of it) but also to Oklahoma, Colorado, and the industrial North.

The era of African Americans as the United States' primary farmers had ended. Most Exodusters, like those who left the South for the North in the twentieth century, wound up in cities, and those who farmed mostly remained in the Deep South, often struggling to hold their land and make a living on it in the face of still hostile local and federal governments.

Had there been a fair redistribution of land in the last third of the nineteenth century, one that acknowledged the rights of Indigenous people, of women, of formerly enslaved people, and of other people of color, the twentieth century would have looked much different, with millions of additional small and medium farms run by families concerned about their land, the food they grew, and the communities around them. Instead, the federal government joined with former slaveholders to establish a system that remained unjust, and that increasingly focused on cash crops and monoculture.

It did so candidly and openly. In addition to the Homestead Act, 1862 saw the establishment of the United States Department of Agriculture and the passage of the Morrill Land Grant College Act, which allotted land for and led to the founding of many still well-known, mostly public universities, all of which existed to further the cause of high production at any cost.

Between them, the Homestead and Morrill acts (the latter was extended in 1890) would ultimately determine the future of agriculture and food in America and around the globe, and the goals were explicit: In 1863, the first commissioner of agriculture, Isaac Newton, declared that "the surplus of agriculture not only allows the farmer to pay his debts and accumulate wealth, but also does the same for the nation. To increase this surplus, therefore, to develop and bring out the vast resources of our soil, and thus create new additional capital, should be the great object of the Department of Agriculture and of legislation."

Newton went further: "It should be the aim of every young farmer to . . . do his best; to make two blades of grass grow where but one grew before." That statement shows a complete ignorance of nature, the world, and even the laws of the universe. Everything is finite, even the riches of land in America. Yet the nineteenth-century decline of European agriculture had created a void, and the world needed a cash crop to step in and fill it. That crop was wheat, it turned out, and in the words of Dan Morgan, author of *Merchants of Grain*, "the greatest market for food the world had ever seen" was ripe for anyone who was willing to grow and sell it.

No one could come close to the United States in doing that. The young country's railroads had expanded from 30,000 miles in 1860 to more than 160,000 miles by 1890, and this helped ensure that the new grain-growing territories would be occupied quickly and their product moved easily. The companies that would become Cargill, Pillsbury, and General Mills began building networks of grain elevators connected to those railroads and coordinating trades and global shipments. American wheat and flour exports more than tripled in the last three decades of the nineteenth century, and that was just the beginning.

Homesteaders, with the very real backing of a nation that wanted to grow at any cost, flooded into Wisconsin, Minnesota, the Dakotas, Nebraska, Kansas, and Colorado—first from Britain, Germany, and Scandinavia, and later from much of the rest of Europe. Between 1860 and 1890, the number of farms nearly doubled, to 4.5 million.

The economic engine that was America became the most powerful the world had seen. It was, in a sense, a vertically integrated version of a traditional colony. In other words, while Europeans drew wealth and power from materials extracted from colonies oceans away, the American homeland and colony were one and the same: The homeland *contained* the colony. Wendell Berry calls us "imperialist invaders of our own country," and although "we" were certainly at first imperialist invaders of someone else's country, it's a good point to make. America turned the traditional colonial model inside out, using its own natural resources to build an export system where all the profits remained at home. That was a first.

Much of the industry was financed by the act of trading itself, and the dramatic fluctuations in price made wheat buying especially attractive. Supply seemed to grow without end, feeding an international demand that was so novel and complex no one could understand it.

This unprecedented planting of millions of acres in such a rapid period created the agricultural surplus that has driven American society ever since, putting farmers in the challenging position of producing more not because demand was ever increasing (it was not), but to counter falling prices and to satisfy the traders who were making money in every instance.

Tariffs protected the budding industry. Liberal immigration policy (still mostly for white Europeans) helped keep the new labor flowing west. And because, as of 1883, grain could be sold as "futures"—meaning you could sell or buy a crop before it was even in the ground—farmers learned to operate on credit.

The developing system ensured that the homesteaders who helped fill new territories—and the void left by slavery—soon became themselves little more than suppliers, a permanently indebted class and a kind of cross between DIY industrialists and serfs.

None of these risk- and debt-ridden farms mattered at all to the new corporations, as long as they kept getting product to trade. Just like smallholders in nineteenth-century China and India, farmers were growing not for their benefit or that of their communities, but for a global cash economy. In the States, the risk wouldn't become starkly obvious until the Dust Bowl and the Depression, and those were now not far away.

The American grain machine, a monster of rail lines and grain elevators, stampeded across the midwestern plains like the buffalo it had replaced. Agriculture, along with railroads and finance, became a primary source of the nineteenth century's greatest fortunes. There were dozens of ways to get rich in agriculture, but farming itself was rarely one of them. Grain mills, elevators, heavy equipment, processing plants, transport companies, and more were growing rapidly, and milled flour was now worth twice as much as cotton. In the forty years that followed the Civil War, general manufacturing multiplied by a factor of six and food production kept pace, until it grew to make up a fifth of all industry.

And all of this needed coordination, a way to bring "rationality" and standardization to agricultural production. Thus was codified the American way of farming—a revolutionary approach that paralleled changes in manufacturing and became a global model for modern agriculture.

Although "modern" is an accurate enough word, in that it also means "novel," a better, if less commonly used, word for the style of farming that was being developed is "extractive." It's industrial-era agriculture that relies on machines to systematically take more out of the earth than can be replaced, and far more than the earth can afford. The pre-war South's reliance on monocropping and the export of cotton and tobacco was now becoming national policy, and the process was becoming mechanized. The field had become a factory, agriculture an industry.

That industry was represented in government by the Department of Agriculture, which had determined that industrialization and commodification, the *business* of food, was to come first. The well-being of farmers was a distant and incidental second. And eaters—well, they would take what the market gave them. Nourishment was barely even a consideration for the people who bought food. Farming to maximize healthy food for humans was never a goal, any more than was minimizing damage to the land and other creatures.

In fact, the goals of American agriculture were as simple as they were cynical: Increase surplus and create capital. From its birth, the USDA was designed to harness the political and economic power that comes with being an agricultural powerhouse. If the people and resources exploited to create that powerhouse were collateral damage, so be it.

PART II

The Twentieth Century

6

The Farm as Factory

W E USUALLY THINK of the Industrial Revolution as a story of factories, one that began in Britain, where steam power was first harnessed for machines that could, for example, run looms at faster rates than ever before imaginable.

But urban factories were only a part of the picture. Far from cities and their huge brick buildings, the farm was also industrializing. As Deborah Kay Fitzgerald notes in *Every Farm a Factory*, there are five characteristics of almost all successful factories: "large-scale production, specialized machines, standardization of processes and products, reliance on managerial (rather than artisanal) expertise, and a continual evocation of 'efficiency' as a production mandate."

The twentieth-century farm ticked all of Fitzgerald's boxes, as more change happened in agriculture in the century following the Civil War than in the previous hundred centuries combined.

And industrialization was moving west: The thick layer of millennia-old sod that covered the flatland over the Appalachians was incomparably productive—once it was broken. The major challenge for the new homesteaders flooding that area, however, was breaking it. The sod was so thick and tough that not only was it difficult to penetrate, but the clods would stick to old-fashioned plows, forcing frequent pauses for cleaning.

John Deere, a bankrupt blacksmith from Vermont who'd moved to Illinois in 1836, attacked the sod-busting problem with a plow that used a new shape and angle, one that featured a steel blade rather than a cast-iron one. He sold them differently, too. Rather than taking orders, Deere rolled his plows off a production line and found customers to buy them off the rack. By 1859 he was making ten thousand plows in a year and he had at least four hundred competitors, and this trend toward simplification and standardization continued.

Americans rapidly altered the ecology of the Plains by revolutionizing machinery. Then they revolutionized the machinery that made the machinery. The "American system" of manufacturing, which combined the might and speed of machines run by semi-skilled labor to replace expert craftsmen, became internationally famous at the 1851 Crystal Palace Exhibition, in London, also known as the Great Exhibition of the Works of Industry of All Nations. There, American manufacturers introduced guns made with interchangeable parts, which could be quickly repaired even on the battlefield. Similarly ingenious farm implements were developed next.

The new system also treated humans as interchangeable. Roles were broken down and systematized by tasks, so almost anyone could take over for almost anyone else without slowing down production. Only a skilled person could make a shoe by hand, but a worker at a shoe-making machine might have only a single task to learn, perfect, and perform. Failure to perform that task meant swift replacement—an operator was as readily replaced as a part from the machine they were operating. The system didn't need skilled individuals; it needed workers, and only as many of them as it would take to get the work done.

The name most closely associated with this "rational management" was Frederick W. Taylor. His work on assembly lines inspired a generation of agricultural engineers, often public employees working at land-grant colleges or agricultural experiment stations, who urged farmers to become "more professional," to treat farming like any other business, and to rely more heavily on machines to produce more goods with less labor.

Deere's plow was a significant invention. But it was the appearance of the steam tractor and, soon thereafter, the gas-powered tractor that was the true game changer. These motorized horses would soon reduce human and animal labor exponentially, while nearly erasing all the challenges inherent in breaking virgin soil.

The first oil well was drilled in Pennsylvania in 1859, and the soon-to-follow combination of gasoline power, increased horse-power, and mass-produced steel drove rapid change. In 1850 it took a farmer and a horse at least seventy-five hours to produce a hundred bushels of corn. By 1930 that same task took as little as fifteen hours. Production grew in parallel, from 173 million bush-els of wheat in 1859 to 287 million by the century's end. The big difference was the tractor.

Like most emerging technologies, the early tractor was a work in progress. It was crude, slow-moving, often malfunctioning, un-comfortable to operate, expensive, difficult to fuel, and dangerous. And, especially in the case of early coal- and wood-fired models, it was prone to starting fires. What's more, it had to be pulled onto the fields by horses, where it took time to gather steam.

Nevertheless, where farmers already had credit and cash, in places like the rich and supremely productive states of Ohio, Indi-ana, and Illinois, early tractors quickly became popular. The pace of change accelerated again in 1892 with the introduction of the first successful gas-powered tractor, which was superior to the steam model in every way: lighter, cheaper, safer, and more effi-cient.

There were 37,000 tractors at work on American farms in 1916, when Henry Ford's model was introduced with great cere-mony in Nebraska. Ford himself was convinced that there would be a market for ten million tractors, and he vowed to sell his for an unbeatable price. He could foresee its impact: "I am going to plow up the Australian Bush and the steppes of Siberia and Mes-opotamia." By 1940, the tractor population was over one and a half million.

Once gas tractors became affordable and started to sell, the prairie was attacked in earnest. The literally groundbreaking ef-ficiency of the new tractors sped up planting and harvesting, with harrowers that made neater rows and seed drills that planted uniformly and quickly. Finally, "combines" merged several harvesting processes into a single machine, cutting the cost of production by more than half, mostly by reducing labor.

By 1960, 4.7 million tractors were working on 3.7 million farms, which themselves had begun to plummet in number as efficiency led to consolidation. There were just over half as many farms in 1960 as there had been in 1940, while the number of tractors had remained fairly steady.

The tractor had another impact, one few of us alive today would likely consider: It freed up millions of acres of farmland that had once been devoted to feeding draft animals. Horses fell in number, from a peak of twenty-five million in 1920 to around three million by 1960, at which point the USDA stopped tracking them.

The impact was profound. According to USDA economist Willard Cochrane, writing in 1958, "the substitution of tractor power for animal power has released some 70 million acres, or one-fifth of our cropland, for the production of marketable crops."

But among the "marketable crops," farmers' options were limited. Since the new machinery was best customized to plant and harvest just one crop, farms became less diverse. On the new farms of the Plains during the first half of the twentieth century, that single crop was most often wheat, which grew from around twenty million acres planted in 1870 to fifty million just thirty years later.

World War I made the world's appetite for wheat temporarily insatiable, and yet, between urbanization and the need for men in the military, there were fewer farmers per capita than ever. This meant that farms had to produce more food—which, thanks in large part to the tractor, they could.

As production soared, the United States, along with other former and present colonies, was shipping enough grain, both domestically and worldwide, to feed the growing ex-farming workforce in the rapidly industrializing cities of Europe and the Americas, and enough to feed armies as well. Meanwhile, rural Europe continued to shrink as people gave up their farms to try their luck at industrial work or business, or to have a go at farming in a place where they might be more successful, like the American West.

The migration of that population was the greatest transcontinental movement of people ever.

But, unbeknownst to this new wave of ambitious immigrants, the agricultural landscape of their imagination was rapidly disappearing.

Farmers have always had good and bad years, and the boom-and-bust economy during this period was particularly volatile, in part because growing global markets meant that a drought, or a war ten thousand miles away, could suddenly and unpredictably affect demand, supply, and prices anywhere and everywhere. And because grains, and even futures, were now traded on financial exchanges, there was a surge in the occurrence of bubbles, panics, price fluctuations, and recessions, all of which were as unpredictable and equally dreaded as bad weather.

While the Homestead Act had been a help to millions — anytime you can get free land, you're doing relatively well — it's no exaggeration to say that even before new farmers began working their homesteads, trends were pointing toward a future that had no need for them. Ever-increasing production and consolidation meant the number of farms in America began to shrink, and support for the homesteaders was disappearing.

To the businessmen who prospered off their labors, individual farmers were annoying. They required specialized attention, they organized for fair treatment, and they were often behind on their bills. If their numbers could be reduced while production was kept at the same level, the whole system would work much more smoothly.

But although they were often called "hayseeds" by city people, farmers knew what was going on. As the nineteenth century ended, they began to protest against economic unreliability, volatile and unpredictable interest and mortgage rates, and deflationary pressure, all of which the government could have remedied but did not. They understood, too, that the country's rich were becoming ever more powerful.

More food was being produced than ever, and yet hunger and the fear of hunger remained. Worldwide, farmers who once grew food for their families and neighbors were forced to instead sell their crop on the market for cash to stay afloat. On that same market, farmers—like everyone else—could buy whatever food they could afford.

But if their cash crop failed, there'd be nothing with which to buy food grown elsewhere. And of course there'd be no locally grown food either. It would be Ireland all over again. Yet agriculture continued to move toward servicing the global market, leaving individual communities behind.

In an attempt to control production and prices, and to remain independent, many farmers allied with labor movements and other forces working for positive change, forming organizations like the National Farmers Union. Striving to escape monopolies' control, these organizations formed independent cooperative buying groups for supplies, financing, and insurance.

Farmers demanded better transportation rates from the railroads, better loan rates (and loan forgiveness) from the banks, better tax rates (including heavier taxes on land speculators), stronger and better-enforced antitrust legislation, and a looser money supply from the government. As these unifying themes emerged, farmers and their representatives united, forming the Populist Party in 1892 and garnering six and a half million votes for progressive presidential candidate William Jennings Bryan in 1896. Unfortunately, William McKinley got seven million.

But even as established farms consolidated, new ones were springing up. In the States, both government and business were eager to get land out of the public domain in order to generate tax revenue and continue to build demand for the products of agribusiness. The need for more farmers and workers meant that federal policies continued to encourage immigration, and the numbers of new Americans continued to climb at a staggering rate. Between 1860 and 1900 the country's population more than doubled, to about seventy-five million people.

After farmers gained a more realistic picture of what life was like in the middle of the country—and after the good land started to run out and it became clear that honest farming was rarely an easy road to riches—stronger incentives than the original 1862

Homestead Act were needed to get people to move out of eastern cities and create farms in the West. Congress passed the Enlarged Homestead Act of 1909, which doubled the allotment to 320 acres for new farmers who would accept western lands that were difficult to irrigate, arid, and windy and had unpredictable rainfall.

For many, that meant Texas, Oklahoma, Nebraska, and Kansas, where, Homestead Act or no, land was essentially free for the taking. Others went farther west in search of literal and figurative gold. "Suitcase farmers" bought thousands of acres on the cheap, visiting their land only to plow, sow, and finally harvest (if they didn't hire out their labor), exploiting the then historically high price of wheat and selling out whenever things turned unprofitable. Speculators hatched get-rich-quick schemes, and land developers and railroad companies set up demonstration farms to show how fortunes were guaranteed to all who took this once-in-a-lifetime opportunity to claim their free land, which was pitched as can't-miss for new farmers.

These land hustlers lured easterners with "guarantees" that wheat prices would remain stable, because demand would never slacken; that western soil was ideal for growing wheat; and that the climate, according to University of Kansas scientists, was changing *permanently* for the better.

Never mind that doubling supply of a product for which demand was inelastic—once people have enough food, it's not easy to get them to eat more—was virtually guaranteed to lower prices. Never mind that wheat, as history had demonstrated, was tough on even the best soils. And never mind that no one can predict long-term climate, and that the weather on the Plains was, as it happened, going through a brief, beneficially wet phase.

In fact the combination of more farmers, more wheat, and changing weather was a recipe for disaster, which was precisely what was to follow. Farmers had always worked hard, but until the twentieth century they'd been working their own bodies, their own animals, and their own land, which had to provide them with the food they and their families needed to live, indefinitely. All of this made them good stewards of the land and savvy farmers.

Now, farmers were producing so much they needed hired labor, they needed machinery instead of animals, and, to thrive, they needed more land. For this, they needed credit, which meant greater risk than ever before. Policy, machinery, and finance were all combining to make farms bigger.

Like the products of factories, those of farms were sold and shipped elsewhere. And, like factories, farms generated new, sometimes hidden, and often extreme costs: pollution, exploitation of workers and animals, soil degradation, and resource depletion — costs that were absorbed by the earth and society without repayment.

Waste, no matter how foul, was considered normal, and a certain amount of pollution was considered "fair use." Scientists assured polluters that "nature" would self-cleanse. Water, like land before it, soon became a commodity in its own right, and its quality deteriorated.

Yet because growth was paramount, the transition to industrial farming, like that to agriculture ten thousand years earlier, was inevitable given the circumstances. But unlike the original agricultural revolution, this new one happened at a breakneck pace — over just a couple of generations.

Perhaps it was impossible to see at the time, but what was needed was support for regional agriculture, for farmers who would steward the land and produce food for their communities rather than for traders. But the protests of nineteenth- and twentieth-century radicals had limited impact in a country where growth and profitability for the few were deemed more important than the welfare of the many.

Innovation made it seem almost as if unlimited growth of commodities were possible. The tractor had led to an extraordinary production boom. The only limitation was soil fertility, an ever more pressing issue.

And it wasn't only farmers who could see that plundering faraway treasure troves of composted manure was only a temporary solution. In 1898, the president of the British Association for the Advancement of Science, William Crookes, echoed Malthus in what became known as "the Great Wheat Speech," issuing a challenge to his organization's members and the scientific community at large.

His chief subject, he said, was the food supply, an issue of "life-and-death" interest to "every human being." And by "human being" Crookes meant "the bread-eaters of the world . . . the great Caucasian race, which includes the peoples of Europe, United States, British America, the white inhabitants of South Africa, Australasia, parts of South America, and the white population of the European colonies.

"As mouths multiply," he said, "food resources dwindle. Land is a limited quantity, and the land that will grow wheat is absolutely dependent on difficult and capricious natural phenomena. I am constrained to show that our wheat-producing soil is totally unequal to the strain put upon it. . . . It is the chemist who must come to the rescue of the threatened communities."

His concern was absolutely legitimate. The population of industrial Western Europe was sustained by grain imports from its colonies and its wheat-rich ex, the United States. The Corn Laws were repealed in part because imported grain was so cheap that the homeland couldn't grow it competitively. This was all well and good until Europe began to realize that, even in wealthy countries, food imports were only as strong as the peaceful trade relations that sustained them. The peace wouldn't last.

Predictably, when the British and other Europeans decided to reinvest in domestic agriculture, there wasn't enough land—or, that is, still fertile land. Competition and tensions grew, and there were skirmishes over colonial territories whose soil was still nutrient-rich enough to produce. As Crookes noted in his speech, "the very first and supremely important munition of war [is] food."

What's more, fertilizer extraction from abroad was also fast becoming a non-option. As traders used kidnapped Chinese people to cart out guano at an ever-increasing rate, supplies dwindled. For a time, two other forms of high-nutrient fertilizer—potassium nitrate, also known as saltpeter, and sodium nitrate (or "white gold")—took its place. These were, and still are, mined worldwide, from India to Kentucky to Chile, but as nitrate supplies also diminished, prices rose. And the demand for usable nitrogen only kept increasing.

There's plenty of nitrogen in the world; it makes up nearly eighty percent of the atmosphere. But nitrogen is inert—plants can't use it in its gaseous form—and there was no known way to remove it from the air and make it beneficial. Useful forms of nitrogen like guano and saltpeter were, in the long run, even more limited than nitrogen-rich cow and chicken manure. If the global cash-crop economy were to flourish, someone would have to rise to Crookes's challenge and find a way to exploit atmospheric nitrogen.

Fritz Haber, a German Jew born in 1868 and a friend of Albert Einstein's, did just that, and he would become one of the most important chemists in history.

In 1909, just a little more than ten years after Crookes's adjuration, Haber found a way to use intense pressure (more than two hundred atmospheres' worth of it) and high temperatures (over four hundred degrees centigrade), along with iron as a catalyst, to combine atmospheric nitrogen and hydrogen, thus producing ammonia.

By pulling nitrogen from the air for the first time, Haber had produced the basis for artificial fertilizer. He had created, as the Germans said, *brot aus luft*—"bread from air."

Widespread use of this new fertilizer wasn't immediate, however. Haber's process was bought by German chemical firm BASF and industrialized by his brother-in-law Carl Bosch. Large-scale production began in 1913, but instead of developing chemical fertilizers, BASF pivoted toward a different booming industry —war. The Haber process opened the world to a new class of nitrogen-based chemical weapons and to more powerful and easily made explosives.

Haber himself was a prolific developer of new weapons for chemical warfare, turning chlorine, mustard, and other gases into weapons. This led to the development of Zyklon A, originally targeted at insects. After Haber's death, the same technology was used to create Zyklon B, the gas Nazis used in extermination camps, where several members of Haber's own family were killed.

After World War I, when ammonia-based fertilizer was finally produced in quantity, grain production doubled and then doubled again within a couple of decades. Cover crops, crop rotation, and manure would go the way of horse-drawn plows as chemical fertilizers were used wherever farmers could afford them. Along with the tractor and soon-to-be-developed chemical pesticides, the new fertilizer was to determine the course of agriculture in the twentieth century and beyond.

Before that could happen, there was a war to win. And although it's seldom remembered, World War I was won by wheat. By the end of the Victorian era, in 1901, both Britain and Germany had transitioned from agricultural countries to the world's great industrial and military powers. Both were net importers of grain, wool, fertilizer, and other necessities, items that could be sent to Britain almost only by ship. Germany, too, depended on overseas imports for crucial products like dairy and wheat.

Supply-wise, the big difference between the two countries was the Atlantic Ocean. While it was always open for Britain to trade with its allies and colonies, Germany's access was (and still is) more limited, moving through either the narrow and easily patrolled English Channel or the North Sea, also usually controlled by Great Britain.

Almost immediately after the war began in 1914, Britain closed both bodies of water to German shipping. Britain's allies France and Italy blockaded the Adriatic Sea, whose northernmost port was Trieste, at that time a part of Austria-Hungary. For the remainder of the war, with few exceptions, Germany could not import food by sea (even the Baltic was partially blockaded), and with most men of fighting age serving in the army, German agriculture had shortages of labor, fodder, fertilizer, and animals (millions of horses were at the front).

According to Avner Offer's *The First World War: An Agrarian Interpretation*, about nineteen percent of the calories consumed in Germany came from abroad, way more than its citizenry could afford to do without. And there were impediments beyond food imports. The German diet was as meat heavy as that of any industrialized country, and raising meat reduces the overall number of available calories, since some of the calories "concentrated" in animals are used in keeping them alive.

Which brings us to the curious case of Denmark. Although Denmark declared neutrality when the war began, in 1917 Germany cut that country off from imports of fertilizer, grains, and other foods when it declared a total blockade on all international shipping it could control.

The Danish diet, like that of Germany, was especially vulnerable. The country raised half as much grain per capita as Germany, and they used much of it to feed livestock. But, in an impressive display of clarity, decisiveness, and unity, the government decided to increase the grain supply for citizens by reducing alcohol production, rationing white bread, ceasing the raising of pigs, and encouraging the consumption of whole grains. As Dr. Mikkel Hindhede, one of the leaders of the campaign, said, "Meat is the last requirement to be met [in the diet]. If the people must wait until pigs and cattle have sufficient food, they will die of starvation."

Hindhede was correct. Any halfway balanced diet with enough calories provides adequate protein. So, by incorporating the grain that had formerly gone to animals, the Danish diet made the most of its agricultural production, concentrating on whole grains, potatoes, fruit, and vegetables.

In fact, Hindhede dubbed the year between October 1917 and October 1918 "the Year of Health." Denmark's mortality rate became the lowest ever. The average death rate from chronic diseases, based on a sample of Copenhagen adults from 1900 to 1916, was one hundred people per ten thousand. During the Year of Health it was sixty-six. The overall death rate in Denmark in October 1917–1918 was 10.4 per thousand, down from its previous low of 12.5.

In fairness, there are other possible explanations for the health improvement. Some called 1917–18 "the Year of Butter," claiming that health had improved because of lowered alcohol intake and the elimination of margarine. But whatever the reasons, and no doubt they're complicated, Denmark's health improved after a controlled dietary "experiment," made possible (and necessary) only by a reversion to an older style of growing and eating. And it's inarguable that the Danes were much better fed — with fewer resources — than the Germans. Their diet was so effective, in fact, that the recommendations of most of today's public health experts are in line with the Danish style of eating during the war.

In Germany, the chemicals that might have been used to make artificial fertilizer were being used for bombs and gas, and the blockade meant that Germany couldn't import Chilean saltpeter, the mined source of nitrogen that had largely taken the place of guano. Its agriculture suffered accordingly, and there were staggering increases in cost and, ultimately, hyperinflation. Germany's response was to create the War Food Office to attempt to fairly ration and allocate food, which meant that much food was sold on the black market.

The malnutrition that followed made Germans susceptible to disease, resulting in hundreds of thousands of civilian deaths, along with long-term damage to a generation of youth raised without enough calories to develop properly. Wartime and postwar hunger fueled social unrest and exacerbated divides between urban and rural dwellers, classes, and ethnicities, not only in Germany but throughout Europe — it was an underlying cause of the Russian Revolution — the Middle East, and beyond.

Meanwhile, America's wheat boom had primed it to become the main supplier of grain for Western Europe. Future president Herbert Hoover was appointed to run the U.S. Food Administration, which established domestic price standards to limit gouging, allocated food supplies for troops, and controlled sales to the allies.

With much of the bounty of the burgeoning agricultural industry shipped overseas to allies and soldiers, Hoover encouraged Americans to become more self-sufficient and fill up on eggs and cheese, both of which were still produced either in the household or nearby. Americans took up gardening too: Three million previously uncultivated lots were planted, an especially impressive number when you consider that the nation's population at the time was around one hundred million.

As a result, wheat exports tripled and meat exports quintupled over the course of the war and its aftermath. By 1919, food products were one-third of American exports. This boom in exports couldn't last, however, and the inevitable crash spelled further disaster for small-scale farmers.

The high grain prices generated by the demands of war led many American farmers to expect that bigger would always be better, that planting more meant more profit, and that the federal government would back this notion.

In a way, they were right: It's easier for government and more profitable for industry to have a thousand farmers each produce a million bushels than to have a million farmers each produce a thousand bushels. Not only did fewer farms and fewer farmers mean a cheaper loaf of bread; it also meant more tractors. The biggest farms were the ones that succeeded, in large part thanks to government support.

An interesting case study was pioneering farmer Tom Campbell, who in 1917 argued that the best use of his time and skill was not to fight but to produce wheat on an industrial scale, using all the tools at his disposal. This included, as Fitzgerald cites in *Every Farm a Factory*, "the same principles of mass production, cost accounting, specialized machinery, and skilled mechanical labor as any great industrial organization in this country."

Campbell presented his case by telegram to President Wilson and J. P. Morgan, and he was rewarded with 100,000 acres of tax-free land leased from the Bureau of Indian Affairs—land that had been taken from the Crow, Blackfeet, and Shoshone—and a two-million-dollar investment from the House of Morgan. Campbell, who went on to be known as the World's Wheat King, also advised Stalin on agriculture, developed an early form of napalm, and became an Air Force brigadier general.

Few stories were as grand, but the trend was widespread. From the moment the gas-powered tractor was introduced, innovations ramped up the scale of farming. Hydraulic lifting systems made changing implements easier, as those implements could now be swapped depending on the crop. More efficient diesel motors were introduced, and four-wheel drive and improved transmissions made all-terrain work possible. Better planters meant that spacing could be adjusted for different types of crops, allowing more efficient cultivation, and so on. As chemical fertilizer increased yield per acre, and as field size increased along with overall planted acreage, owning the newest machinery became critically important.

Early adopters of tractors and other new technologies gained a decided advantage by selling huge quantities at the existing high prices. Those prices would inevitably fall as everyone else caught on, as mass production led to more surplus, and as margins became so thin that only the biggest producers could remain profitable.

"In the long run," wrote the USDA's Cochrane, who became the agency's chief agricultural economist in the sixties, "by the time most farmers have adopted the technology, the income benefits that the first farmers realized have vanished. Mr. Average Farmer is right back where he started, as far as his income position is concerned." This has held true for every major innovation in industrial farming, from tractors to genetically manipulated seeds. Each has benefited the biggest and penalized the smallest.

Before long, it took more land, more equipment, more chemicals, and more financing to become a successful farmer in the most prolific crops, like corn, soybeans, and wheat. And as it developed, buying mechanized farm equipment did not guarantee prosperity, but rather debt, putting farmers on what Cochrane called the "Agriculture Treadmill." This was true even in Campbell's case. The House of Morgan didn't just *give* him two million dollars; it *loaned* it to him.

Expanding production and specializing in commodity crops was the only way to stay alive. Most benefits went to equipment manufacturers, chemical producers, and seed companies, and the successful names from this era remain well established: General Mills, Cargill, Deere, DuPont.

As so many forces aligned against old-style family farmers, the struggle against rampant development became hopeless. Overproduction from the war years led to a more or less permanent surplus, and prices fell so low that all but the biggest farmers were in the red. The push to grow bigger and focus on one crop came from every direction, and even those entities that had been set up specifically to help family farmers survive, like the land-grant colleges and their agricultural experiment stations, were pushing smaller farms to ramp up cash-crop production.

When, in 1922, the USDA formed the Bureau of Agricultural Economics (now the Economic Research Service), it officially joined in encouraging the states to guide their farmers to produce to certain standards using similar techniques. In doing so, the bureau established a de facto national agricultural production policy. The feds would help farmers, either directly or indirectly through the states, to move toward a uniform system of production. Farms continued to become fewer, bigger, and more similar.

It wasn't an entirely cynical process, and some might even call it an innocent one. "Experiment station scientists and administrators never considered the possibility that insofar as their work proved successful it might help enrich the rich, impoverishing and ultimately forcing many worthy if less entrepreneurial farmers from the land," wrote historian Charles Rosenberg. "Nor did they foresee potential conflict between their advocacy of an increasingly sophisticated government-support research effort and the gradual demise of a self-sufficient, decentralized world . . . Only the most efficient could hope to survive."

Whether it was intended or not, the tragic result of the push to standardized monoculture was that scientists and researchers became allied not with farmers but with bankers, equipment manufacturers, and sellers of seeds and chemicals. As Wendell Berry writes in *The Unsettling of America*, "colleges of agriculture" became "colleges of 'agribusiness,'" as "an institution that was supposed to protect rural life is now its greatest enemy: an educational subsidy given to the farmers' competitors."

The deck was stacked. Big companies wanted farmers to hold more land, produce more crops, and fall further into debt. At the same time, supposedly impartial advisers believed that, if small farmers were going to inevitably disappear anyway beneath advances in machinery and chemicals, why not simply help those who could grow bigger to do so? To hell with the millions of farmers who produced food for their communities.

In the aftermath of World War I, farms began to die at an accelerated rate. From 1920 until 1932 — *before* the environmental disaster we call the Dust Bowl — twenty-five percent of farms were lost to debt or taxes.

Mechanization and growth made the farm economy more erratic, as more debt, more income, and more crops meant higher highs and lower lows. By 1930, when Deere & Company and its main competitor, International Harvester, dominated agricultural equipment sales, John's grandson, CEO Charles Deere Wiman, bailed out the local bank and extended lenient credit during the Depression, realizing that showing generosity to insecure farmers was not only good marketing but also good business. Eventually, credit purchases became the norm, and in 1958 the company established the John Deere Credit Company, which became one of the largest finance institutions in the country.

Large-scale equipment is essential to industrial agriculture, but it's also prohibitively expensive as an outright purchase by anyone we might think of as a "family" farmer. A modern but far from top-of-the-line combine costs half a million dollars. A purchase like that requires complex financing, owning massive acreage to justify the expense, and monocropping to produce cash crops most efficiently. In 1945, when as many draft animals worked American farm fields as did tractors, the average value of a farm's machinery was $878, equivalent to an investment of $22,000 in 2020; now that average is six times higher.

That financing tied farmers to equipment, chemical, and seed producers — and to bankers as well. And while Deere & Co. showed good will toward struggling farmers, its success in financially bonding those farmers virtually ensured that creditors remained profitable in the long term. It's also among the chief reasons why industrial agriculture is so difficult to change today.

Today the company's margins are almost four times as great from providing credit than they are from sales. But it's the combination of the two that keeps it powerful. If farmers do well, they buy new equipment, perhaps on terms that aren't ideally profitable for the finance arm. But if they struggle — and almost all do, eventually — they buy that new equipment on far more onerous terms. Either way, Deere wins. Its 2019 profits were eleven billion dollars, a bit more than ten percent of the combined profits of all two million–plus farms in the United States that same year.

7

Dust and Depression

FOOD HAS ALWAYS been political, but as time has passed, our relationship with food—how it gets into our hands—has been shaped more and more by government and policy.

Sometimes governments stand by while farmers large and small do their work. That passivity usually means failing to protect the poor against the rich and results in consolidation. But policies can determine kinds and levels of production, improve (or hinder) nutrition, foster a surplus for trade, or even create scarcity. Policy shapes all of these outcomes.

The impact can be painful. From the Potato Famine onward, the modern era has seen negligence, cruelty, and a lack of compassion starve millions to death. In some cases, governments have even weaponized food to commit genocide.

The shining example of genocidal food policy is Joseph Stalin, who rose to absolute power in 1924, when the Soviet Union was barely industrialized. Stalin's admiration for America was no secret. He believed that "the combination of Russian revolutionary sweep with American efficiency is the essence of Leninism." Many supporters of the revolution would disagree with that, but Lenin himself was in no position to argue: He was dead. And Stalin wanted few things more than an economy that could compete globally with that of the United States.

In 1861, Tsar Alexander II abolished serfdom, a type of near slavery that had existed in Russia and parts of Eastern Europe for hundreds of years. After emancipation, serfs became peasants, which meant they could own land. (Throughout the world, "peasant" still means "small, poor farmer"; it's not derogatory.) They were free—free to become relatively well-to-do if they could and, if not, free to starve. It's safe to say that almost all continued to lead hard lives.

Stalin believed that in order for the revolution to succeed and the Soviet Union to become a world power, it had to increase efficiency and productivity at any cost. And by that time, the burgeoning American model of agriculture made it clear that big farms had to swallow smaller ones. Stalin followed suit with no regard for the lives of individuals.

Stalin both encouraged and forced peasants to move to manufacturing centers, where the industrial workforce doubled in just a few years. Meanwhile, farming began to mechanize and focus on cash crops. But lack of equipment, lower crop prices, and what was effectively a tribute tax—peasants were required to give a percentage of their production to the state—led to a grain shortage in the late twenties. The state's response was the first Five-Year Plan, which gave Stalin complete control over economic policy and commenced a war between the state and the peasantry, who mostly wanted peace, land, and independence.

Stalin, however, pushed collectivization, the transformation of individual farms into larger, group-managed operations where farmers would, in the now familiar pattern, produce commodity crops like sugar, beets, and cotton—crops that could be sold but were all but useless for subsistence. He simultaneously reduced the price that the state paid for these crops, so farmers couldn't live on the cash they fetched.

What was supposed to be rational, science-backed central planning was, in practice, arbitrary, cruel, and largely unsuccessful. Fields were sown with the same crops year after year, a surefire recipe for soil depletion that echoed what was happening simultaneously in the U.S. heartland, with equally disastrous results.

Powerless, landless, and living in grim conditions, the peasants revolted, slaughtering their livestock and destroying their equipment. Production fell even further. There was, however, still food to export—in large part because prices were too high for many people to afford the collectively produced crops, making domestic demand artificially low—which improved the country's balance of trade. Thus, Stalin could claim that collectivization had been successful.

That was not your perspective if you were starving. But, like the nineteenth- and twentieth-century colonialists, Stalin felt no sympathy for the peasants, and no obligation to remedy their plight. Instead he actually used hunger as a lesson for the "esteemed grain growers,"—as he wrote sarcastically to novelist Mikhail Sholokhov—whom he believed to be waging a "'quiet' war against Soviet power."

Full-fledged famine followed. In his book *Stalinism, Collectivization and the Great Famine*, my friend the Italian historian Andrea Graziosi notes the four key elements of this famine. First, Stalin and his regime executed policy with the express goal of breaking the peasantry. The state itself, Graziosi says, was essentially built upon a "protracted war with the peasantry." Second, although the famine was not caused intentionally, it was willfully manipulated once it began. Third, Stalin used hunger as a punishment, terrorizing people who threatened his power and deporting millions of people to Siberia. Finally, in Ukraine and Kazakhstan, this policy developed a genocidal quality. More than a million Kazakh nomads died of starvation in 1931 and 1932 after their herds were seized by the state.

Most sources put the number of people who starved to death in the Stalin-generated famine at around seven million, although some estimates range as high as twelve million. Something like forty percent of the Kazakh population and, in some areas, up to a third of Ukrainians perished. Stalin's "agricultural prosperity" left the Ukrainian countryside's fields of rich black soil bereft of crops and people alike. Everyone who could have worked the fields had either died or fled to the cities or abroad.

This was the first instance of a modern government using food as an internal weapon against a rebellious citizenry. But a trend was established. From then on, as economist Amartya Sen contends, famines didn't just strike without warning. They happened only in the context of civil unrest, the absence of democracy, and outright war. In his analysis of famines in Bengal (1943), the Sahel (1972–74), Ethiopia (1972–74), and Bangladesh (1974), Sen concludes that *food availability had no correlation with onset of famine.* Political freedom did.

Imitating the Soviet Union a generation later, Mao's Communist Party drew up and executed a plan to turn China into a steel superpower, transferring more than a third of all peasants to mining and irrigation projects while leaving untold acres of grain unattended. Meanwhile, production of food for personal consumption was banned entirely, and all grain was shipped to the cities; grabbing a handful of grain or digging up a potato could earn you a death sentence.

Bad agricultural practices and a willful ignorance of existing science, especially plant genetics, only compounded the crisis, which was masked as harvest records were systematically falsified, for fear of angering Mao and his agents. Believing he had doubled production and therefore increased surplus, Mao cut grain acreage in 1959. The result was a sudden and severe shortage. People in rural communes died twice as fast as urban elites, and the corpses that weren't fought over and eaten for survival were buried in mass graves.

The worst of the famine, which was known by many names (including the official and tragically risible "Three Years of Difficulty"), took place from 1959 to 1961, during Mao's Great Leap Forward, and killed, by current estimates, more than forty million people, nearly six percent of the Chinese population.

In hindsight, it's easy to judge the cruelty of Mao's revolution. But like many other world powers, the United States was largely indifferent to the struggles of its own "peasants"—its small farmers—and the parallels are obvious. When America mechanized its agriculture and, on its foundation, built the most powerful economy ever, it created migrants in its wake. That no true famine resulted was in large part thanks to the presence of a limited but real democracy.

You can wreak havoc in many ways, among them a laissez-faire attitude toward unchecked corporatization. Although nothing approaching widespread famine occurred in the United States, the government's failure to intervene—as usual, there was no plan for helping the millions of people whose skills the new technology would render obsolete—amid the ever-increasing push to increase the size of farms and grow one cash crop at a time led to the suffering, involuntary displacement, and eventually even death of many Americans.

The need to feed a huge Allied army during the First World War had propelled thirteen and a half million new acres—four times the size of Connecticut—into wheat production. Over the next ten years, commonly called the Roaring Twenties, new and powerful tractors had turned over something like forty million more acres of sod, an area about the size of Georgia.

Unusually steady rain and still nutrient-rich soil allowed for ever bigger harvests, and American farms were harvesting more than enough wheat both for the country's own population and for exports. Even when the stock market collapsed in 1929, many grain farmers continued to do well. When commodity prices rose, farmers planted as much as they could. And when those prices eventually and inevitably fell, farmers still plowed and sowed even more, hoping to pick up the slack in income.

But a market flooded with cheap grain wasn't the only problem. In the midst of this economic collapse, the ecology of the Great Plains was unraveling.

Rainfall virtually ceased, and the winds began to blow harshly. In the early 1930s, "black blizzards" of dust swept over fields, roads, and towns. Trains missed their stations and crashed because of low visibility, children were lost and even smothered in the storms, and adults, unable to see, were forced to crawl home at night. Some quoted Deuteronomy: "The Lord shall make the rain of thy land powder and dust; from heaven it shall come down upon thee, until thou be destroyed."

Yet unless you refused or were unable to look beneath its surface, the Dust Bowl—like most tragedies of modern agriculture —was neither an act of God nor inevitable. Rather, it was a direct result of the actions of settlers and the government programs that had directed them.

The thirties were hardly the first time dryness and high winds combined to rake the Great Plains. They were, however, the first time they assaulted land that had been scraped and plowed by speculators and farmers who understood next to nothing (and didn't bother to learn) about that land's ecology.

Thousand-year-old buffalo grass had stabilized and protected soil against the frequent droughts and howling winds. By some estimates, bison had been grazing the Plains for a hundred thousand years. Now farmers were tearing up that grass to plant wheat, almost exclusively, for years on end. The bison had been removed, along with the land's Indigenous stewards, by trappers, hunters, and traders, who shipped furs and skins back east; by the military, which supported the slaughter of the animals to reduce the Native people's food supply; and by railroad companies, who wanted the bison gone because they slowed and even damaged trains. Sometimes trains were slowed to the pace of passing herds so passengers could conveniently shoot the animals.

As the twentieth century approached, the bison population was next to nil, and, as the land was plowed for wheat, the deep-rooted grass was next to depart; the soil itself would follow.

The rate of destruction of this unique and massive ecosystem, about the size of Alaska, was not only unprecedented, it was inconceivable—until it happened. If anyone had caught on to the damage that was being done, it was already too late.

The tractors had been running day and night. In 1931, almost forty percent of the entire land area of southwest Kansas was planted with wheat. The area surrounding Dodge City and adjacent parts of Texas, Oklahoma, New Mexico, and Colorado were similarly overextended; when the winds hit, this region became the heart of the Dust Bowl. By that time, the wheat that had once brought close to two dollars per bushel would get you fifty cents —in a good year. Even that price might've worked for the struggling farmers, except that the frequent rains abruptly stopped and the weather returned to normal—arid. In fact, the moderate weather that "experts" had predicted would last more or less forever had been an anomaly. And with the Great Depression leaving tens of millions of Americans unable to afford food, wheat prices plummeted even further.

Even as they became desperate, many farmers remained hopeful. Believing that their land would continue to yield prodigiously in perpetuity, they continued to clear more acreage and double down on planting to compensate for falling prices. President Hoover approved more credit for farmers, and on better terms, allowing them to invest in more land and more equipment, and making farming hundreds of acres feasible for each now heavily equipped and increasingly indebted family.

But no matter how much they harvested, no matter how much they sold, lower prices forced farmers to borrow more, to plant more, and to grow more—just to try to service their debt. Those farms that folded were swallowed up by their neighbors, whose debt grew. (Some kindly souls, in some cases having bid pennies at auction, returned the farms to their bankrupt friends.) Using the techniques encouraged by inexperienced government agents who could offer no substantive warnings about the risks, they continued to unceasingly "plow, sow, harvest, plow."

Many proponents of USDA agricultural experiment stations love to talk about their heroic efforts to save American farmers during the Dust Bowl. But the USDA's failure to anticipate the dangers of the plowing frenzy is infinitely more telling. Agents had little or no training in soil management, water conservation, crop rotation, or erosion protection—the very practices that might have averted the Dust Bowl crisis. Rather, they were champions of industrialized monoculture, encouraging mechanization and reckless planting.

It was a perfect setup for disaster. Soil became untethered as the mild and wet weather returned to the norm of hot, dry, and windy. The combination created fearsome dust storms, failed crops, foreclosed houses, hunger, and illness, including "dust pneumonia." By 1933, previously prosperous families had lost their homes and were living in chicken coops, and all that remained was glimmers of hope and persistence. Farmers became "next year" people: "Wait till next year."

Through the early thirties, the plight of the Plains farmers was largely invisible to most back east, who had problems of their own. But on May 9, 1934, a storm swept more than three hundred million tons of dust from the Plains tens of thousands of feet up into the air and carried it over Chicago, Detroit, Cleveland, and Buffalo. Two days later, New York streetlights were turned on at noon, and topsoil settled on President Roosevelt's desk in the White House.

When Franklin Delano Roosevelt became president in 1933, farm income was a third of what it had been in 1929. The McNary-Haugen Act, introduced in 1924, would have enabled the federal government to purchase surplus at an artificially high price and then sell it on the world market, thus floating the West's struggling farms. But it was twice vetoed by the laissez-faire president, Calvin Coolidge. With processors paying less and manufacturers charging more, it was costing farmers more to produce crops than those crops were worth.

The new president's much-praised brain trust, a group comprising mostly Columbia law professors, came to believe that the Depression had its roots in agriculture: If farmers struggled, so did the economy. That, at least, was sensible.

But with trends in farming leaving more and more farmers broke and miserable, writes Dan Morgan in *Merchants of Grain*, "the mood in America's farm country was sullen and rebellious. Protesting farmers burned their grain, dumped their milk, slaughtered their livestock, and in one case dragged a judge from his courtroom during a farm foreclosure hearing and threatened to hang him on the spot if he did not stop the proceedings."

Some farmers tried to raise agricultural prices by physically keeping produce off the market. In Iowa and Nebraska, a group known as the Farmers' Holiday Association adopted a jingle:

Let's call a "Farmers Holiday"
A Holiday let's hold
We'll eat our wheat and ham and eggs
And let them eat their gold.

They established roadblocks on highways outside Omaha, Sioux City, and Des Moines, dumping milk into ditches and refusing to move cattle.

Other strikes increased the pressure on Washington to relieve the crisis. Farmers begged lenders to halt farm foreclosures, and indeed there were statewide moratoriums on foreclosures in Nebraska, South Dakota, and Minnesota, lasting a couple of years. But although the president of the conservative American Farm Bureau Federation warned that "unless something is done for the American farmer we will have revolution in the countryside within less than 12 months," no national uprising of farmers materialized.

Roosevelt talked a big talk. In a radio speech in 1936, he said, "No cracked earth, no blistering sun, no burning wind . . . are a permanent match for the indomitable American farmers . . . who have carried on through desperate days, and inspire us with their self-reliance, their tenacity, and their courage."

But it was just bluster. No farmer is truly indomitable, nor have they ever been, and encouraging them to try and beat the pants off of nature rather than working with it was a recipe for failure as old as agriculture itself. In fact, the United States, like Sumer and Rome, started to crumble under a failed farming system. And only the most meager government support arrived for small farmers and their families.

Indeed, the dream of the American family farm was fading. The value of all farmland and buildings declined by one-third between 1930 and 1935, and the average farm's value was cut nearly in half.

Up to a third of the regional population, like the Joads in Steinbeck's *The Grapes of Wrath*, was compelled to move. The migration this time was mostly to California, where the weather was perfect, water was abundant, and everything was green—precisely what had been said about the Great Plains fifty years earlier.

Some of the widely denigrated "Okies" and "Arkies" used horses to pull their cars west, because they couldn't afford gas, stopping to beg or work for food. Like the formerly enslaved Americans who left the South after the end of Reconstruction in the 1870s, they were called Exodusters. Like many millions who are forced to migrate today, they were fleeing ecological disaster brought on by land-killing agriculture, all to satiate the hunger of trade.

Washington's first substantive response was the Agricultural Adjustment Act of 1933, also known as the "first farm bill," which introduced income support for farmers that has continued, in various forms, to today. In the short run, this meant limiting production by paying famers to reduce acreage. Once production reached a certain level, farmers were paid to either stop planting or dig their crops under—destroying rather than harvesting. Some land was even "retired." "Parity" prices were also negotiated for each crop as the government spent to keep prices in line with the cost of production and the rest of the economy.

From the farmers' perspective, this support worked for a while (if you consider burying your crops to keep prices up "working"), but it failed to address the big picture. The USDA's Willard Cochrane described this "farm problem," in which the ever-increasing supply of crops outpaces the relatively steady need for them. (So much for Malthus, really.) In a well-fed society, he explained, only population growth can increase the demand for food. So when production increases faster than population, falling prices are guaranteed.

Cochrane determined that the years 1900 to 1914, the period used to determine the price floor when setting parity prices, had been "a time of extraordinary population increase. Immigration reached an all-time high in this decade, and the rate of expansion in agricultural output slackened considerably. So in this peacetime period we have the demand for food products outpacing total supplies, causing farm prices and incomes to soar."

The fundamental basis of our agricultural support system was a misguided attempt to replicate a farm economy that existed when the population was increasing at what turned out to be a unique pace—a pace that created demand that could be manufactured only through war or policy. And since population has never grown like that again (and in all probability won't), commodity supports have become permanent, now mostly in the form of insurance.

But the problems went deeper than oversupply. The well-being of farmers was threatened more by massive debt than by flagging income, and a flood of foreclosures made that all the more clear. Farmers, as John Deere recognized, had become vehicles for doling out debt. Machinery, seeds, chemicals, and interest charges were all new and increasing burdens, and more income merely gave farmers the cash flow they needed to keep paying the bills. Foreclosures meant new loans to expand operations—not only to buy more land but to buy new, larger equipment.

In response, Roosevelt and Congress funded a barrage of programs to ensure a solid agricultural future on the Plains. The Soil Conservation Service (now the Natural Resources Conservation Service) trained and paid growers to adopt better techniques, with the assistance of actual soil scientists, who focused at least a little bit on soil conservation. At the same time, a hundred-million-dollar federal buyout allowed farmers to sell cattle and land for cash. About half of those cattle were slaughtered for food, canned, and distributed to the nation's hungry.

Roosevelt also started the Works Progress Administration, and many of the farmers who stayed on the Plains resorted to performing manual labor for the program in exchange for lifesaving wages. The Civilian Conservation Corps planted a "shelter belt" of more than two hundred million trees, improving the ecology of the Plains, though coming far short of restoring it. The real goal of transforming the landscape into a crop-production factory remained.

By 1938, wheat was again being planted in the Great Plains. The weather improved, the newly planted trees blocked the howling winds, and better pumps harvested a new, more reliable source of water: the massive Ogallala Aquifer, which will eventually empty as a result.

But all these "solutions" addressed symptoms, not causes, and no one in power was interested in a conversation about the long-term goals of the agricultural system. Was it to create healthy families, communities, and economies? Was it to sustain the land? Or was it to exploit every resource imaginable, including humans, so that flour millers, tractor manufacturers, fertilizer producers, banks, and so on could sap farmers' income?

It would not be articulated, but the evidence shows that it was (and is) the latter, at least for those in power. The conversation never happened, largely because those out of power—the vast majority of Americans—couldn't force it.

From the end of World War I to the Depression era to the New Deal, government policies were of little to no help to farmers. But they were especially unhelpful, even actively destructive, for small-scale southern farmers, tenant farmers, and sharecroppers, especially those who were the descendants of enslaved people.

In fact, the worse you were treated by American policy in the eighteenth and nineteenth centuries, the worse you were treated in the twentieth. For example, the Social Security Act of 1935 and the Fair Labor Standards (*sic!*) Act of 1938 both excluded agricultural and domestic, thanks to influential southern Democrats who refused to protect the Black people working in those sectors.

This meant that the New Deal disproportionately excluded people of color from the most vital government protections—social security; the right to collective bargaining and worker organizing; the minimum wage, the maximum workweek, and time and a half for overtime; and the ban on child labor. States were even allowed to set a lower minimum wage for tipped workers, a direct affront to railway porters and maids, almost all of whom were former slaves or their children. That policy shamefully continues to this day.

Historians have long acknowledged that enslaved people, freedmen, and their descendants built the cotton industry and the rest of southern agriculture, and therefore a large part the wealth of the United States. Yet despite post–Civil War promises, Black Americans were still, for the most part, not given the opportunity to become landowners, as white Americans were. Rather, they were largely pigeonholed as tenant farmers and sharecroppers, struggling to make rent and often forced back into the cotton-growing business.

Cotton is a food as well as a fabric crop. Its seed is used for oil, animal fodder, and fertilizer, and there's a 1,500-mile-long stretch from southeast Texas to southern Virginia that's known as the Cotton Belt—yet another huge expanse of rich American soil devoted almost entirely to one crop. In the thirties, this area, essentially the southeastern quadrant of the country, was home to just a quarter of the national population but almost half of the rural population. At the time, half of the farmers in America were southern, and about a quarter of those were Black.

That the Department of Agriculture served big business better than small-time farmers was hardly news. Nor was it surprising that Black farmers suffered most under the department's policies. Although the USDA is a federal agency, its programs are administered locally, often through county extension offices. And local governments in the South were blatantly, even proudly, racist. So when New Deal farm programs actually did step in to save farms, they were typically, conveniently, white-owned farms. Black farmers were shut out, denied loans, deprived of information about farm-saving programs, and of course excluded from management positions in local USDA offices.

African Americans faced several other unique challenges. Commodity support programs increased the price of farmland, creating a further barrier to ownership for non-landowning Blacks. Racist storekeepers and manufacturers' representatives upcharged them for equipment, seeds, and chemicals, while crop buyers bid low on Black farmers' harvests.

What's more, as they were typically laborers instead of landowners, few Black farmers received any of the cash incentives associated with cutting back production. And, predictably, Blacks were still discriminated against even as farming began to recover. Between 1930 and 1935, the number of white tenant farmers increased by 146,000, a ten percent increase over just five years. Meanwhile, the number of nonwhite tenant farmers *declined* by 45,000, a ten percent decrease in their ranks. The numbers were going in equal and opposite directions, always penalizing Blacks.

Ownership in acreage followed the same pattern. As millions of farms went bankrupt during and following the Depression, the total number of farmers fell by fourteen percent. Among African Americans, it fell by thirty-seven percent. The number of Black-owned farms peaked in 1920 at almost a million (all but ten thousand were in the South), when Blacks made up fourteen percent of the U.S. farming population. They now make up about one percent of it.

None of this happened without resistance. The Colored Farmers' National Alliance and Cooperative Union, founded in the 1880s, and the Southern Tenant Farmers Union, led by African Americans and organized across race lines, initiated strikes, lobbying, and publicity efforts. These groups grabbed Eleanor Roosevelt's attention and resulted in the 1935 Resettlement Administration, which in 1937 became the Farm Security Administration, which attempted to move farmers from soil-exhausted land to somewhere they might prosper.

But the help was too late and way too little. Despite promises that began with Sherman and continued on through Roosevelt's administration, a disproportionate number of Black farmers and workers remained landless, discriminated against, and without work or money. In the Great Migration, which took place roughly from the end of World War I until 1970, six million African Americans left the South for the industrial cities of the North, the biggest internal displacement of Americans fleeing their homes in history. Racism, Jim Crow tyranny, and perceived opportunity are most often cited as the main drivers of this migration. But it's crucial to remember that Black Americans had been mostly farmers: at the beginning of the century, three quarters of Black households were in rural areas. So by depriving millions of Black farmers of their land, the government had used food as a tool to force them to flee.

The work of much of the remaining Black population was replaced by machines. Harvesting cotton was notoriously tricky, making mechanization slow. But in 1948, International Harvester, aided by funding by the USDA, came up with a functioning mechanical cotton picker that quickly became ubiquitous. Predictably, the USDA took no action to retrain, relocate, or otherwise support the millions of displaced workers who were no longer needed to pick cotton. Over the course of the 1960s, two-thirds of Black farmers defected to other occupations. The decline was three times as steep as the decrease in white farmers.

As farming in the South deteriorated, farmers white and Black alike were forced to look for new horizons. And while most went north, others turned to the gilded West.

As everyone knows, California's combination of climate and natural riches is unmatched, and long before it was settled by the Spanish, California was a haven for Indigenous people. Its first boom as part of the United States, however, was not centered around farming, but mining. For a flash in America's history — in recently annexed California and in the larger American Southwest — gold was king.

But gold mining was difficult and dangerous, and sported lottery-like odds. It didn't take long for most new Californians to realize that "land mining" — American-style agriculture — could produce more money, more reliably.

Much of California's farmland was already in big holdings. Between 1821 and 1846 — during which time California was part of Mexico — the land was divided among friends and family of the governors. These haciendas, massive tracts that made up more than ten percent of all the land in California, ran along the coast from the then capital of Monterey to San Diego, and were mostly used to raise cattle for tallow and hide to be sent east by ships sailing around Cape Horn. (The trip was too long for fresh beef.)

That landholding character was largely maintained, so that by the late nineteenth century real estate was concentrated in the hands of land developers and speculators, along with the railroad companies. "By 1871," as Mark Arax writes in *The Dreamt Land*, "nine million acres of [California's] most fertile land were in the firm grasp of 516 men." By 1889, the small family farm was already becoming irrelevant. Measured by value, one-sixth of the state's farms produced two-thirds of the crops.

In fact, almost as soon as white settlers arrived, they began work on changing the Central Valley from a diverse natural grassland dotted with wetlands and forest to a vast expanse of dusty monoculture. What evolved was a bizarre combination of production and destruction—both a marvel of twentieth-century engineering and a nightmare of ignorance about the balance of nature and its ability to sustain human life.

California's main crop, as elsewhere, was wheat, much of which was shipped straight to Europe. And, as elsewhere, wheat exhausted the soil. Every cash crop has its heyday in California, and wheat's was typically short: The crop tallied fifty-four million bushels in 1884; by 1900 it was down to six million.

But this brutal blow to California's farmers was a victory for its developers. "With bonanza wheat vanquished," says Arax, "the barbarism of the frontier could now give place to a real civilization." The only barrier to "real civilization" was water. As commercial demands increased, it became clear that water coming from the aquifer, rain, and snowmelt wasn't enough, especially as the remaining farmland relied increasingly on monoculture, which in general needs and wastes more water than multicropping.

Sustaining California's never-before-seen farming scale required novel contingency plans. As a result, water from the Kern, San Joaquin, and Sacramento rivers, among others, was diverted toward the state's parched fields, in what Arax calls "the most extensive and intensive farming experiment in the world," when Californian fertility was "supercharged by irrigation and the science of the Agricultural College at the University of California."

The federal government was eager to help. In 1902 it founded the Reclamation Service, later and more commonly known as the Bureau of Reclamation, though it was hardly "reclaiming" land— a more appropriate name might have been the Bureau of Transformation. The bureau orchestrated the massive irrigation projects that would water much of the American West, the most famous of which was the Hoover Dam, begun in 1931, which stabilized agriculture in the Imperial Valley. That region, formerly desert, now calls itself "the winter garden of the world."

Grand irrigation schemes have been part of every agricultural power from the Sumerians onward, and California was hardly the only place that needed large-scale irrigation to enable large-scale agriculture. But nothing matched the scale at which California bent ecosystems to the needs of its primary business. In the twentieth century, irrigated land in California grew by an overall factor of seven.

Today, about twenty-five million acres in the state, an area almost as big as Kentucky, are arable land, and another fifteen million are grazed. California grows half of the country's fruits and vegetables, and almost all of its almonds, figs, olives, and other Mediterranean crops. It's also our largest dairy-producing state. Almost none of that production could happen without irrigation.

Irrigation is the key to most superior farmland, and that's especially true of the Central Valley, the 450-mile stretch that runs from Bakersfield to Redding, and the heart of California agriculture. It contains the world's largest patch of Class 1 soil — the best there is. The roughly twenty-five-degree temperature swing from day to night is ideal for growing plants, and the sun shines nearly three hundred days a year. With irrigation, the state needed only one more ingredient to make this the most productive patch of land in the world: labor.

High-value, labor-intensive cash crops like citrus, stone fruit, nuts, and vegetables in general became the most profitable use of the soil's wealth. (Cannabis came later.) But unlike midwestern farming, which was dominated by the tractor, these crops also needed large influxes of manual labor during certain seasons. From that need, an innovatively oppressive, elaborate, and modern system of temporary employment developed. Predictably, it depended on the exploitation of seasonal migrant and often imported workers.

Through the nineteenth century and into the twentieth, Chinese workers, who had already built the western segments of the

railroad, migrated to toil in California's new farms, canals, ditch-
digging sites, and dams. At one point in the 1890s, they represented half of all California farmworkers. Japanese and Filipino
migrants also played important roles, as did Dust Bowl "Okies" and "Arkies." "The ill wind that was dusting the plains of the
lower Mississippi began to blow providently for agribusiness,"
wrote Ernesto Galarza. The arrival of the Dust Bowl migrants,
according to the anthropologist Walter Goldschmidt, for the first
time brought white families to join "the army of cheap labor that
is requisite for the continued functioning of the industrialized agriculture of California."

The workers who have driven agriculture in America have long
depended on that truism. But at the same time, they've almost
never fairly benefited from it. Especially in post-slavery America,
the agriculture industry's tried-and-true trick was to find laborers in circumstances so intolerable — like the Dust Bowl, for example — that they were willing to endure the most grueling jobs.

Black Americans and Indigenous people have each suffered
uniquely, but class divisions and disenfranchisement went beyond
race. The burgeoning, mostly white middle class depended on an
ever-growing underclass of immigrants. Filipino, Mexican, Chinese, and Japanese migrants, as well as the original Exodusters
who arrived in California, may have escaped famine and death in
their homelands, but they were hardly guaranteed better lives in
the United States, where they were denied landownership and became embroiled in the regime of disaster-prone mass production
of crops destined for distant markets. For the most part, these
workers would arrive desperate, realize the extent of their exploitation, then leave. If they stayed, they would often eventually
be expelled in favor of a new source of labor willing to take even
lower wages. Whether they came from another state or another
country didn't matter much, at least at first.

That changed with the onset of World War II. The resulting
general labor shortage was especially acute in California, where
the internment of Japanese Americans, two-thirds of whom were
citizens, had "the double effect of removing field workers who
were notably industrious, and of displacing farm families whose

labor contributed importantly in certain crops," notes author and organizer Ernesto Galarza. Even though more than a million Mexicans (many of whom were of Californian ancestry) had migrated north between the end of the nineteenth century and the beginning of the war, the shortage gave remaining farmworkers a bit of bargaining power. The industry didn't like that. Searching for solutions, it found an ally in the federal government, which was willing to regulate a seasonal labor force of immigrants who would be signed on to work in agriculture when and as needed.

Thus began the Bracero Program (the word means "one who uses his arms," or simply "worker"), agreed upon by the U.S. and Mexican governments. In 1947, the agribusiness capitalists wrote in their recommendations to the governor of California that in their ideal world, "Mexican workers . . . should constitute a flexible group which can be readily moved from place to place where local help falls short of the numbers needed to save the crops. These workers should be in a sense 'shock troops' used only in real emergency as insurance against the loss of valuable production." Workers, in other words, were hired on a seasonal, as-needed basis and then sent home when there was no need for them.

Without oversight, wage theft became routine, as did beatings, sexual harassment, overwork—just about every kind of abuse short of actual slavery. (There's a reason the Bracero Program is often called "rent-a-slave.") In other words, the status quo survived. The often skilled braceros were hideously underpaid for exactly as long as they were needed, and no longer. They were segregated from the greater society and were sent back to Mexico when their jobs were finished. This continued in one form or another until 1964, peaking at nearly 450,000 workers in 1959.

Little changed when the Bracero Program ended and migrant labor became technically illegal. Even general campaigns for workers' rights, which were spearheaded largely by European immigrants, usually excluded farmworkers, both because of their isolation and because of the organizers' racism. Progress came when the farmworker organizing of the late fifties attracted the attention of national labor unions like the United Auto Workers and the AFL-CIO, as well as racial justice groups like the Black Panthers and the NAACP. That progress continued with the merger and transformation of several different organizing groups, most notably the Filipino Agricultural Workers Organizing Committee and the National Farm Workers Association, led by Cesar Chavez and Dolores Huerta. (The modern name, United Farm Workers of America, or UFW, was formally adopted in 1972.)

Organizing itinerant workers was, as you might imagine, tough going. After years of struggle marked by only occasional success, Huerta proposed first a union blockage of table grapes and then the famous consumer boycott, which led to a successful contract in 1970. Yet even now, fifty years after some of the UFW's greatest victories, farmworkers in particular and food workers in general—the people who create, process, cook, and deliver the food we eat—often still go hungry.

Meanwhile, California farmland continues to yield high profits, in large part thanks to cheap labor, and it likely will continue to do so. Because, although California grows its crops one at a time on vast spreads—as anyone who's seen a thousand-acre farm of romaine in the Central Valley can verify—it produces a wide variety of crops, just about every edible plant imaginable. Growing hundreds of types of crops makes it more difficult to mechanize California's agriculture, and also makes it more difficult to sell that agriculture. It's fairly easy to sell boatloads of wheat to entire countries overseas. But to sell tomatoes and peaches and walnuts and rice and broccoli and lettuce and so on to individual markets within your own sprawling country—that's a whole 'nother ballgame.

The solution to California's ag problem was just as complex. Everyone wanted to get rich selling apricots, almonds, broccoli, and carrots. And the best way to do so was often freezing them or sealing them in a metal can. As a result, a new industry was built—the "food" industry—and technological innovation was its bread and butter.

8

Food and the Brand

USING YIELD AS the only metric, American agriculture was a roaring, overflowing success. The American farmer was growing a superabundance of wheat, corn, sugar, rice, cotton, and later soybeans. And yet, despite producing this surplus, farmers still continued to bear tremendous risk.

Then there was the question of what to do with this bounty. Such levels of surplus all but guaranteed cheap food. But more increasingly, the surplus was used to invent new versions of foods: Industry learned to process and manufacture almost everything, from butter and cheese and ketchup to breakfast cereal and bread and burgers. It was a new, revolutionary way to make money, and one that fundamentally changed the dinner table and how we eat.

For eaters, the results were a mixed bag. The new foods were time-savers in the short run — in this new era, almost no one was a farmer, and few had time to make pickles or milk a cow, but store-bought foods were affordable and convenient. In the long run, however, they caused ill health and brought with them hidden costs, like pollution and resource exhaustion, that negated the evident savings. As usual, the system most benefited the middlemen: traders, millers, equipment and chemical dealers, processors, wholesalers, and retailers.

Nevertheless, the surplus, and the production techniques that came with it, resulted in a wondrous slew of new offerings. Take the symbol of twentieth-century American eating: The cheeseburger. Topped with a flap of reduced and dyed milk paste ("American" cheese) and a generous drizzle of over-sweetened tomato jam (ketchup), then sandwiched in a sad simulacrum of bread, replete with painted-on "crust" (the bun), the all-beef patty became iconic.

We have all said — or at least heard — "There is nothing like a burger." In my pre-adolescence, I ate twenty-five-cent burgers. Better still, two burgers — fresh patties, juicy, crisped on a grill — fries, and a Coke for fifty-five cents. I remember sacks from White Castle in that same period. Several years later, in high school, I drove ninety miles with some friends in an old Ford to my first McDonald's, listening to the Beach Boys on AM radio.

It's likely that you have similar stories — the best, the local, the most memorable, and so on. Burgers have replaced "Mom and apple pie" as central to American life.

Yet there is nothing intrinsically fabulous about a burger, and many are, in fact, disgusting. But that doesn't reduce their significance: The burger is fundamental to our national consciousness, the embodiment of that huge area of beautiful, well-watered, nearly virgin land that allowed for ever-increasing production, discovery, invention, cunning, and a ruthless, ignorant exploitation of resources. Those resources yield fifty billion burgers a year in America alone, around 150 per person.

The story of how that all happened is the story of American beef itself.

The mid-nineteenth-century cattle drives were slow and risky. Drought and winter were deadly obstacles. By the 1880s, rail expansion and barbed wire fencing began to reduce the number of drives as cattle were shipped in railroad "stock" cars.

These shipments made the railroads a fortune, but the process was inefficient. The yield from a live cow was about forty percent, which means that for every hundred pounds of cattle that were crowded into a car and shipped, only forty pounds of meat could be sold after the cow was slaughtered and butchered. What's more, each cow had to be tended to, fed, and kept alive — not always an easy task, as disease spreads quickly in crowded cattle cars.

At first there was no way around it. A slaughtered carcass didn't keep well during shipping, a constraint that was handcuffing the entire beef-packing business, keeping it local and small, and limiting profit. Fresh pork kept a little better, and many of its popular finished products, like ham and bacon, were already preserved. Thus beef accounted for only three percent of the meatpacking industry as a whole.

These challenges were profound, but demand and the potential for profit were nearly unlimited. There had to be a solution. The breakthrough came in 1880, when Gustavus Swift built a fleet of refrigerated railcars that could reliably transport freshly butchered ("dressed") beef from Chicago to New York. What had once been many discrete, local, and decentralized beef industries became a unified national business with no limits on growth.

Swift quickly built his own stockyard and slaughter facilities in Chicago, St. Louis, and other critical rail junctures in the Midwest, and a new network of distribution centers all across the country. By 1900 the dressed-meat business, controlled by just a few firms, was the second-largest industry in the country, after steel. The leaders formed a trust, fixing both prices and freight rates, while the railroads gave the monopoly preferential pricing.

Teddy Roosevelt famously attempted to bust the trusts, but the industry was so heavily capitalized and infrastructure-based that there was no hope for a new competitor. As a result, though their names have changed since 1900, there are still only four major meatpackers in the United States.

At the time—the early twentieth century—the boom doubled the country's cattle in twenty years, to the point where there were almost nine cattle for every ten people in this country, a proportion as high as we've ever seen. (The ratio is about a third of that today.) Some of this meat—maybe ten percent, but not more— was exported, which left a *lot* of beef for domestic consumption, about a pound per person per week. And about forty percent of the yield from a typical cow is ground beef.

That meant there were a lot of burgers.

Guessing when and where the hamburger was invented is a fool's game, since it's likely that spiced ground meat on bread was eaten wherever bread and meat first intersected, thousands of years ago. (It certainly wasn't in Hamburg.) Although there's some evidence that the first dedicated burger joint in the United States was Louis'

Lunch, in New Haven, Connecticut, founded in 1895 and still there, the burger became popular in late-nineteenth-century New York and elsewhere. The zeitgeist really caught on just after World War I.

The White Castle System of Eating Houses was founded in 1921, and its first hurdle was convincing consumers that ground beef was safe. Upton Sinclair's *The Jungle* was published in 1906, and its tales of poisoned rats being tossed in the meat grinder were, er, unsettling.

But ground meat was suspect even before *The Jungle*. No one knew what was actually being ground, and people generally believed that ground meat was about-to-spoil meat. White Castle's founder, Edgar "Billy" Ingram, addressed that by grinding fresh beef directly in front of customers. He also made his buildings out of stainless steel and white enamel, and even his choice of name was a tactic, since the color white symbolized purity and cleanliness in a society tainted by racism.

Ingram created a standard of architecture, menu, and quality, as well as a standardized form of takeout: the sack. These strategies, combined with a five-cents-per-burger price, made his first restaurants an instant success. White Castle saturated the Wichita market in less than two years, and by the end of the decade it was national. And profitable: Managers used company biplanes to cover their massive territories.

Hundreds of copycat entrepreneurs followed, building small white buildings in which burgers were cooked and sold, and coining names like White Tower, Red Castle, and White Palace. Meanwhile, Ingram continued to innovate: He created a proto–Betty Crocker, hiring a woman he renamed Julia Joyce and sending her out to promote White Castle to groups of women.

He also foreshadowed the movie *Super Size Me*, by funding an experiment in which a medical student named Bernard Flesche ate nothing but hamburgers — an average of more than twenty a day — for thirteen weeks. Flesche was pronounced in good health at the experiment's conclusion, but he reportedly tired of the diet and never ate a burger willingly again. He died of heart issues at the age of fifty-four.

For several reasons, the rise of cheese into the apotheosis of burger toppings was inevitable. The thin beef patty could be dry, and few would argue with a creamy and salty topping in any case. Even without any added preservatives other than salt, cheese keeps well. (The writer Clifton Fadiman charmingly called it "milk's leap toward immortality.") Some natural cheeses, like Parmesan, can last for years without turning bad.

And, not surprisingly, given all those cattle, there was a surplus of milk. Production had grown by a factor of ten between the end of the Civil War and the beginning of World War I. During the latter war, milk — canned, condensed, and powdered — was shipped overseas. And, as with wheat, demand stimulated supply. From 1914 to 1918, canned milk production increased from 660 million pounds to more than 1.5 *billion* pounds. The market seemed unlimited. Farmers responded, as per habit, by producing more and more.

When demand slackened at the end of the war, the first great dairy surplus followed. Falling prices brought more milk to more people than ever before, processing plants closed daily, and industry soon consolidated. According to Harvey Levenstein, in *Revolution at the Table*, "In one week alone, Borden's [dairy company] purchased fifty-two concerns."

Next came imaginative marketing. In Wisconsin, the dairy capital of the most dairy-productive country in the world, selling milk was paramount. In 1919, the National Dairy Council —formed in 1915 to convince the public of the safety of milk after an outbreak of foot-and-mouth disease—targeted childhood nutrition with its first pamphlet, "Milk: The Necessary Food for Growth and Health." It was written by the era's best-known pusher of cow's milk, Elmer V. McCollum, a biochemist at the University of Wisconsin's Agricultural Experiment Station.

In 1918, sounding much like William Crookes in his Great Wheat Speech twenty years earlier, McCollum advanced the gospel of milk as part of a campaign to convince the public to drink more of it: "The peoples who have made liberal use of milk . . . have been more aggressive than the non-milk using peoples, and have achieved much greater advancement in literature, science and art."

Before long, children were "educated" to drink four glasses (a quart!) each day. And pasteurization (widely mandated by 1909), refrigeration, and declining adulteration made fresh milk readily available nationwide. It became even more popular with the introduction and mass marketing of chocolate milk, perfected by Nestlé, and ice cream. Then, in 1940, schools in Chicago began providing milk for students, and most of the rest of the country followed, selling milk for a penny a serving.

The USDA compensated dairies for the difference between the penny and their costs, including profit. In 1946, when the National School Lunch Program began, meals were *required* to feature milk. This mandate continues, as do other forms of government support for dairy, including for advertising.

Today we take this all for granted. But although milk is indeed healthier than soda, water is the preferred routine beverage for most non-nursing humans. Cow's milk isn't the ideal food for babies, children, or anyone else.

In fact, milk has never been essential. It's high in protein, but almost all Americans get more than enough protein without trying. It's also high in saturated fat, which, unfortunately, the American diet also has in abundance. Whether overall it's harmful or helpful, milk is far from a necessary food, and even farther from the wonder food that early marketing campaigns peddled.

What's more, the *majority* of humans, as many as sixty-five percent, are lactose intolerant. Milk gives them intestinal distress, or worse. (I was a perfect example of a milk-sick child, encouraged if not forced to drink several glasses a day and chronically intestinally woeful. When I grew up and virtually stopped drinking milk, those ailments disappeared.)

Nevertheless, the National Dairy Council's marketing scheme was a success, and then some. By 1925 the average American consumed about a gallon of milk a week. And yet, no matter how much the government and industry promoted milk consumption, there was always a surplus. With the average dairy cow producing more than four hundred gallons of milk each year, and with more than twenty million dairy cattle in the country, there were billions of gallons of the stuff to be consumed. The solution to this problem was more cheese.

As the best way to preserve excess milk, cheese making has been common in dairying areas for as long as they've existed. What's more, even before the twentieth century, cheese had been a steady source of income for many farmers. An average pre-1900 family milked five or six cows, as Bruce Kraig describes in *A Rich and Fertile Land: A History of Food in America*. By the early nineteenth century those families produced an estimated hundred million pounds of cheese per year.

Eventually, households banded together to hire a common cheese maker and began pooling milk in a centralized facility. Some of these became factories, which bought milk from local families—sometimes hundreds of them—and produced cheese at scale.

Eventually, these factories replaced hand-hewn cheesecloth and massive wheels that required two people to rotate with steel vats and mechanical presses. For quicker turnaround and more profit, cheese wasn't aged as long, which stunted flavor, which was in turn boosted by the addition of other ingredients, plus coloring of course. Thus virtually ended cheese-making artisans and good cheese made by Americans.

Responding to the increased need for a product that could be produced fast and in bulk, and last more or less forever, James L. Kraft patented his processed cheese—what we think of today as American cheese. His techniques involved grinding a variety of quickly made, low-grade, cheese-like paste, adding salt and other ingredients, and pasteurizing the resulting glop, resulting in cheese with a long shelf life and an even, low-temperature melting point.

Like so many others, the company got its break with wartime government contracts. By the end of the 1920s Kraft sold forty percent of the cheese in the United States. That number climbed even higher when the company conquered the technical challenges of developing Kraft Singles, a process that sent cheese sales through the roof—and helped standardize the modern cheeseburger.

But even with cheese, burgers need fixins. Enter Henry J. Heinz and his wonder condiment: ketchup.

In his rise to dominance, Heinz had the help of Harvey Wiley, an Indiana-born doctor and chemist, a charismatic zealot who became head of the USDA's Division of Chemistry in 1883 and made a mission of rescuing the American people from harmful chemicals and fraud.

There was plenty of each. Before the railroads were built, food was usually locally sourced. But by the end of the nineteenth century, it was processed, preserved, packaged, and shipped on a never-before-seen scale. Manufacturers, distributors, and marketers could move and sell food *anywhere* without government regulation, largely flying under the radar.

Fraud was common and profitable, and consumers knew that food was hardly guaranteed to be "pure." An official estimate put tainted food at about fifteen percent of the total market. Milk, for example, was often watered down, thickened with starch or plaster of Paris, and finally preserved with formaldehyde. Mushrooms were bleached. Peas were kept green with copper sulfate, a pesticide. Flour was mixed with sand, and bread was baked with sawdust.

Everyone suspected that beef was doctored or tainted, too. There was *The Jungle*, which had followed soon after the "embalmed beef scandal" of the 1898 Spanish-American War, where soldiers claimed to have been fed meat that caused an epidemic of illness. As the issue became bigger, President Theodore Roosevelt wrote to Sinclair, "The specific evils you point out shall, if their existence be proved, and if I have power, be eradicated."

Wiley was on board with that. Among his devotees was a group of young employees dubbed the "Poison Squad," a tight-knit band whose motto was "Only the Brave Dare Eat the Fare." They ingested chemicals like sulfuric acid, formaldehyde, and copper sulfate in an attempt to provide evidence to ban new food additives.

But Wiley had a number of other, less extreme allies in appealing to Theodore Roosevelt to join the chemical fight. Eventually, Henry Heinz jumped into the fray, albeit with less-than-righteous motives.

Heinz was one of perhaps two thousand commercial makers of ketchup, a bastardization of what had originally been a British attempt to mimic the dark, fermented fish sauces of Asia. In America, ketchup had become an efficient way to use the bits of tomato rejected during the canning process, whether because they were too small, too ripe, not ripe enough, rotten, worm-eaten, or otherwise unacceptable. Often, these bits were collected into a slop on the factory floor, boiled down, skimmed, seasoned, and bottled.

It took skill to make ketchup appetizing, and that skill involved the use of a variety of "food colorings, including cochineal, carmine, eosine, acid magenta, and various aniline coal-tar dyes," as well as preservatives, including boric acid (until Germany banned imports containing it), and salicylic acid, which is safe only at low levels. (Made from the willow tree, it's the basis of aspirin but also is useful in removing skin.) Almost all existing brands of ketchup — the condiment was already ubiquitous — also used sodium benzoate, which was an effective preservative, tasteless and (probably) harmless.

Heinz reckoned that if he could eliminate sodium benzoate from his ketchup while also getting the chemical banned, he would be the only legal ketchup maker left. This, however, meant an overhaul of the production process: Heinz needed a new recipe — one that would ensure that ketchup would keep more or less indefinitely without chemical preservatives — as well as a more sanitary factory environment and a more reliable transportation network.

His most important modification was doubling the amount of sugar. This preserved the concoction more naturally and gave it the stronger body with which we're now all familiar: One tablespoon of this new ketchup had as much sugar as a typical cookie. And, oddly, while he made the ketchup much thicker, Heinz failed to change the narrow-necked design of the bottle, resulting in decades of people banging their palms against the bottom of the bottle.

It remained for Heinz to make sodium benzoate illegal. Food safety legislation had been continually introduced in Congress for more than a decade, usually at Wiley's behest. But food processors joined with whiskey makers and drug companies, which were making a killing selling snake oil, to keep their deceits and poisons outside the jurisdiction of law.

Roosevelt made food regulation a priority in his second term, however, and Wiley (with support from Heinz, who worked on details) was the primary author of the bill eventually known as the Pure Food and Drug Act of 1906. It reached the House just as *The Jungle* was published, which helped tilt the scales.

But Wiley and Heinz fell short of their dream policy: The new law didn't ban any food ingredient outright. It did, however, require transparency in labeling, forcing manufacturers to disclose the presence of everything used in the production process, including chemicals. That was good enough for Heinz, at least, who simply wanted government to endorse "pure food," a marketing term that allowed him and other large manufacturers to slander and bankrupt smaller ones.

The act was a victory for Heinz, who mounted an innovative "public information" campaign against the dangers of preservatives. "Shall Your Foods Be Drugged or Not?" read one advertisement. "Benzoate of soda is a coal tar drug. If there is any good in it when used in Ketchup, why doesn't the manufacturer who uses it blazon it in great letters on the label instead of whispering it in the smallest type he can find?" Heinz ketchup took over the market.

Thus, a law that aimed to protect the public resulted in a dangerous precedent that reigns to this day. By providing consumers with the name of every ingredient in their processed food and letting them decide what's good and what isn't, the government dodges all responsibility under the pretense of "freedom of choice."

Since then, some ingredients have been banned, but thousands more have been either "generally recognized as safe" — a category established in 1958 to signify approval by the Food and Drug Administration (FDA) based on assurances by manufacturers — or simply ignored by regulators. This effectively empowered corporations to propagate disinformation and deceptive marketing. It also marked the beginning of manufacturers adding sugar to virtually everything. Sugar almost universally heightens flavor and has the added benefit, from a manufacturer's point of view at least, of being habit-forming.

There were national brands in the nineteenth century: Nestlé was founded in 1866, Heinz and Campbell's in 1869, Coca-Cola in 1892, and United Fruit (later Chiquita) in 1899. But Heinz's successful bid to anoint its ketchup above all others brought branding's importance to the fore. Dozens of manufacturers were mass-producing hundreds of foods that either didn't exist before or now existed in a new form. These foods were distant from nature, less nutritious, but certainly more shelf-stable. How to make each of them stand out?

With competition becoming national and stamping out most local products, branding was essential. "Soup" and "bread" and "green beans," products that had no identity in and of themselves, would lose out to those that did — Campbell's and Wonder Bread and Birds Eye, which had "brand appeal," like Oldsmobile and Colgate.

Successful branding is more than just a cute name, but sometimes not much more. In essence, it's as simple as adding distinctive, though often meaningless, characteristics to a product — color, packaging, a catchy slogan or jingle, sometimes even claims of quality. In many cases, dreaming up a successful branding and marketing campaign for a new product is enough to create the product itself. In the words of the *Harvard Business Review*, "Brand is everything, and everything is brand."

To win at marketing, advertising, public relations, and sales, you have to have the best brand. This might be a matter of luck, of manipulation (as with Heinz's ketchup), of hiring brand-building experts, or simply through purchasing existing brands. Which is why, during the rise of the brand, the most successful companies were conglomerates like General Foods and Standard Brands.

For food processors, developing brands is imperative. This became clear more than a hundred years ago, when shoppers began to select a box or a can or a bag whose contents were entirely hidden. The quality of the items in these containers was impossible to determine until they were brought home, so shoppers had to be "educated" about their distinguishing features. That education came about through marketing and advertising.

Producers might be able to market broccoli: It's beautifully formed—a miniature tree!—with a pleasing color and a strong but likable flavor. It even prevents cancer. But producers can't *own* broccoli. The broccoli I sell can't be much different from yours. And even if I find an awesome new variety—one that's purple or has great flavor or prevents cancer better—you can grow it, too. I could freeze broccoli and label it with my brand—say, Green Giant—but even that doesn't add much to its profit margin.

If, however, I create broccoli chips, which keep forever, contain added fiber, and are loaded with soy protein and perhaps some sugar and a few chemical enhancers for extra flavor—*that* I can brand. Bitty's Broccoli Bites!

Distinctive brands soon went national. In the twentieth century, people began to eat the same brand of bread as their cousin in Syracuse or their friend in Des Moines. They saw the same ads in magazines and newspapers and heard the same commercials on the radio. The same was true of television in the coming decades, and on the web a half century after that. People became loyal to these brands, and they looked for them everywhere. And they found these brands with ease.

As brands became dominant, they determined what crops got planted and how those crops were processed and sold. More than ever, crops were grown for their potential as derivatives, not as actual food sources.

In a very real way, this led to the standardization of the American diet. Beginning with the food-processing giants and their brands that emerged in the 1920s, corporations like Standard Brands and General Foods—eventually subsumed by Nabisco and Kraft, the first in turn absorbed by Mondelez International and the second joined with Heinz—had created a pantheon of food-by-formula, scientifically engineered, "easy-to-prepare" products, then brought them to life with marketing.

Campbell's Soup led the charge by demonstrating the profit potential of bold advertising, producing large and colorful magazine displays and bringing out that iconic tomato-red-and-white label, with its recognizable typeface. (No one thought color was worth the marketing money until then.) They targeted housewives, too: "I Couldn't Keep House Without Campbell's Tomato Soup" and "Wouldn't I Be Silly to Make It Myself?" Between 1899 and 1920, Campbell's multiplied its marketing budget one hundredfold, reaching a million dollars. During the Depression it ballooned to $3.5 million.

In 1904, Campbell's became an early adopter of the now staple industry technique of marketing to and about kids, creating a cartoon series where plump and red-cheeked darlings were kept wholesome and healthy through eating soup. A few years later, the company published a small cookbook, a style of advertising that soon became commonplace. Even though canned foods hardly require preparation, this augmented their value by pushing the processed foods—like Campbell's Cream of Mushroom soup—as needed ingredients to produce other dishes, like "casseroles."

Of course, convenience food like Campbell's Cream of Mushroom soup is "processed," or even ultra-processed, a term that I'm going to use frequently from this point on to describe those foods morphed beyond recognition, and one that's coming into common use. Few ultra-processed foods (UPFs) are natural (in the real sense of the word, not the marketers' sense) or nutritious. Some, such as Froot Loops and Coke, are even anti-nutritious. Food manufacturers combat such truths with statements like "Almost all food is processed!" This is convincing enough for many people, since even whole-grain flour has to be ground and refined, and nothing like bread exists in nature. How's the buyer supposed to know what's real and what isn't?

Michael Pollan famously recommended that you not eat anything your nineteenth-century ancestors wouldn't recognize as food, which is sound advice. It's also easy enough to say of hyper-processed food what Supreme Court Justice Potter Stewart said of obscenity: You know it when you see it. Plain oatmeal is "processed" food, just like all breakfast cereal. But it doesn't take a genius to see that it's a far cry from Froot Loops.

It's wrong to argue that women, who were trying to hold their homes together while effectively working full-time jobs with no official pay, shouldn't take advantage of every shortcut that they could. Still, deception was needed to convince many women to adopt a diet that commodified taste, relied on artificial nutrients, and thumbed its nose at tradition. Among the foremost early deceivers was the beloved Betty Crocker, who in 1945 was named the "First Lady of Food" by *Fortune* magazine. It also dubbed her the second most popular woman in America, behind Eleanor Roosevelt.

Of course, Betty didn't exist.

She was born fully formed, or at least thought up, in 1921 by staff of Washburn Crosby (later General Mills) and developed by home economist Marjorie Husted, who would write Betty's radio scripts and serve as her voice. A good-looking, charismatic, and all-knowing puppet, Betty normalized and glorified the new ultra-processed foods: "Who could ask for anything better than white cake with chocolate ice cream and marshmallow topping right out of a jar?" Betty pondered.

Betty received marriage proposals and gave advice. She shifted with the times, from housewife Betty to business Betty. And even when that same *Fortune* article revealed that the First Lady of Food didn't exist, her popularity continued unabated, as did industry's ability to normalize food coming from a box or a can, and not from the earth, with little more than a catchy mascot.

But not all brand building was done through creating new foods or fake people and then marketing the hell out of them. Some stemmed from political and military manipulations involving food, actions that profoundly affected not only the global food system, but the sovereignty of entire nations. The best symbol for this is the banana, and the banana's own indomitable symbol: Miss Chiquita, the ubiquitous "First Lady of Fruit." Her eponymous produce empire was an amazing and unprecedented example of branding that made a household name out of a product that was not even remotely distinguishable from its competition except by its label.

United Fruit—one of the most important players in the banana world, along with Standard Fruit (later Dole)—was formed in the late nineteenth century, in a merger between an enterprising fruit shipper and the son of a global railroad tycoon. The company became known as "El Pulpo" (the octopus), because it had a tentacle in just about every country in Central America, and its power extended even farther south.

United Fruit operated with more than impunity: It had the protection of the U.S. government and in particular the CIA, which enforced the company's colonial power by funding agitators, performing elaborate cover-ups, stoking civil wars in El Salvador, Colombia, and Honduras, among others, and even engineering entire regime changes. In 1954, the CIA–United Fruit team overthrew the government of Guatemala.

By 1929 United Fruit owned three and a half million acres globally—about the area of Connecticut—as well as major railroads. Bananas became cheaper than apples, and they remain so. In fact, they're now the world's fourth-largest crop, after wheat, rice, and corn—a hundred billion of them are shipped every year.

As its international capers ate away at United Fruit's reputation, the company turned to marketing and public relations prophet Edward Bernays, who'd seen what propaganda was capable of during World War I and wanted to test its power in peacetime business. Shunning the manipulative and sometimes evil implications of that word, he rebranded the practice of changing people's minds as "public relations." Whether he was selling soap or cigarettes or changing the public image of a nefarious corporation, Bernays deployed a tried-and-true operation of "defining goals, allocating resources, strategizing, and finally determining the best course of action."

Throughout the twentieth century, Bernays, who lived to 103

and became known as the father of public relations, worked with organizations as diverse as Procter & Gamble and the NAACP. His work only rarely touched specifically on food, but he had some notable wins. One of those was his clever rebranding of United Fruit, bestowing the company with the outward face of Señorita Chiquita Banana (originally Miss Chiquita), who has carried the company's reputation admirably despite its brutal attempts throughout the years to preserve utter control in Central America.

In the fifty years following the Civil War, American cities went from containing one-fifth to one-half of the country's population. As more people left farms, the majority of Americans relied on others to supply them with food. So the final piece of the brand dominance puzzle was technology, which was rapidly revolutionizing food accessibility. Railroads could bring food from almost anywhere to almost anyone, but advances in food preservation and cooking itself were equally crucial.

When the twentieth century began, most cooking was done on massive cast-iron stoves that burned coal or wood, which are heavy and cumbersome. The stoves themselves required a great deal of maintenance and tending, and they were the source of frequent and sometimes horrible burns. ("Mind the stove" didn't just mean "Stir the pot.") They also coated nearby surfaces with smudgy soot and sometimes started fires that could burn a house down.

Anyone who could afford to transition to gas did so. With easily adjusted flames and thermostatically controlled ovens, the new kitchen ranges were immeasurable improvements—so much so that they haven't changed much since.

Canning had also become common. In 1795, the French government (where Napoleon, who famously said, "An army marches on its stomach," was a rising commander) offered a reward to the French person who could find a way to make his troops' food last longer. The winner was Nicolas Appert, who invented canning technology in 1804.

Appert didn't understand why canning works, but we do. A

hot-water bath kills bacteria and builds steam in the closed container. As the steam cools, it condenses, and the internal pressure reduces; the now greater external pressure seals the lid. With the contents and their internal surroundings sterilized, and the seal preventing new bacteria from entering, the food itself was safe to eat at any time, so long as the seal held. It's bacteria, not time, that cause spoilage.

Canning became an industry of its own at the time of the Civil War, and soldiers from the North and the South alike got a taste of canned food. (The South had few canning facilities, which was a real problem, but its troops often raided the Union's supplies.) By the 1890s, cans were ubiquitous in middle-class American households, where urbanization meant smaller or no gardens. The gap between eaters and food was growing wider, and the quality of food in general was deteriorating. Sugar was often added during the canning process as well.

Home refrigeration and freezing changed things even more. Before refrigeration, ice was a commodity, brought down from the mountains or cut out of frozen lakes and stored—often buried —for as long as possible. In the States, most nineteenth-century northern towns had their own large insulated icehouse, like a walk-in cooler, from which individuals could withdraw or buy. The first home refrigerator was a small version of this: the icebox. In those places not cold enough to produce it, ice was often shipped in. Keeping food cool was just that important.

The early twentieth century brought mechanical refrigerators, which first became common in meatpacking plants and breweries in the late nineteenth century, and then in homes after the end of World War I, where the ability to keep food "fresh"—or at least fresher—reduced the need for daily market trips.

From a preservation perspective, cold was good, but colder was even better. Clarence Birdseye, a bankrupt New York taxidermist trying to make a go of it in Labrador in the 1910s, was inspired by the Inuit method of freezing just-caught fish on the ice.

Birdseye was determined to create a way to freeze food without the Arctic climate. He began experimenting with freezing green vegetables, and in the twenties he developed a new method

—pressing food between two metal plates kept frigid using an ammonia-based refrigerant. Later, he changed the metal plates to belts, and the ammonia to calcium chloride spray. This worked even faster, and preserved the food better, because slow freezing bursts cells.

In 1929, General Foods owner Marjorie Post was served what turned out to be a previously frozen goose, and enjoyed it enough to purchase Birdseye's company. The alliance spurred the improvement of his technology, and, as freezers became smaller and cheaper, they were installed in supermarkets, in three-way alliances between the stores, Birdseye, and the appliance manufacturers.

The pace of technological change was astonishing. Suddenly there was electric lighting, washing machines, and vacuum cleaners, while countless other items that were formerly made at home, from clothing to soap, were churning out of factories. As a result, people became increasingly used to buying what they needed.

The next stage of the revolution involved the buying process itself.

By the end of World War II, canned food, refrigerated food, boxed food, and frozen food were all ubiquitous in the United States. With production, marketing, and transportation all modernized, it was inevitable that stores, the establishments that interacted directly with shoppers, would change as well.

Until the twentieth century, people in cities and towns walked from shop to shop, often daily, buying vegetables and fruits here, meat there, dry goods elsewhere. Grocery stores with larger selections weren't self-service at the time. Customers asked a clerk for items or handed over a list, then waited while their order was assembled, or left and had their order delivered to their home.

From the customer's perspective, it was a mixed bag. The full service was nice, but the process was slow. Discounting was virtually unheard of, and supply was erratic. For grocers, it was wildly inefficient. They relied on a world of wholesalers, salesmen, and jobbers to fill their inventory. And with each customer being waited on personally, labor costs were high.

Between the car, of which there were three times as many in 1930 as there had been in 1920, and the refrigerator, which virtually eliminated daily trips to the market, food shopping was clearly destined for change.

One pioneer was the Great Atlantic and Pacific Tea Company, founded in 1859 as a retail tea company and converted to a chain of grocery stores by its second generation of owners. The new shops, standardized with a white-and-red A&P logo, were greater in number and lesser in service. The chain created its own factories for store-brand goods, centralized ordering for third-party merchandise, built or bought warehouses, and assembled fleets of trucks.

In short order, shopping moved toward self-service. Credit was no longer an option, and delivery was offered only in dense urban centers. A&P used scale to reduce the number of middlemen, cut costs, and make supply more reliable. In no time at all it was wildly successful, the Walmart of its time, with 650 stores on the eve of World War I and almost ten thousand just ten years later. By 1930 it had sixteen thousand. Today's two biggest grocery store chains, Walmart and Kroger, have half that many combined.

But the paradigm changed again in 1916, when a Memphis businessman named Clarence Saunders opened the first Piggly Wiggly, which advertised discounts, an appealing feature given inflated wartime prices. To remain profitable, Saunders ruthlessly reduced labor costs. Instead of having clerks help people, he employed some workers to deal with stock and others to operate cash registers. He also created a one-way pattern that guided shoppers through the aisles and forced them to see every brightly colored box.

Self-service, where food and packaging did the talking, created a new connection between customer and brand, a connection that was forged by national ad campaigns that encouraged people to browse and buy—not because an item was on their original list, but just because it was on the shelf and looked good.

This was a seismic shift. Food shopping once involved patronizing several businesses, locally owned and operated, with relationships and services that provided many jobs. Those services and jobs were factored into the cost of food itself, which was relatively more expensive.

With supermarkets came a race to the bottom. Services declined, as did the quality and actual *value* of the food being sold, until later generations took it for granted that all food was branded, and often completely contrived. (Reflect, for a second, on the existence of the frozen entity called Lean Cuisine Casual Cuisine Wood Fire Style BBQ-Recipe Chicken Frozen Pizza.) They took for granted the presence of supermarkets, too, soulless venues for marketers to push their wares. For many people, real food became little more than an afterthought.

9

Vitamania and "the Farm Problem"

AT THE TURN of the twentieth century, the economy was becoming increasingly nationalized and commodity-based, and impoverished, mostly Black southern farmers and sharecroppers, desperate to make money, were still growing cotton almost exclusively. This meant they had to buy their own food, and the staple they most often turned to was corn, which, grown in unprecedented quantities in the Midwest, was almost as cheap as dirt.

When Columbus brought corn from Mesoamerica to Spain in 1498, the crop spread like crazy. It's easy to grow, yields in abundance, and keeps well, which is what every cash-hungry farmer wants.

But without nixtamalization—the process of treating dried corn with slaked lime—corn is a poor staple, not nearly as good as whole wheat and brown rice. And while the Spaniards had spread the crop throughout Europe and among many of those Europeans who ultimately became Americans, including (both directly and indirectly) enslaved people, they all but abandoned the process that maximized its nutritional benefits. Relying on unnixtamalized cornmeal mush (grits, in the South) to the exclusion of other foods, as southern farmers were forced to do, led to niacin deficiency. That in turn caused widespread cases of pellagra and "the four Ds" that accompany it: diarrhea, dermatitis, dementia, and death.

Eighty-seven thousand people died from pellagra in the

American South at the beginning of the twentieth century. More than half of them were African American, and more than two-thirds were women.

It's been known for millennia that diet has a central role in health, and that different foods prevent different diseases. A number of cultures, including the Maya and the Vedic (the Indian culture that developed Ayurvedic medicine), used "hot" foods and "cold" foods—referring not to temperature but to supposed effects on the body—for different groups of ailments. The Egyptians identified scurvy five thousand years ago, and British sailors were called "limeys" because they were given limes to prevent the disease. Neither, however, knew about the key nutrient: vitamin C.

At about the same time as the American South's pellagra crisis, half a world away in Java, a Dutchman named Christiaan Eijkman uncovered the science behind nutritional deficiencies. Searching for the cause of beriberi, Eijkman conducted a series of experiments on chickens and linked beriberi to a diet of white rice, which is stripped of many of its nutrients during processing. When he fed the chickens nutritionally whole brown rice, they were cured. And so were humans. It was later determined that beriberi is caused by a lack of thiamine (B_1), present in the bran layer of whole grains.

One by one, vitamins were isolated and named, and by 1948 thirteen were deemed essential, in this case a term that means not only necessary for health, but not produced by the human body. Other essential nutrients not considered vitamins have since been identified. In 1941, the National Academy of Sciences and the National Research Council, working together to determine suitable rations for troops, issued the first Recommended Daily Allowances (RDAs), which attempted to quantify the optimal intake for calories and essential vitamins and minerals.

That same year, the recently established FDA issued standards for enriching white flour, beginning what became known as the "quiet miracle," the eventual near elimination of vitamin-deficiency-related diseases like beriberi and pellagra through the addition of synthetic nutrients to common foods. Iron and B vitamins were added to flour, vitamin C to orange juice concentrate, and vitamin A to margarine.

Nutrient fortifying seemed like a good solution to a problem that hadn't existed when bread was brown. It promised a quick and marvelous fix for the developing system of food processing, and without the legwork needed for structural change. But the true nature of food and nutrition isn't that simple.

You may remember Justus von Liebig, who defined the trinity of plant nutrition: nitrogen, potassium, and phosphorus. Since plants needed only three key nutrients, according to Liebig's erroneous writings, it should follow that the laws of human metabolism would be analogous. All we are is the sum of the plants we eat, he reasoned, and those plants eaten by the animals we, in turn, eat. Recall the reductionist maxim: Everything can be understood as the sum of its constituent parts.

Since humans understood very little about nutrition at the time, not much stood in the way of Liebig's confirmation bias. And so, in his mid-nineteenth-century *Researches on the Chemistry of Food, and the Motion of the Juices in the Animal Body,* he described the "dietetic trinity" of human nutrition: proteins, carbohydrates, and fats.

Just before 1900, German researchers began to measure the ideal amount and type of food humans need. Wilbur Olin Atwater, a professor at Wesleyan who'd spent time in Germany, was inspired to develop a kind of respiration chamber called a room calorimeter. These were sealed, and well-appointed rooms in which subjects would live for days, performing whatever activities one would consider normal in a twenty-eight-square-foot room. Energy expended was measured by heat exchange, and, through this, Atwater was able to determine the caloric values of thousands of foods. He also pioneered the understanding that the human body metabolized calories of macronutrients—fat, carbohydrate, or protein—differently, and that all three were needed for nutritional balance.

But the calorie reduced food to a measure of heat, and the tautological statement "A calorie is a calorie"—meaning all food was of essentially the same quality—gained authority. Thermodynamically speaking, it's true. A calorie is defined as the amount of energy required to increase the temperature of a gram of water one degree centigrade, no matter where or in what it's found. (That amount of energy is 4.2 joules.) But from the standpoint of nutrition, it's an incomplete statement, harmful, cynical, and fodder for nefarious propaganda from producers of nutritionally bereft foods.

Liebig and Atwater's findings were reducing the complexity of food to some components of nutrition, and making the latter more important than the former, a fundamental mistake we live with today. Just as soil needs more than potassium, phosphorus, and nitrogen, human nutrition is more complex than the calories contained in proteins, fats, and carbohydrates, along with whatever micronutrients we've managed to analyze.

The simplistic approach, however, dominated. Nutritionists and others everywhere began addressing the symptoms of malnourishment rather than the causes.

For example, although eating brown rice prevents beriberi, white rice has a better shelf life and can stave off beriberi as long as it's dosed with synthetic thiamine. Yet brown rice is more than white rice plus thiamine, and by failing to recognize this complexity (and even mystery), producers have degraded our diets in ways nutritionists don't fully understand.

That argument has not been a match for expediency; it was easier and more profitable to address deficiencies by adding micronutrients in chemical form. Furthermore, vitamins provided a novel selling point to deliver peace of mind: Think, for example, of the staying power of orange juice's vitamin-C-laced reputation. People called this new marketing obsession "vitamania," and it became a fad that never ended. In 1942, the vitamin market was worth two hundred million dollars a year; today it's thirty billion dollars.

In the early twentieth century, vitamania changed no traditional food more radically than bread. Until then, white flour had been difficult to produce. It was associated with wealth, and believed to be more pure than actually pure ground whole wheat. (In America, this association took on racial overtones: white loaves were "chaste," and dark ones "defiled.") But without added nutrients, white flour offers little besides calories.

"Grains" are actually a subset of fruits. As a category, they include a long list of some of the world's most widely consumed foods: rice, quinoa, fonio, and more. (Corn is included, although it's technically a vegetable. None of this taxonomy is as precise as Linnaeus, the eighteenth-century Swede who developed modern taxonomy, believed.) Whole grains have been providing the bulk of calories for humans since just after the birth of agriculture; they've been the most reliable source of nutrition for entire civilizations. And near the top of the list of civilization-sustaining grains is wheat.

The bran of whole wheat—the tough outer layer—contains the fiber that few of us get enough of, as well as some B vitamins and minerals. The germ, the most nutrient-rich part of the kernel, has the greatest share of vitamin E, folic acid, phosphorus, zinc, magnesium, and thiamine. Take those away and you're left with the starchy endosperm, which makes up the bulk of the grain and contains most of its carbohydrates. It's a good source of calories, but it's not a whole, nourishing food.

In addition to nutrients, though, the bran and germ contain oil, and that oil can go rancid with time, ruining the flour. Get rid of those pesky elements and the resulting white flour keeps more or less forever. So wheat producers were faced with a choice: local production, which required quick sale and consumption of a higher-quality ingredient, or mass production, with a long shelf life and a nutritionally inferior product. For large producers, the choice was an easy one.

Separating bran and germ from endosperm had always been challenging. Even simple milling requires that a dried wheat berry, sometimes almost as hard as a pebble, be finely ground so as to make it palatable when mixed with water. "Stone-ground" means just that: pulverizing grains between two stones, traditionally moved and turned by humans, animals, or water- or wind power.

Historically, discarding bran and germ took more steps, more

time, and more work; it was also wasteful. Hence the limited availability of white flour and, again, the tendency for milled grains to
be sold locally, before the flour could spoil.

With the mid-nineteenth-century invention of the steel roller
mill in Budapest, powered by steam and later electricity, the
process of producing white flour sped up immeasurably. In the
United States especially, the sheer amount of flour produced,
along with the great distances it traveled to market, meant that
never-spoiling white flour quickly became the norm. Industrially
produced white bread followed soon thereafter.

Until a hundred years ago, the major problem with commercially
made bread was that buyers didn't know what was in it. Flour was
often extended with filling but non-nutritious ingredients, and
sometimes dangerous ones like chopped leaves and straw, sand,
plaster of Paris, and who knows what else. (In the nineteenth century, sawdust was sometimes dubbed "tree flour.")

When white flour became widely available, the industry followed Heinz's model, using public fear to its advantage and selling "purity," as if whiteness was a guarantee. And then white flour
became even whiter, through bleaching with chlorine, benzoyl
peroxide (now an ingredient in acne medication), calcium peroxide, and chlorine dioxide. All of these are banned from food processing in the EU, though they're still allowed in the U.S.

With new machinery, super-duper yeast, and a host of acceler-
ants, a loaf of bread could be produced way faster than ever before.
To protect it from tampering or contamination, the new factory-
made white bread was sealed in "hygienic" waxed paper. Because
wrapping machines were expensive, smaller local bakeries struggling to keep up with the trends were driven out of business.

And since this packaging also eliminated the ability to see
or smell the bread, brands promoted the notion that softer was
fresher, and therefore better. But the softer bread was nearly impossible to slice by hand, which led to the slicing machine, giving
mass production yet another advantage. (So successful was sliced
bread — the "greatest thing," many have said — that a World War
II ban on slicing machines, for the sake of rationing steel, was

quickly revoked after nationwide protest.) Bread, the "staff of life," had been an important calorie source for wheat-growing civilizations forever; at its twentieth-century peak, it constituted twenty-five percent of calories for Americans.

The paradigm — Wonder Bread — was introduced in 1929. And although it and its hundreds of clones were lacking in nutrition, they were supported by the USDA, of course, and the American Medical Association, too.

Many experts had other notions. Even the vitamin pioneer and milk pusher Elmer McCollum spoke confidently about the lack of nutrients in white flour: "The American public has been educated to like white bread and white flour by skillful advertising," he said.

McCollum was later bought off by General Mills, who paid him to promote the healthfulness of white bread on the Betty Crocker radio show. He then appeared before a congressional committee to condemn "the pernicious teachings of food faddists who have sought to make people afraid of white-flour bread." So much for integrity.

And yet no one could deny that *something* was going wrong with America's diet. Physical exams of men entering the armed forces for World War II revealed vitamin deficiencies like scurvy, a variety of B-vitamin-related issues, and night blindness, which results from a lack of vitamin A. All this on top of twenty thousand people dying of pellagra in the previous few years.

After a decade of depression and hunger, this might not have been a surprise, but it had to be dealt with. The government may have been fine ignoring Black women dying of pellagra, but when it became a military matter and therefore "important," official concern was aroused. Thus, the scientific community, the food industry, the government, and especially the military "solved" the problem by adding chemical nutrients to white flour. The armed forces announced in 1942 that they would buy only enriched flour.

That was that. In the postwar years, as marketing increasingly shaped people's tastes, industry representatives and policy officials collaborated to create the ideal loaf, which was sweeter, softer, and more pillow-like, thanks to more sugar and chemically strengthened gluten. Wonder Bread, which helped "build strong bodies 12 ways," remained the standard. All twelve ways in which it built strong bodies were through synthetic nutrients.

Bread had become a vitamin pill in the form of a sponge cake.

Bread baking had become a thing of the past in most homes. By the early 1900s, there was a "servant problem" as factory work became more common and fewer workers were available for domestic labor. Furthermore, cities were becoming more cramped, making it more difficult to house domestic workers.

Until then, as Helen Zoe Veit says in *Modern Food, Moral Food*, "housework had very recently connoted not just servitude but also slavery, and to some degree middle-class women who did housework risked muddying their own social standings." The work was exhausting and never-ending, "a symbol of bondage," in the words of a home economist from the time. Nevertheless, there were soon millions of middle- and upper-class women — women who'd grown up with enslaved or domestic workers — doing the majority of domestic labor themselves. Cooking was among the most important and time-consuming of those chores.

New cooks were critical participants in the burgeoning mass-market economy. They were shoppers, yes, but they were also managers, and their domain was the home, which was evolving with the same kind of efficiency that was being applied to farm and factory. Time-and-motion studies were even performed to analyze housework.

The homemaker was both manager and worker, responsible for absorbing the information offered by newspapers, radio, and magazines, information that urged her to prepare new foods, obey newly discovered scientific rules dictating good "nutrition," and in general take full responsibility for her family's health and well-being. It was up to her to both parse that information and execute behavior based on it.

These true heads of households needed a new kind of training. Enter the home economist.

"Home economics" was founded by Ellen Swallow Richards, who graduated from MIT in 1873 with a degree in chemistry. She was the first woman to be admitted to a science university, although she was asked not to pay tuition so that, if questioned whether any women were enrolled, the university could deny it. By the time she joined the faculty in 1884, there was much cutting-edge science about sanitation, germs, and nutrition, but the avenues open to women primarily involved domestic life. Among Richards's early work was the publication of *The Chemistry of Cooking and Cleaning.*

In 1899 she organized a meeting in Lake Placid, where a mostly female group of biologists, chemists, sanitation experts, and others working under the "domestic science" umbrella began discussing how technology and advances in their disciplines could improve the home and the life of the homemaker. Home economists were the result—experts who were there to affirm that housework was not only an expression of love and intelligence, but also a true job that could be done efficiently and with skill.

The original home economists were well-intentioned. But once they demonstrated their influence, Big Business swooped in to harness it, making home economics a marketing machine for American processed food, the equivalent to what agricultural economists were for farmers. Both existed to teach people how to acclimate to a shifting economy that no longer valued growing or cooking food. As Harvey Levenstein writes, "prime consideration was to train women in consumption, rather than production."

Opening a can is no challenge, nor is using a refrigerator. Distinguishing among brands of new "foods" and how to use them, however, took some help. Women needed advice in learning how to manipulate these new fruits of mass production. The key to selling it all was its purported efficiency: maximizing your family's health and nutrition while minimizing the money you spend.

The coming-out party for home economists was World War I, when Food Administrator Herbert Hoover relied on them in his "Food Will Win the War" campaign. Through pamphlets, newspaper and magazine articles, and other materials disseminated with the government's seal of approval, the campaign positioned home economists as authorities on recipes, best practices in the kitchen, and shopping. They had become trainers of women in the ways of the modern nuclear family.

The role of home economics won further support in 1923, when the USDA established the Bureau of Home Economics (BHE). Congress charged the bureau with helping to create markets for agricultural products, while supplying home demonstration agents who worked for the Cooperative Extension (renamed the Cooperative Extension Service in Agriculture and Home Economics) with ways to improve rural home life. This could mean anything from informal get-togethers to training in "scientific" methods of cooking, childcare, and farm management. Shortly, land-grant colleges were churning out trained instructors to teach housewives about the modern food system.

The BHE had an identity issue: It was trying to educate young consumers about nutrition while supporting unhealthy, post-agricultural products that encouraged home cooks to ignore real, nutritious foods. This conflicting mission mirrored that of the USDA as a whole. The agency was meant to promote healthier foods, all while supporting an industry that systemically degraded food quality.

It would be naive to think that the USDA was equally devoted to these dueling missions. Its first loyalty has always been to the ag/food industry and to destroying any knowledge that would jeopardize the industry's profits. And that tendency would be enhanced by another world war.

Three times as many Americans served in the military during World War II as for its predecessor. As mostly men shipped off for combat, women tended to work on farms, in factories, and in offices. Nevertheless, production continued to climb and, relative to most European and Asian countries, the United States barely suffered.

In fact, it thrived. Wartime production ended the Depression, and there were virtually no limits to the methods at America's disposal. Fossil fuel extraction skyrocketed, as did factory production, especially of munitions and weaponry. War was raging, and everything went into winning it.

The causes of World War II are so complex that historians still argue about them. But the role of food in the territorial ambitions of Japan, Italy, and Germany is often bypassed.

It's a surprising omission, since it's no secret that empty stomachs often drive ideology. The German and Japanese governments were justifiably concerned about their lands' ability to feed their growing populations, especially relative to the empires of the classic imperial countries of Western Europe and, of course, to the impressive landmasses of both the United States and the Soviet Union.

At the time, Holland ruled over Indonesia. The Belgian Congo was seventy-seven times larger than Belgium itself. France controlled much of Southeast Asia, and although Great Britain's empire was less extensive than it had been a hundred years earlier, it still included India. Europeans ruled nearly one hundred percent of Africa, and these colonies provided their mother countries with land, food, and markets.

Meanwhile, the Axis countries controlled little territory other than their own. Although Italy had colonized Ethiopia, it was struggling to maintain it, and Germany's African colonies had been divided among the victors of World War I. Japan, a non-European latecomer, was shut out, and its position had only worsened after the protectionism that followed the Crash of '29. Oil was hard to come by, yet Japan was increasingly fuel-hungry, gaining population and striving to transition to heavy industry. Beefing up its military to prepare for colonial domination seemed to be the answer.

Global trade was largely controlled by the British. Many German citizens spent up to half their income on food alone even before the war began, and the high cost of imports was largely to blame. As in World War I, the effects of blockade, damaged and commandeered train lines, and general chaos were catastrophic for food supplies.

Around twenty million civilians died from starvation and associated diseases worldwide during World War II, the majority in China. The Soviet Union saw huge losses, too: A million people starved to death during the Siege of Leningrad. More Japanese soldiers died from hunger and its effects than in battle, and starvation in Nazi camps led to the deaths of untold numbers of Jews, Romani, gays, and leftists, since their ration was about a tenth of subsistence level. Millions of others were gassed, which was easier and cheaper for the Nazis than feeding prisoners.

Much has been made of wartime rationing in Britain, and there was certainly inconvenience and even hardship, but thanks to the abundance of the empire, no one starved to death. It was the colonies that suffered disproportionately, as they were providing food and troops for their colonizer while their own civilians went hungry. The wartime famine in British-controlled Bengal killed an estimated three million people, and deaths in Vietnam likely totaled more than a million.

Given all of that, it's awkward to point to the positives, but there were a couple. In the United States, rationing was real enough that many people took Victory Gardens seriously. There were around twenty million of these, grown by almost half of all households, in backyards, neighborhood lots, and nearby countryside — as well as on Boston Common, the National Mall, and the grounds of the White House — and they produced around forty percent of all vegetables by the end of the war.

Thanks in large part to civilian restraint and discipline, no wartime diet was more abundant than that of American soldiers, who ate about twenty percent more than their French or British counterparts. Back at home, the United States didn't see any benefits as dramatic as what Denmark experienced during World War I. But deaths from cardiovascular diseases did dip during the war to roughly 1935 levels. With peace, they immediately began climbing again.

While wartime tractor production was scaled back to boost that of tanks and other armored vehicles, need led to innovation in tractors and hydraulics. A company named Massey-Harris, for example, introduced a new generation of self-propelled combines and convinced the federal government to allow it to build five hundred over its quota and create a wartime "Harvest Brigade." The invention pushed the company to the leading position in the industry, and by 1947 the number of self-propelled combines had increased tenfold.

Post-war, European agriculture was in rough shape. Farmland had been bombed, overrun, ignored, and badly used. Many farmers had died on the battlefield, moved to cities, or just given up. But with their abundant fuel, machinery, and land, American farmers produced unprecedented amounts of commodity crops. In fact, 1945 saw the biggest wheat harvest in history. Global demand was sky-high, too, and, as Harvey Levenstein reports in *Paradox of Plenty*, "Total food production was one-third more than in the last prewar years. [America] was now producing fully one-tenth of the world's food."

The country was poised to rule the world—politically, militarily, economically, and agriculturally. The main question for the industry was how to keep selling the bounty.

Farmers faced a different dilemma: how to transition to a new life. As the trend toward fewer farms only worsened, and as returning soldiers found new jobs, Stephanie Ann Carpenter reported that "between April 1940 and July 1942, more than two million men left the farm, and by the end of the war, the agricultural population had decreased by six million." It wasn't only the G.I. Bill, which encouraged former soldiers to go to college; it was the now common issue of farm consolidation.

The wealth of the family farm was never the fundamental pillar of American life that we've been encouraged to believe. By war's end, five percent of farms were selling a third of all crops. In the wake of the war, these trends took hold in Western Europe as well. The numbers of farms, farmers, and farmworkers were dropping while machinery and yield were increasing dramatically.

With the machinery and chemical industries both highly dependent on fossil fuel, and with human labor increasingly displaced, the heartland became a producer of what might as well be called "petrofoods." As Wendell Berry wrote in 1977, "That we should have an agriculture based as much on petroleum as on the soil—that we need petroleum exactly as much as we need food and must have it *before* we can eat—may seem absurd. It is absurd. It is nevertheless true."

The petrofood industry continued to invent new products at record speeds. In 1938, the USDA funded four regional "crop utilization research" labs in which well-meaning scientists worked to discover uses for every part of every crop, in order to determine ways to use the surplus for economic and public good. They developed hundreds of products, many beneficial, many not. Both high-fructose corn syrup and penicillin (also a by-product of corn milling) are examples. Over the years, they have gradually increased food's role as an industrial resource.

These changes rocked every level of the agricultural system, including seeds.

Hybrids, or crosses between two varieties of plant or animal, were nothing new. Until the mid-nineteenth century, when Gregor Mendel established modern genetics by observing heredity and trait patterns in pea plants, hybridization (or cross-breeding) was an often random process as old as biology itself. The classic example is the mule, which can result from mating a male donkey with a female horse. Cross-breeding varieties of plants was less dramatic, but far more important historically. The first crosses were of non-hybrid plants—called "open-pollinated," or "species," or (these days) "heirlooms." But hybrids can be crossed also, as can hybrids of hybrids, and so on.

Some hybrids can reproduce; others cannot. Almost none can reproduce accurately—that is, retain all the characteristics of the parents' genes. In other words, if you breed two of the same hybrid, whether plant or animal, you get a different hybrid. That hybrid may have more or fewer desirable characteristics—it's a toss-up. But even if the outcome is ideal, it won't replicate itself again. To get that same outcome, you'd have to breed those same two original hybrids.

It's an arduous process, but sometimes it's worth it. A mule is better suited to some tasks than either horses or donkeys, and a hybrid chicken may lay more eggs or grow faster than a non-hybrid. Hybrid corn may grow to be more productive, taller, and straighter, and therefore easier to harvest. It can be drought- or pest-resistant, tolerant of chemicals like fertilizer and pesticides, tastier, longer-lasting, higher in protein and other nutrients, easier to dry, better for making high-fructose corn syrup or corn oil or ethanol, and just about anything else you can think of within reason.

If you had been growing the same seed as your parents or neighbors for a couple of generations, and someone came along and said, "I have a seed here that will be twice as productive as yours is, it'll be easier to harvest, and it will live an extra week without rain," you probably wouldn't think twice about buying it.

And that's what happened. By 1924, innovators like Henry Wallace—future secretary of agriculture and of commerce, vice president under FDR, and 1948 presidential candidate—understood hybridization well enough to cross-breed and sell seeds with characteristics so desirable that farmers who had never paid for seed in their lives ponied up. At the same time, other hybrids were being developed at agricultural experiment stations throughout the country.

So quick was the transition that hybrid corn seed went from ten percent of the market in Iowa to ninety percent in just over four years, beginning in 1935. Nationally, the corn crop went from one percent hybrid in 1930 to thirty percent by 1940. It's now around ninety-five percent hybrid.

This only quickened the pace at which farms were forced to commercialize and lose their independence. A field of hybrid seeds may produce a crop with predictable and presumably more desirable characteristics, but its seeds will almost certainly produce inferior results. Not only that, but, once hybrids were patented, planting them without a license was technically illegal.

Because higher yield is usually first on the list of desirable characteristics for crops grown in our monoculture-ruled world, entire industries have come to rely on just a few hybrid varieties that do it best. Where there were once literally millions of permutations of corn, every individual plant born of its own combination of open pollinators, the U.S. corn industry whittled its diversity down to a small number of genetically uniform hybrids.

(The exact number of species is so proprietary that even the industry itself probably doesn't know. But it's certainly fewer than a thousand.)

All hybrids — not just corn — follow this pattern, and many are destined to produce something other than food for humans. They don't adapt to their native environments, or become hardier with each harvest, as open-pollinated plants often do. Rather, they stagnate. This lack of resiliency and adaptability to local conditions threatens food security, especially since widespread planting of just a few hybrids produces an extremely vulnerable crop.

What hybrids do is give high yield. And the records set by the 1945 harvest were soon broken. In the next fifteen years, yields of corn, wheat, cotton, and milk increased by fifty percent or more, and over the coming decades they would increase steadily. By 1960 the government held in storage almost two *billion* bushels of corn, and the price was as low as it had been at the beginning of the war. This wasn't a surplus in the truest sense of the term, whereby all excess crop is put away in case of emergency. In this case, there was too much excess to be saved. This was a super-surplus, the result of overproduction.

In farming, supply continues to increase even as prices fall, because many farmers plant more hoping to recoup lost income. This became even more common after the federal government extended price supports after the war to try to keep farming profitable. It was — as the USDA's Willard Cochrane noted — a treadmill of more machinery, fewer workers, higher yields, and falling prices.

Disposing of the super-surplus — commonly referred to as "the farm problem" — usually involved schemes to limit production and "reduce excess supply," in hopes of raising prices and therefore farm incomes. In a perfect or even somewhat better world, it would have been the USDA's job to engage in agricultural planning, fund new research, and monitor and manage pricing. But in a 1972 report, Jim Hightower, who later became Texas's commissioner of agriculture, noted that less than two percent of the time spent in improving plant-growth efficiency was invested in maintaining or improving the income of rural people.

Privately held companies were calling the shots, and things were going well for them. Fewer farmers, more machines, and lower prices were fine. Farmers, after all, weren't even important: "Agriculture's chief need is the reduction of the number of people in agriculture,'" wrote the Committee for Economic Development, a business planning group formed by the Department of Commerce, with members from General Foods, Quaker Oats, Hormel, Coke, and others, in 1946.

The farmers of our fantasies — families who worked the land to produce food for themselves and local markets — were faster than ever becoming extinct. Where the farm population once made up half of the total in the United States, by 1960 it had fallen to below ten percent. And despite repeated promises to ensure that small farmers would continue to thrive — twenty percent of full-time farmers in the mid-fifties made $1,200 a year (about $11,000 in today's money), so "thriving" is relative — there was no policy that encouraged or supported the kinds of growth farmers needed to be viable competitors on the market.

Farming is not for everyone, but society chooses what kinds of farmers to support, and what those farmers get to grow; they're part of a larger system. For more than a century, some government agents have tried to make that system better for farmers and for eaters, and proposed concrete policies to improve the situation. Cochrane, who first diagnosed the "treadmill" of machine dominance, suggested the government buy land from farmers and put it to better use than growing commodity crops. (It was a good idea then, and it's a good idea now.) Charles Brannan, a lawyer and a veteran of the New Deal–era USDA, who became Harry Truman's secretary of agriculture, recognizing that two percent of farms sold more than the combined output of two-thirds of all others, suggested that farms in that two percent "be not eligible for price support." His plan included supporting soil conservation and hinted at subsidizing real fruits and vegetables instead of commodity crops. It received widespread grassroots support but was doomed to failure when faced with Big Agriculture's interests and the money behind them.

What happened instead was a creative scheme in the Eisenhower years that extended the use of surplus as a political tool. There were many nations outside of Europe whose people needed food and supplies but couldn't afford them. The United States agreed to help these nations — to "feed the world" — but only on its own terms. Predictably, these terms were more about market development and political power than actual food distribution.

First up was the Marshall Plan, which followed the wartime pattern of providing European countries with food and supplies, whether in the typical form of loans or the rarer form of grants. The United States produced yet another super-surplus of wheat in 1947, and funneled much of it into the initial grant to Europe. Fertilizer, fuel, and animal feed were too precious just then to give away.

Initially, the plan focused primarily on America's closest allies: The UK, France, and West Germany received more than half of the aid. It received a great deal of publicity as a key factor in aiding European recovery and — as the common phrase would have it in the late forties to the early sixties, "preventing the spread of Communism." In truth, at something less than fifteen billion dollars (a precise amount is difficult to determine), it was better than a kick in the pants but probably not a huge difference maker. But because it was accompanied by the Truman Doctrine, aimed at countering the influence of the Soviet Union, it did set the precedent of offering U.S. goods in exchange for influence, preferential trade treatment, market development, and recommendations regarding national economies.

The country most profoundly affected by the Marshall Plan was, counterintuitively, the United States. The demand for wheat was again seemingly unlimited as exports multiplied by a factor of ten in the middle four years of the forties. Almost all of that wheat (and many other varieties of food) was purchased by the federal government and exported as influential figures in government and business recognized the value of a global food system centered around the influence and agricultural might.

What followed was PL (Public Law) 480, or the Agricultural Trade Development and Assistance Act, routinely called "Food for Peace." Beginning in 1954, this installment plan shipped commodities abroad while providing the destination countries with loans from the U.S. government to pay for them. The program subsidized commodity farmers to continue to overproduce, and to give that surplus to—or rather foist that surplus upon—developing nations, hooking them on wheat, corn, soy, and other grains and, ultimately, processed food. Grain traders and shippers, including familiar names like Cargill and Continental, quickly saw unprecedented sales and profits.

The idea was that food would become a way to show developing countries how functional and generous capitalist countries were, while preventing the USSR from showing them how functional and generous "socialist people's states" were. But, as Raj Patel says in *Stuffed and Starved*, "any US-aligned government that found itself battling worker-led organizing or, indeed, any plausibly left-wing political opposition could gain access to the US strategic grain reserve. Those countries abutted by socialist ones were bumped to the front of the queue." Thus, South Korea, Taiwan, and South Vietnam were primary clients. Grain was showered upon India as well, which was then in danger of "going communist."

Two years after the signing of PL 480, American aid accounted for a third of the world's wheat trade. No other country, save possibly Canada, could compete price-wise, and small-scale farmers all across the globe recognized the futility of growing commodity grain without government support. Former net exporters of agricultural products became net importers as the United States wove a web that would keep former colonies and other "underdeveloped" countries dependent upon them. The imported grain might have helped short-term shortages, but it also discouraged self-sufficient agriculture.

The General Agreement on Tariffs and Trade (GATT) institutionalized these grants and loans, guaranteeing a way for the world's rulers to once again establish the have-nots as markets for the wares of the home countries. Although GATT was ostensibly designed to prevent "dumping"—the trading of commodities at a price lower than the cost of production—and to develop agriculture and industry in the nonindustrialized world, its effect was the opposite. Dumping, whether in the form of aid or trade, became the norm, and agricultural self-sufficiency declined worldwide. The United States had the global agricultural industry in a stranglehold, and its grip was strengthening.

10

Soy, Chicken, and Cholesterol

E VEN WHILE THE United States was exporting tens of millions of tons of grain through PL 480 and other programs, an equal amount was left. And as if that weren't enough, another ingredient was arriving on the scene that would further boost the production of grains and help change the American diet.

That game changer was soy.

The soybean is productive, almost incomparably nutritious, and nitrogen-fixing. Grown in rotation with other crops, soy helps keep soil alive. It contains two and even three times the protein of most other beans and grains and as much as or more than most animal products, as well as fiber and micronutrients. Grown sustainably, it could contribute mightily to the health of perhaps a quarter of the world's eaters.

But when producers discovered that soy and animals were the perfect combination to create surplus-eating, protein-concentrating profit centers, soy took on a new life, joining corn as a foundation of twentieth-century agriculture, grown primarily to be processed into junk and overfeed animals for slaughter.

The postwar years brought true mass production of animals. By the seventies, half the arable land in the United States was planted with grain to be fed to animals, and the vast majority of all corn, oats, and soybeans were used as animal feed.

Chickens led the revolution.

Until mass production arrived, chicken hadn't been the staple it is today. It was originally popular mostly among enslaved people, as it was the only animal they were permitted to raise for meat. Their descendants carried on the culinary tradition, and they were joined by chicken-eating immigrants, especially those whose religion ruled out eating pork.

Chickens have the best conversion ratio—producing the most meat per pound of feed—of any common land animal. But until midcentury, most chickens were bought live for egg-laying purposes, with hundreds of thousands of Americans raising the birds for themselves and their neighbors.

The commercial broiler industry ("broilers" are bred to be eaten, "layers" to produce eggs) is said to have begun with Cecile Steele, a Delaware woman who, in 1923, raised a flock of five hundred chicks that she sold for sixty-two cents a pound, almost ten dollars a pound in 2020 money. By 1926 she had built Mrs. Wilmer Steele's Broiler House, which could house ten thousand birds at any given time, and Delaware was producing a million birds a year.

But as Lu Ann Jones points out in *Mama Learned Us to Work*, there are other contenders for the title of sparking the mass production of chickens, at least one as early as 1919. They're all women, largely because raising poultry was "women's work." But as chicken farming became a major industry, corporations and the men who ran them took over.

By 1930, Ralston Purina, Puritan, and other leading feed producers were providing feed straight to farmers on credit. Since the most expensive part of chicken farming was feeding the birds, the industry was built largely by debt-ridden farmers. This wasn't unlike sharecropping, the system by which merchants and landowners gave credit or land to cotton farmers in exchange for a share of the crops.

There was much talk about chicken production during the Great Depression (including the "chicken in every pot" line, widely attributed to Herbert Hoover, but uttered in a similar form by France's Henry IV more than three hundred years earlier). The industry boomed soon thereafter, during World War II.

Chicken wasn't rationed like other meats, so demand was high and profit was nearly guaranteed. In fact, the government program Food for Freedom encouraged civilians to eat chicken and eggs, in order to save red meat for the troops abroad. As a result, the number of broilers nearly tripled in the war years.

At the same time, the federal government paid well above the cost of production for its own purchases, which were massive. The Army sucked just about every available chicken out of the Delmarva (Delaware, Maryland, and Virginia) Peninsula, where production was concentrated. This gave a huge boost to producers in the South as well, men like Jesse Jewell and John Tyson, who were able to ramp up their operations significantly. These men were the first "integrators," as they're called, controlling almost every step of the chicken-producing process and using hundreds of farmers as independent contractors.

Jewell, who might be thought of as the father of the modern chicken industry, followed the feed companies' lead and began settling chicks with farmers while providing feed on credit. Working first in Florida and later in Georgia, where the hill country was called the "Chicken Triangle," Jewell bought a fleet of trucks to bring feed, chicks, and supplies to farmers—and to bring chickens to market. He also built a processing plant, complete with freezers.

The industry exploded and consolidated in the next half century, when, according to a 2008 Pew Commission report, "the number of chickens produced annually in the United States . . . increased by more than 1,400 percent while the number of farms producing those birds . . . dropped by 98 percent."

Drugs paved the way. In the late forties, a researcher named Thomas Jukes began lacing chicken feed with aureomycin, an antibiotic, which he found prevented disease in large, crowded, and confined populations—and possibly promoted growth. This coincided with the USDA-sponsored "Chicken of Tomorrow" competition, in which a bird was raised to twice the weight in half the time (using half as much feed!) as before the war, and with a higher percentage of breast meat. It didn't take much to convince the industry to cram bigger flocks into smaller spaces, and profits rose even as retail prices stagnated or fell.

The era of cheap chicken had arrived. By the mid-fifties national production topped a billion birds, and, soon after, there were fewer than ten percent as many poultry farms as there had been just fifty years earlier. The remaining farms produced ten times as many chickens, at prices that, adjusted for inflation, had done nothing but decline.

The deregulation and consolidation that defined the 1980s — the "decade of the deal" — spurred a more tightly controlled chicken industry, dominated by Holly Farms, Perdue, and Tyson. These companies began branding individual chicken parts and, most crucially, creating and converting them into more profitable products. In 1960, eighty-three percent of all chickens were sold whole, and just two percent were used to make value-added products like strips, tenders, burgers, or other processed foods. (The rest were sold as parts.) Today, only ten percent are sold whole; fully fifty percent of chicken makes its way into value-added products. (Again, the rest is sold as cut-up chicken parts.) Most notable among these processed wonders is the true paragon of the chicken-derived junk food: the McNugget.

McDonald's has become a leading symbol of everything that's gone wrong with food, but its creation was as inevitable as the "discovery" of America or the invention of the Model T.

By the sixties, women were reentering the workforce in increasing and significant numbers. Most men had never cooked and weren't about to start, and, with women more overworked than ever and the industry's marketing machine focusing on selling "convenience" food, cooking was increasingly seen as a nuisance. The slippery slope might have started with chips and TV dinners and cake mixes, but it reached its nadir with the family outing to a fast-food restaurant.

The particulars of McDonald's story have been told well and at length in Eric Schlosser's deservedly famous *Fast Food Nation* and the lesser-known *McDonald's: Behind the Arches*, by John Love. But briefly: In 1940, Dick and Maurice "Mac" McDonald opened McDonald's Bar-B-Q, their second restaurant. (Their first was a hot dog stand.) With car service, pulled pork, burgers, and drinks, it quickly became the most popular place in the growing town of

San Bernardino, just east of Los Angeles. A few years later, they were successful but bored. Seeing a way to streamline the business, they shut down for three months and redesigned the restaurant.

The new concept, McDonald's Speedee Service, lowered prices, eliminated service, and cut the menu down to burgers, fries, shakes, soda, coffee, and milk. John Love quotes Dick McDonald: "We were going after big, big volumes by lowering prices and having the customer serve himself. . . . It was obvious the future of drive-ins was self-service."

The resulting assembly line would've done Ford proud. Customers ordered at the counter, to which their food was delivered. In the "kitchen," one person cooked hamburger patties. Another assembled the burgers using ketchup, mustard, chopped onions, two pickles (there were no alternative options), and, if ordered, cheese. One wrapped the burgers, another made shakes, another fried potatoes, and so on. All containers and utensils were disposable in order to virtually eliminate washing up. The idea was to minimize employees' learning curve and pay, make the food as simple and uniform as possible, and have customers take on much of the burden of service.

A nineteen-cent cheeseburger with ten-cent fries and a twenty-cent shake or dime soda was the perfect meal to eat in a car, and the scene had already been set. The roads were there, the cars were there, the kids were there, the cheap white flour and the means to mechanically produce buns were there, and the same was true of the cheese and the milk and the sugar and the Coke and the beef and, before too long, the chicken.

In the coming years, the McDonald brothers would develop the stores' sleek look and iconic golden arches, and sell more than twenty local franchises. In 1954, a milkshake-machine salesman named Ray Kroc, wondering why the McDonalds were buying so many, paid a visit. Kroc determined to buy out the entire operation. He'd completed the deal by 1961, and quickly took the chain national.

The most formidable fast-food chain in history had been born. By 1970 there were three thousand franchises, and growth was unprecedented. Today there are hundreds of thousands of fast-food franchises. Subway has the most outlets, but McDonald's, whose annual sales are in the range of thirty billion dollars, is the most valuable.

Fast food originally catered to the commuting, suburban, middle-class white family. But the corporate need for growth, combined with the impact of increasing concerns about our diets as well as other factors like increased costs because of rising gas prices, made finding new markets a necessity. So fast food moved to cities, where it could call out to people passing on foot, and where it could be marketed to urban people of color.

When, in the mid-twentieth century, southern Black Americans migrated to northern cities, they quickly reached a higher concentration in those cities than their share of the national population, at the time about twelve percent. But African Americans were still paid less for performing the same jobs, and owned just two percent of all businesses; the expansion of political freedoms brought about by the civil rights movement didn't do much to advance economic justice.

That *everyone* had rights, and that domestic and global institutions had a duty to protect those rights, were novel concepts among most white people and their institutions. By the sixties, as U.S. civil rights groups began to focus on economics, uprisings in major U.S. cities shook the white power structure. One cynical response to these demonstrations was then–presidential candidate Richard Nixon's 1968 pledge to "get private enterprise into the ghetto," promising African Americans the "freedom of choice they do not have today."

The Small Business Administration, whose ostensible goal was to provide assistance to Americans wishing to start or boost their companies, had granted a staggering total of seventeen loans to Black business owners in its first ten years of operation. Nixon was aware of this, and saw an opportunity to find a way to gain favor with both Black communities and large corporations, directing the SBA to prioritize loans to minority populations through the Equal Opportunity Loan program. The money flowed — twenty-five million dollars in all.

Distributed among new would-be business owners, that would've been significant, but much of it went to the country's twenty-five largest franchise operations, mostly gas stations, auto dealers, and fast-food chains. Nor was the agency alone: In 1996, Burger King joined with the Department of Health and Human Services to open new franchises in Washington, Chicago, Detroit, and other cities, with the idea of promoting "comprehensive urban renewal." In fact, "the lion's share" of businesses created through these programs, according to Chin Jou in *Supersizing Urban America*, were inner-city franchises of fast-food chains.

This was not an economic development project for minority neighborhoods but rather a subsidy for fast-food companies, which in turn were a boon to Big Ag. Even better, from the corporate perspective, was that Black-owned franchises paved the way for further entry into the inner-city marketplace, where profits were higher than in most suburban stores.

Fast food skyrocketed from a six-billion-dollar industry in 1970 to well over two hundred billion dollars in 2015. The per capita number of restaurants more than doubled, and calorie consumption from fast food quadrupled. Fast food also doubled its share of the money that Americans spent on food outside the home, and in 2018 it generated global revenue of over $570 billion—more than the economic value of most countries. A third of Americans now eat fast food daily.

Did this benefit African Americans, or cities in general? No and no. Even those new businesses that succeeded brought limited benefit to the franchise owners, who had little say in how they operated their businesses, set their menus and pricing, sourced materials, or paid their employees. And, as everyone knows, fast-food jobs are hardly the key to individual success or healthy, prosperous communities. In fact, even as McDonald's grew using federal funds, it actively fought to keep teenagers exempt from minimum-wage laws, guaranteeing that the new jobs it brought paid poorly.

Dietwise, the expansion of fast food has been a disaster. In 1965, African Americans had been more than twice as likely as whites to eat a diet that met the recommended guidelines for fat, fiber, fruits, and vegetables. But the growth of fast food eroded diets everywhere, and especially in vulnerable communities, where money was short and safe public gathering spaces were sparse. Sugary foods and drinks have one negative impact, fatty red meat another, ultra-processed pseudo-foods like McNuggets yet another.

Combined, they've led to an increase in diet-related deaths, many premature, affecting BIPOC (Black, Indigenous, people of color) communities more than others. Although today fast food symbolizes the modern American diet, its expansion was just one among a pattern of food trends that became global during the twenty-first century.

Before the war, food processing was simple and understandable, usually some combination of cleaning, sorting, cutting, chopping, pureeing, and grinding, followed by canning, freezing, or other packaging.

Deconstructing food into its components began in the thirties, accelerated during the war, and took off in the fifties. Using combinations of heat, chemicals, and pressure, food was broken down and recombined into novel forms. Some of these—Trix, for example, or Cheetos—were outright inventions. Others were mock versions of familiar foods: Think of Cremora, which is intended to resemble half-and-half, or I Can't Believe It's Not Butter.

Transforming surplus rather than trading it was not exactly new; it's how cheese became a household item. But new government support and new technology took processing to another level. USDA scientists were developing cheese that would keep more or less forever at room temperature. Later sold as Velveeta and the like, this "pasteurized process cheese food" must by law contain no less than fifty-one percent real cheese. The rest may be artificial coloring, flavoring, dairy ingredients, water, salt and mold inhibitors. As ingredients, variations on this stuff allowed the creation of Cheetos, Kraft Mac and Cheese, Cheez-Its, Doritos, and other never-before-seen "snack foods."

What began as time-honored techniques for preserving or extending the harvest, like brewing, pickling, and wine- and cheese-making, were transformed beyond recognition. A good deal of these new production practices concentrated calories while adding sugar and fat, much of it from corn and soybeans, which, not coincidentally, are primary sources of the chemically processed oil used in frying.

The challenge lay not in getting Americans to eat these new foods. Sugar, salt, and fat are all found in foods we need, and we're hardwired to crave them. Rather, the challenge lay in getting Americans to eat these foods in increasing quantities, to solve the problem of the super-surplus by force-feeding the masses. The solution would come through selling Americans on chronic overeating of foods that would make them sick. And the marketing machine was up to that task.

"Available calories"—all production minus all exports—increased by thirty percent per person in the second half of the twentieth century. We ate most of them, the result being that the average American man weighed twenty-five pounds more in 2002 than he did in 1960, while the average weight for women is now what it was for men fifty years ago. The marketing of junk amounted to an organized attack on our collective health.

Almost every postwar change supported the industrial food system. Support for the auto industry (especially the interstate highway system), new suburban housing, and accelerated depreciation for new business construction, including shopping centers, all combined to give the nascent fast-food system and mega-centers like Walmart a natural home. Televisions became ubiquitous at the same time, and the sophisticated advertising that developed with it gave marketers the opportunity to reach millions of eaters at once with messages of fun and happiness.

It's easy to imagine that the big food processors could hardly believe their luck. By introducing a product on television and giving it a colorful, slogan-splashed package, you could sell practically anything, no matter how divorced it was from real food. And with the creation of brand mascots, ever-increasing minutes of television time were devoted to selling to children. Think of the genius behind Frosted Flakes: crunchier, sweeter cornflakes, with Tony the Tiger right on the box telling kids the cereal is "*grrrreat.*" Now imagine presenting Tony and his product on a new medium, to the biggest generation in history, all primed to nag their moms into buying dessert disguised as breakfast.

By 1970 we had seen the introduction of high-fructose corn syrup; Cheez Whiz, Fritos, and Pringles; countless television commercials pushing breakfast candy ("cereal") to four-year-olds, and yogurt with ice cream levels of sugar; TV dinners; self-basting turkeys; Tang (an orange-colored breakfast drink containing only sugar and "flavorings") and Nestlé Quik; frozen waffles; Pop-Tarts; packaged donuts (not "doughnuts"), Hostess Twinkies and Sno Balls; more margarine (and its incumbent trans fats, now virtually illegal) than butter; "diet" soda; "Minute" Rice, "instant" oatmeal, "Instant" Breakfast; Froot Loops and Lucky Charms; cake mix and canned dough; "creamer"; Gatorade; and thousands more.

As for profit, corn cost $1.44 per bushel in 1954. Even assuming an entire box of cornflakes was made of corn and not cheaper ingredients, eight ounces of cornflakes could be made from 0.0089 bushels, or about 1.3 cents. Add the sugar and you have two cents of raw ingredients. The retail price was more than ten times that. And of course, less than one percent of that profit went back to the farmer who grew the corn in the first place.

Then there's calorie concentration. Corn contains twenty-five calories per ounce; cornflakes, more than one hundred. For comparison, grits, a traditional breakfast cereal, has seventeen calories per ounce.

Considered in its entirety, the new food system centered around fast food and junk food, along with previously unimaginable quantities of animal products. It ignored the quality of food it produced or its effects on the world at large or its people, and thus created a never-before-seen form of malnutrition that would sweep across the country and later the world like a plague. To single out the Department of Agriculture would be extreme. But its role was ongoing, evident, and damaging.

In 1916, the USDA divided food into five groups: cereals, fruits and vegetables, meat and milk, fats and fatty foods, and sugar and sugary foods. Two decades later, the agency issued what are now called Dietary Reference Intakes for nutrients, by adding fifty percent to what it believed was the average requirement for "normal adult maintenance"—thus setting overeating as a government standard from the outset. The agency prescribed only minimum nutrient requirements, ignoring upper limits on intake, lest they inhibit sales. As supply grew, overeating—usually of hyperprocessed grains—became official policy. And processors had free rein to market their foods.

For a half century, the USDA ignored sugar entirely, and gave equal weight to the "four major food groups": meat, dairy, fruits and vegetables, and bread and cereals. They assured the three big food lobbies—milk, meat, and grain—that Americans would understand the importance of consuming plenty of each. The government made no recommendation that we eat legumes (the world's most important protein source) and saw no distinctions among carbohydrates. Whole grains, cookies, and white bread were portrayed as effectively equal sources of nutrition.

The most important work on contemporary nutrition is *Food Politics*, published in 2002 by the biologist and nutritionist Marion Nestle. In it, she noted that a 1923 USDA publication specifically set the stage for overeating: "The number of different food materials available . . . is constantly increasing as a result of improved methods of agriculture. . . . There is no one of all these many foods that cannot be introduced into the diet in such a way as to contribute to its wholesomeness."

That is bullshit. Unless you're literally starving, sugar is not a useful nutrient, and neither are thousands of other twentieth-century creations that contain either empty or harmful calories, and the failure of government to regulate those creations amounts to criminal negligence. Because as the combination of overproduction and marketing made overconsumption of hyperprocessed foods the norm, diet-related chronic diseases increased. And heart disease doubled.

At that time, heart disease was considered a normal function of aging. Autopsy studies often determined that the cause was coronary atherosclerosis, also known as hardening of the arteries. But why, then, was the problem reaching epidemic proportions? That question caught the attention of the medical community.

One early researcher was Ancel Keys, a physiologist who'd helped to develop K rations for the World War II troops. The K ration was an adequate-calorie, long-shelf-life meal, usually composed of canned meat, a canned fruit or vegetable, a chocolate bar, and a variety of items like gum, cigarettes, and bouillon powder, packed in a box that fit in a uniform pocket. The "K" might have stood for Keys, or not; no one seems to know for sure.

After the war, Keys ran a study on hunger and found that well-fed American businessmen had higher rates of heart disease than their food-deprived counterparts in Europe. This was consistent with epidemiological research, which also found that, given adequate rations, food-deprived Europeans were healthier than they were during periods of prosperity. Remember Denmark in World War I.

Keys investigated the role of diet in the escalating rate of heart attacks, contending that these killers were not "natural" after all. And he came to believe that "the outstanding characteristic of atherosclerosis is the presence of lipid deposits, mainly cholesterol, in the walls of the arteries. And both in man and animals the most obvious factor that affects the blood lipids is diet." There had been research and evidence implicating high cholesterol levels as early as the mid-nineteenth century, but they were largely ignored by the medical establishment.

More or less simultaneously, in 1948, President Truman signed the National Heart Act, which allocated funds to begin work on what became known as the Framingham Heart Study, centered in the small city of that name near Boston. Similar studies took place or would soon take place elsewhere in the country.

To this day, definitive nutrition studies that make scientific claims about causation are difficult, mostly because manipulating and recording people's diets in the kinds of numbers needed to produce accurate statistics is impossible.

Imagine a practitioner trying to answer these questions regarding people whose cholesterol level went up, and whether it mattered: Did the subjects eat more cholesterol? Did they eat more foods that raised their cholesterol? Which ones? Or did they eat fewer foods that reduced it? Or did they just get older? Did they gain weight at the same time? Why? Did they exercise, or stop? Were other, unforeseen factors involved? Was there a detectable result of the cholesterol rise? Did they develop heart disease? Did they have heart attacks? Die? And so on.

By the late forties, randomized controlled trials (RCTs), which tried to isolate and answer questions like these, were common — when it came to drugs. They simply dosed one group and not another (the "control"), then measured who got sick, or well, and who didn't. Food is way trickier. Controlling or eliminating the factors noted above (and there are more; they're effectively countless) is difficult enough, but if it's to be statistically significant, you must do this across huge populations. Hundreds or thousands of people must be fed the same diet, accurately, while stabilizing ("controlling for") many other factors. And these trials would have to last at least fifty years, if not a hundred, to be definitive.

Furthermore, RCTs can answer only the questions we pose. We may ask them to compare a bad low-carb diet (say, one high in saturated fat) with a very good low-fat diet (one largely dependent on fruits and vegetables), or vice versa. Or we may ask them to tell us the health effects of a vegan diet. But it's the study's designers who determine the quality of that diet. A plant-based diet, for example, may be optimal — comprising mostly plants with little or no processing — or it could be based largely on Coca-Cola, fries, and vegan cupcakes.

As it turns out, the broad, "observational" route, as seen in Framingham (which is still going on), is more useful. You collect a whole lot of data on naturally occurring events, including diet, and try to tease patterns from them. And sometimes you strike gold: In 1957, the U.S. surgeon general concluded that a study of

British doctors had found the causal link between smoking and lung cancer.

But observational studies have challenges. For starters, they're completely hands-off. You can't set up a subject's diet the way you want to, nor can you control for anything. That makes conclusions more evasive. On the flip side, the massive sample sizes and inability to shape the experiment make it harder to manufacture an intended outcome to support a desired result, as drug companies sometimes do with RCTs.

In the early fifties, Keys initiated the observational Seven Countries Study (SCS) to try to understand connections between diet, high cholesterol levels, and heart disease. The study involved nearly thirteen thousand men and looked at both diet and lifestyle. Its most fundamental finding, now widely accepted, was that Northern Europeans and Americans had much higher rates of disease than Southern Europeans and Japanese. Among the first indications that Keys was on the right track was a visit to hospitals in southern Italy, where, according to a colleague, "coronary disease was non-existent."

Gradually, studies began to reveal apparent connections between high blood pressure and heart disease and stroke. Equally important, two decades after the start of Framingham, the complicated relationship between cholesterol and heart disease began to unravel. Eventually some cholesterol (HDL, or high-density lipoprotein) was actually found to be good, while high levels of another (LDL, or low-density) were associated with heart disease. Framingham also found relationships between obesity and high blood pressure, diabetes, and heart disease.

That this information existed did not translate to benefit for eaters. Instead, decades of dietary confusion, bad advice, and wrong information followed—all disseminated both accidentally and intentionally—much of it sown by the food industry and supported by the government, including campaigns against dietary cholesterol and fat in general. But the information from Framingham and other studies also led to the recognition of the dangers of saturated fat (most easily defined as fat that's solid at room temperature) and, most definitively, trans fat, a lab creation found in margarine, Crisco, and many baked goods, whose use is now all but prohibited. If the studies had been better supported, if their findings hadn't been contested at every step by industry and its supporters, and if the resulting science had been taken more seriously, scientists would have been able to talk freely about what generally makes for a healthy diet long ago. The obstacles, however, have been great and many, and they remain so.

11

Force-Feeding Junk

S OME AMERICANS MAY remain willfully ignorant of the effects of a hyper-processed, meat-heavy diet, and others (though probably not many) may legitimately remain in the dark. The vast majority understand the risks of overeating fat, animal products, junk food, and so on, despite the lies of Big Food's marketing machine and government policies that help make unhealthful foods the most widely accessible. Countering those lies and policies has been among the great challenges of public health advocates.

In 1957, the American Heart Association concluded that diet may play an important role in the development of atherosclerosis, the deposits of plaque that narrow arteries. Furthermore, it found that the fat content and total calories in a diet may be the dominant contributing factors, and that the type of fat, or the balance between saturated and certain unsaturated fats, also may be important.

But the well-intentioned AHA made a couple of crucial mistakes. The first was that, in fine reductionist tradition, its experts didn't talk about food as whole. Rather, they talked about food broken down into individual nutrients: fat, saturated fat, polyunsaturated fat, carbohydrates, and so on. It would have been simpler (and more accurate) to talk about meat, or even "animal products"—the source of almost all saturated fat.

The second mistake was that there were other factors besides "fat" contributing to the increase in chronic disease. Important among them was sugar, which was critically missing from the AHA summary and downplayed or ignored for decades.

We have long known that sugar isn't good for us. Aristotle figured out that it causes tooth decay, and we've since learned that it contributes to insulin resistance and obesity, diabetes, heart disease, hyperactivity, and more.

Annual per capita consumption of sugar in the U.S. food supply had increased relentlessly, moving from around ten pounds in 1821 to 108 pounds in 1931. But during World War II, when the medical consensus about the nutritional deficiencies of sugar aligned with the military's desire to keep the troops happy with a steady supply while rationing it for civilians, sugar was officially deemed unnecessary on the home front. The American Medical Association advised "that even a substantial curtailment of sugar is likely not to injure the nutrition of the American people." The government put it better. One official pamphlet screamed, "How Much Sugar Do You Need? None!"

We might have needed "none," but by the seventies, the development of high-fructose corn syrup (HFCS)—a sugar equivalent that's virtually identical in taste, habit-forming properties, and treatment by the human body—allowed for a significant increase in consumption.

HFCS was created by a novel wet milling process (most grain is milled dry), which Archer Daniels Midland (ADM) invested in heavily. Its production yielded a by-product, ethanol, and together these went on to become complementary industry boondoggles.

Corn ethanol, a form of alcohol, powered some early automobiles, including the Model T. But it truly started to gain traction when ADM began producing high-fructose corn syrup in quantity while the Nixon, Ford, and Carter administrations were pursuing energy independence after gas prices rose following the OPEC embargo. Finally, after three members of ADM's executive team were imprisoned for price-fixing a feed additive in the nineties, the company hired an ex-Chevron executive to rebuild its business around ethanol.

Not only does ethanol contain less energy than gasoline, but by some calculations (they're complicated, and controversial) it takes more energy to produce ethanol than the fuel yields, which is kind of ridiculous. Nevertheless, through intense lobbying, ADM convinced Congress of the fuel's worth. It then became a gold mine for processors, who received direct subsidies of up to fifty-one cents per gallon (they now stand at forty-five cents), and virtually guaranteed a market for all the corn that industry could grow. Currently, forty percent of the United States' corn crop is used to produce sixteen billion gallons of ethanol per year, which means that around thirty-five million acres, an area close to the size of Iowa (itself ground zero for industrial agriculture), is devoted to growing corn destined to make inefficient fuel. Once again, the union of business and government has found a novel way to use some of the best farmland in the world to produce goods that benefit only the biggest farmers and the industry dependent on them.

The high-fructose corn syrup industry is arguably even worse. In 1981, when domestic sugar prices tripled thanks to protectionist price supports, ADM (which lobbied for those very same price supports) swooped in to promote HFCS as a cheap alternative. Per capita consumption went from insignificant in 1970 to around forty pounds per year now. Since white sugar numbers dropped only slightly, the overall amount of sweetener we ate increased.

Without fanfare, HFCS made its way into a variety of ultra-processed foods, including those not thought of as "sweet." It's in bottled tomato sauce, restaurant French fries, every baked good imaginable, just about all salad dressing—you name it, it's there. Massive amounts went into soda, consumption of which peaked in 1999 at more than fifty gallons per person per year, more than a pint per day. Soda was always profitable and never expensive to make, since water is nearly free for processors and even price-protected sugar is cheap. But HFCS made it even more so.

"Supersizing" followed. The original McDonald's offered a seven-ounce soda, an ounce shy of what today's nutrition facts would call a serving. Today, twelve ounces is "kid's size," and the sixteen-ounce cup—officially, two servings—is "small." A "large" is forty-two ounces, well over a quart.

This unregulated upselling, along with trends like dessert sold as coffee beverages—many of Starbucks's drinks contain more sugar than Coke, upwards of a hundred grams (or around twenty teaspoons, or close to four ounces, or about half of a cup: horrifying by any measure)—led to a total increase in sweetener consumption of more than twenty-five percent.

This had consequences: People got sick. So sick that curtailing the consumption of sugar is a public health priority, and it's likely that sugar will be thought of as the tobacco of the twenty-first century.

This could have been foreseen, and it was by some. As early as the postwar years, John Yudkin, a physician who was dubious about Keys's assertion that fat consumption was the sole dietary cause of heart disease, began to research the role of sugar. Yudkin reasoned that humans had been carnivorous for eons, while sugar was relatively new. Why would something like meat, which humans had always eaten, suddenly start killing them? Why not the newcomer?

That reasoning isn't entirely sound. There can be more than one bad actor, and indeed there certainly are. But, convinced of his analysis, Yudkin began advising people to avoid sugar altogether, arguing that they'd be "less likely to become fat, run into nutritional deficiency, have a heart attack, get diabetes or dental decay or a duodenal ulcer, and perhaps . . . also reduce your chances of getting gout, dermatitis, and some forms of cancer, and in general increase your life span." He has since been proven right on most counts.

Yudkin's book *Pure, White and Deadly* was first published in 1972. It was influential, but his theories didn't gain the same kind of traction as those of Keys, in part because Keys was working with the American Heart Association and the National Institutes of Health. With their backing, his theories were becoming the standard, and he derided Yudkin's work as "a mountain of nonsense." Science was and is, among other things, a series of turf wars.

At the same time, Yudkin was being sabotaged by the Sugar Research Foundation (SRF). Afraid of more damning findings, SRF vice president John Hickson decided to ramp up efforts to steer the scientific community away from sugar and back toward saturated fat. He funded research into heart disease with the goal of uncovering discrepancies, or at least dissenting opinions, that could be useful in "refut[ing] our detractors." He commissioned a literature review and asked Mark Hegsted, a Harvard nutrition professor who was also a director of SRF's initial research project on coronary heart disease, to write it. Hegsted did, and had it published in the *New England Journal of Medicine*.

The review pushed the conclusion that cholesterol and saturated fat were the sole causes of heart disease: "An overall reduction in the levels of circulating lipids will, in fact, be accompanied by a reduction in the risk of atherosclerotic vascular disease." Replacing sugar with complex carbohydrates had "no practical importance."

In other words: Don't worry about sugar. Fat is the culprit.

The review, which neglected to share that the SRF had initiated and funded the study, was subtly but deeply flawed, prejudiced, and unscientific. It wasn't the first hoax that a medical journal fell for, nor would it be the last. But it was successful: Although the actual science shows that high doses of sugar and saturated fat both contribute to bad health, the sugar industry succeeded in its efforts to paint saturated fat as the leading, if not sole, culprit in congenital heart disease (CHD). Sugar's role in CHD was underplayed and outright ignored. Nor was it that simple: With saturated fat propped up as the sole villain, other highly processed carbohydrates that are almost, if not equally, as harmful as sugar flew under the radar.

Salt did not escape attention. Like sugar, salt makes almost any food more palatable, and our craving for it is hardwired into our bodies. However, unlike sugar, sodium—which, along with chloride, makes up the molecule we know as table salt—is an essential nutrient: We can't make it ourselves, and we can't live without it. (We do not *need* dietary sugar. Our bodies can and do convert carbohydrates and even other nutrients into sugars we can use.)

Salt was once hard to come by and extremely valuable. (As you probably learned in high school, "salt" and "salary" have the same Latin root.) Even now, low blood sodium, or hyponatremia, is not uncommon, although it's usually the result of some other condition (endurance athletes drinking too much water may develop it) or a side effect of a drug. A healthy person with a decent diet is extremely unlikely to suffer from it.

But the industrial mining of salt made it cheap and ubiquitous, and it began to appear, along with sugar, in most processed foods, and in quantities that most public health experts believe to be unhealthy. Salt may cause high blood pressure in formerly healthy individuals and exacerbate it in those with existing high blood pressure. (That "the pulse will stiffen or harden" with too much salt was recognized in China around 4,500 years ago.) Eating less salt, generally speaking, causes blood pressure to drop.

Since the seventies, when fast and junk foods took their places as staples, American sodium consumption has steadily increased from just above recommended limits to around double, and hypertension rates have increased accordingly. It's not that we're using the salt shaker more aggressively. Three-fourths of the sodium we eat comes from ultra-processed foods, including food served in restaurants. We're being fed salt by those who want to sell more food.

None of this means that salt is poison, and neither is sugar.

Natural sugars are everywhere. The lactose in breast milk is sugar, fructose is in every bite of fruit and many vegetables, and various foods are converted to glucose that flows in our blood.

Sugar isn't inherently bad, but the amount matters. No amount of sugar is essential to our diets. A little is probably harmless, and a lot is often damaging. The form that sugar takes is important, too. When it's found in fruit, fructose is teamed with absorption-slowing fiber, and therefore rarely a problem. In Coke, it's a straight shot that hits the bloodstream like a jolt. There's a difference in the body's response.

Because Yudkin first explained this, his work has regained currency—*Pure, White and Deadly* was republished in 2012. His fundamental contention was that sugar is processed in the liver and converted first to glycogen, a kind of energy storage. At the point that glycogen levels max out, further intake of sugar is converted to fat. That's now a widely accepted concern.

What we're really talking about here is the often overlooked, misunderstood, or totally ignored difference between simple and complex carbohydrates. Simple carbs are refined sugars and white flours and other highly processed grains like white rice; complex carbs are found in fruits, vegetables, legumes, and whole grains.

Simple or refined carbs cause a spike in blood sugar that stimulates an immediate and sizable release of insulin. Insulin's job, once an appropriate amount of glucose is present in the bloodstream (it doesn't take much), is to first store that sugar as glycogen and, at a certain point, to convert it to fat.

But the stored-fat problem is just the beginning. The more often our bodies use insulin to convert sugar to glycogen, the more insulin it takes to get the job done. The need for more insulin is called insulin resistance, which doesn't always result in weight gain, but which is a precursor to diabetes and liver disease.

Complex carbs, on the other hand, take longer to digest, are easy on the pancreas (your body's insulin monitor), provide essential nutrients, and keep you full longer. It's increasingly clear that the refined carbohydrates in processed foods put us at risk of heart disease and diabetes. It's equally clear that a high-fiber diet of whole grains, fruits, and vegetables can prevent and even reverse these diseases in most cases.

This is why, when people say they're limiting carbs, they mean —or at least should mean—they're limiting *refined* carbs. As Dr. David Katz writes in *The Truth About Food*, "Find me the person who can blame obesity or diabetes on an excess of carrots or watermelon, and I will give up my day job and become a hula dancer!"

No matter who you are, you know how difficult it is to reform your diet. Your eating preferences, formed before you were old enough to know the difference between truth and lies, are as hard to shake as a chemical dependency, and maybe harder. That's in part because ultra-processed food is engineered to be as addictive as possible, as was initially described in *The End of Overeating*, by David Kessler, and *Salt Sugar Fat: How the Food Giants Hooked Us*, by Michael Moss. Kessler, who served as FDA commissioner under Bush Sr. and Clinton, is a man of impeccable integrity. Moss is a former *New York Times* colleague of mine whose brilliant work led to a Pulitzer Prize.

In the half century beginning in 1950, the surplus produced by the United States amounted to an additional seven hundred calories per person per day, according to USDA estimates. Americans reported adding an additional two hundred calories a day to their diets, so the truth likely lies somewhere in the middle. Regardless, overproduction provided the opportunity for overconsumption, and marketing made it happen.

Refined carbs—grains, stripped of nutrients and processed in ways that could not have even been imagined before the twentieth century—make up the bulk of ultra-processed foods. And it's these hyper-refined carbs, along with salt and fat, that in the second half of the twentieth century made it so just about every American knew the pleasures of high-calorie, highly satisfying food that was created in a lab and scientifically engineered (not just a phrase, a real description) to be irresistible.

The food industry became the junk-food industry. Sixty percent of the calories we eat are in ultra-processed food. Sugar, salt, and fat were added to just about *every* processed food as soups, sodas, crackers, pizza, pastries, breads, chips, yogurts, chicken fingers, and thousands of others were engineered for maximum appeal.

In the last quarter of the century, the number of calories consumed in snacks doubled, while calories eaten at dinner decreased by a third. Cooking declined to the point where fifty percent of food was eaten outside the home, and even much of what was eaten in became hyper-processed. The result was an average weight gain of nearly twenty pounds between 1970 and 2000.

As Kessler writes, companies strove to create food that was "energy-dense, highly stimulating, and went down easy. They put it on every street corner and made it mobile, and they made it socially acceptable to eat anytime and anyplace. They created a food carnival, and that's where we live."

Food engineers made people the subjects of algorithms and sought to find what Moss describes as the "bliss point," the precisely calibrated optimal meeting place of sweetness and/or savoriness and/or richness, the combination of sugar, salt, fat, and "flavoring" most likely to produce a state of euphoria. This bliss point is not random, but determined through a series of tests and measurements, including MRI data, that charts human responses to different ingredient combinations.

Even today, subjects are asked to taste endless variations while engineers gather and analyze neurological responses. That data is then used to manipulate ingredients, and, once a product is engineered to maximize craving, another set of data is used to determine the best audience for it—the perfect marriage of marketing and hard science.

The playbook for junk food in general, and sugar in particular, was almost identical to that of tobacco. Both included advertising strategies that focused on young people. Both obstructed research on their products' effects on human health. Both lied about or hid the results of this research whenever possible. Both shirked responsibility for poisoning entire populations, instead emphasizing individuals' responsibility for their own health. And both prevented or interfered with remedial policymaking.

Edward Bernays—the mastermind behind Señorita Chiquita Banana—is perhaps best known for his 1929 "Torches of Freedom" campaign, which destigmatized smoking for women. One core part of his strategy (and legacy) was the "engineering of consent," which sought to change the culture to fit the product, not the other way around. An example of this is when General Mills used Betty Crocker to meld parents' acceptance of processed foods with their desire to nurture their family.

When scientific consensus began to threaten the tobacco giants, they pretended to care about people and took out ads claiming, "We believe the products we make are not injurious to health. We always have and always will cooperate closely with those whose task it is to safeguard the public health."

At the same time, they purposefully created controversy and injected doubt into the public conversation with obfuscations like "We don't know all the facts," as if anyone has ever made a decision with *all* the facts. They funded misleading and reductionist science designed to provide industry rebuttals that, to the untrained eye, appeared scientific. As the Sugar Research Foundation funded "science" aimed at clouding the consensus on sugar's contribution to disease, Coca-Cola paid Harvard's chair of nutrition to ridicule indisputable evidence of Coke's cavity-causing characteristics.

Sugar may not have precisely the same addictive properties as caffeine or nicotine, but eating it stimulates dopamine, the same reward-confirming neurotransmitter triggered by cocaine, nicotine, and alcohol. We love sugar because it makes other food taste good, but it's more than that: Many of us use sugar as a replacement for alcohol (candy sales skyrocketed during Prohibition), and anyone who has ever tried to actually stop eating sugar knows that it's more than a bad habit or an "I just like it" relationship. The dependency is conspicuous.

Lab tests have shown that animals can be addicted to sugar, so it's hardly a stretch to believe that humans can be as well. Furthermore, argues Robert Lustig, the San Francisco–based M.D. and author of *Fat Chance*, "dopamine also down-regulates its own receptor (which generates the reward signal). This means the next time round, you're going to need more sugar to generate more dopamine to generate less reward, and so on, until you're consuming a whole lot of sugar, and getting almost nothing for it. That's tolerance," a marker of addiction.

Even non-caloric sweeteners make us want to eat more, sharpening our sweet teeth into fangs — thank you, Dr. David Katz, for the image — and leading to weight gain. And sugar goes hand in hand with other nutritional vices: *Ninety percent* of Americans (including me) use caffeine daily, whether in sugar-laced drinks like soda, iced tea, a variety of "sports" and energy drinks, or coffee, which has increasingly become a fat-and-sugar bomb. Even some bottled water is enhanced with caffeine and sweetener.

Whether *all* junk food is physically addictive may not matter. What matters is that it's everywhere, and that we're constantly prodded to eat it. What matters is that, while it isn't good for us, it *is*, in fact, satisfying. What matters is that eating it is a habit that's difficult to break. That much is inarguable, and important.

As ultra-processed foods became cheaper to make, the biggest costs left were marketing, advertising, and sales. Inevitably, these initiatives became increasingly technological, cynical, and amoral. And although they targeted all segments of the population, children were the primary focus.

Food preferences begin to be shaped in utero. Mothers with varied diets who breastfeed and wean their children with normal food create much different eaters than mothers with standard Western diets who rely on formula and baby food. Yet in the twentieth century, we began to feed our children as marketers dictated, and marketers dictated foods with high profit margins. If breast milk were as profitable as formula, almost all mothers would be nursing.

The need for a breast-milk substitute was legitimate. There was always a small percentage of women who, for one reason or another, couldn't breastfeed. Traditionally, the solution was either a wet nurse—a substitute breastfeeder, traditionally a family member or an employee, servant, or slave—or a mixture of bread or cereal soaked in water or cow's milk. The glass nursing bottle and rubber nipple were invented in the nineteenth century, as wet nurses were becoming rare for the same reasons domestic servitude in general was declining.

Our old friend Justus von Liebig—who played such an important role in plant nutrition—patented the first commercial formula, a mixture of cow's milk, potassium bicarbonate, and wheat and malt flours. More or less simultaneously, the Swiss pharmacist Henri Nestlé created a formula made of rusks (twice-baked bread, like biscotti) and sweetened condensed milk, which did not cause as many digestive problems in babies as straight cow's milk. Thus, gradually, began the widespread replacement of breast milk with a laboratory creation.

For many reasons, breastfeeding—as natural as breathing— is essential. Yet since, according to Liebig, breast milk was, like other foods, no more than a combination of carbohydrates, protein, and fat, it could easily be duplicated in "formula." A function that was older than humanity itself became a marketing opportunity, as cow's milk was pushed as being more nutritious than mothers' milk — produced for their own human babies!

Young human mothers had been taught how to breastfeed by their elders for as long as motherhood existed. But those days were gone, and both formula and its marketing were fast evolving: Various fats and sugars were added, then nutrients like calcium and vitamins, all to mimic breast milk. Meanwhile, mothers were "educated" about infant care by advertising and the (male) doctors who were increasingly replacing midwives. Through a combination of ignorance, disinterest, prudishness, misogyny, and encouragement from formula companies, these doctors all but ignored breastfeeding and touted the "modern" alternative. More and more, new mothers switched from the most important and natural nourishment to a manufactured substance.

Yet breast milk cannot be reproduced through any "formula," because it varies from one mother to the next, one child to the next, even one feeding to the next, as the child's needs are "reported" through saliva and other means. It isn't clear just how, or how much, formula sets the stage for later food preferences. But since many formulas contain added sugars, it's impossible to imagine that the influence is a net positive.

In the twentieth century, many people started to lose the battle for nutritional health at birth. The third most abundant substance in breast milk is an oligosaccharide. Babies don't digest it directly. Rather, it nourishes a bacterium called *Bifidobacterium infantis*, transmitted through vaginal birth and wiped out by antibiotics, and now thought to be missing in most American babies.

B. infantis is essential in programming our metabolic operations. Those who maintain a healthy population of the bacterium are less likely to become overweight, experience allergies, or have Type 1 diabetes. But the majority don't, which leaves them prone to numerous autoimmune diseases, colon and rectal cancers, allergies, asthmas, Type 1 diabetes, and eczema. All of these conditions have increased as breastfeeding has declined.

There are many other, better documented reasons for nursing. The international humanitarian organization Save the Children sums them up, saying that breastfeeding "is the single most effective intervention for the prevention of deaths in children under five years old." For most mothers, it's actually more convenient and more sanitary. It's certainly less expensive.

Yet formula makers took over the education and caregiving process of young women throughout the world. Maternity wards were stocked with formula paraphernalia, coupons, and samples. Formula representatives dressed as nurses encouraged women to ignore nature, and doctors were bought off to become formula pushers.

Marketing initiatives targeted anxious moms, too. Nestlé reminded new moms that "millions of babies have come to their teeth easily and naturally with the help of NESTLÉ'S FOOD." Similarly, Carnation assured women that "for generations Carnation has been recommended by famous baby specialists and used in America's leading hospitals."

By the fifties, more than half of American babies were fed formula, and yet many formulas list sugar or an equivalent among the ingredients, often a primary one.

Nor did the marketing end at our borders. The coercion and manipulation of poor mothers all across the world is among the worst crimes committed by private corporations since the colonial era. There was some resistance as formula went global, worsening nutrition and domestic economics, especially in developing countries, where a direct correlation was found between bottle feeding and infant mortality.

In the seventies, Nestlé was forced to battle an international boycott begun by a group of American activists called Infant Formula Action Coalition (INFACT). An article in *Fortune* labeling INFACT's campaigners as "Marxists marching under the banner of Christ" was commissioned and reprinted by a right-wing think tank, of which Nestlé was a quiet but generous donor. The company did manage to stop the slogan "Nestlé kills babies," but not before INFACT caught the world's attention. By 1981 the World Health Organization had attempted to establish a semblance of regulation.

Its solution was the International Code of Marketing of Breast-

Milk Substitutes, also known as "the Code," a series of internationally agreed-upon marketing recommendations, one of which was that all formula marketing "should" (note that this does not read "must") provide information regarding "the benefits and superiority of breast-feeding," as well as instructional information about nursing and the downsides of formula.

Notably, the United States was the only country that didn't accept the Code, which, had it been made international law, would have been effective in clamping down on irresponsible marketing campaigns. But because it was just a series of recommendations, it's been predictably and continually ignored, a pattern we see whenever government (or, in this case, intergovernmental) agencies "recommend" instead of mandate. (Similarly, tame as it is, the Paris Agreement has done little to slow the climate crisis.) Producers continue to distribute free formula samples in hospitals, to label their formula in languages other than that of the country in which they're selling, to pay health professionals to recommend formula, and to advertise recommendations that run counter to Code guidelines. Save the Children estimates that Code violations result in the preventable deaths of almost four thousand children *a day*.

The problem doesn't even end once infants are off formula. Up until the twentieth century, children gradually went from nursing to eating the same food as their parents. But with the invention of commercial "baby food," another novel, ultra-processed food form, parents began to transition their children to a concoction of mashed-up, often sweetened foods sold in bottles. As Kristin Lawless notes in *Formerly Known as Food*, even our belief in children's preferences for "bland white foods . . . has no historical precedent or scientific basis . . . We never stop to consider why these children are picky eaters."

And as children transitioned from formula to baby food, from one ultra-processed food to the next, they were primed for a lifelong sugar-rich diet. Boxed breakfast cereal was next, and whole empires of new sugary foods invented specifically for kids would soon follow. There was, however, ongoing resistance.

After Yudkin, most of the science establishment was silent on

sugar. But a few mavericks stepped into the void. One was Robert Atkins, a cardiologist who in 1972 began pushing the Atkins
Diet, the first of the extreme low-carb diets, which makes sense
only in its purported avoidance of junk. (Almost every food contains carbohydrates, protein, and fat. When people talk about cutting "carbs," what they usually mean is hyper-processed grains,
not real foods. To equate Wonder Bread with wheat berries and
potatoes is silly, ignorant, or willfully misleading.)

Atkins was convinced of sugar's ties to chronic disease, as was
Robert Choate, the once famous Nader-style crusader against
breakfast cereals. Although Atkins's name is familiar today—
most "Paleo" and "keto" diets are based on the Atkins diet—few
remember Choate.

He was a firecracker, though, a self-described "citizen lobbyist"
who argued that sweetened cereals comprised nothing but "empty
calories" and therefore were a dangerous rip-off. He testified before Congress that many popular cereals lacked any nutritional
value, citing a University of Wisconsin study that found that rats
fed shredded cardboard boxes mixed with milk, sugar, and raisins
got more nutrients than those fed about half the popular cereals
on the market. Many of those cereals, the study found, promoted
"little or no growth" or would "not support life even when supplemented" with vitamins and minerals.

Choate's 1970 testimony included a chart outlining the patheti-
cally low nutrition content of forty of the sixty leading breakfast
cereals. When told that he hadn't factored in milk, Choate did just
that, and returned to the Senate in 1972. The results were still
dismal.

As sales began to drop, General Foods's response, besides beginning to load up cereals with vitamins, was to simply say that
kids won't eat what they don't like, a line repeated to this day. For
years, the slogan of Apple Jacks was "We eat what we like," spoken by a child. The truth says otherwise, though: We tend to learn
to like what we eat. Choate parried that marketing was being directed at children, who were being "counter-educated away from
nutrition knowledge." He characterized advertisers as hucksters

and described a war between grown men and still-developing children.

Like Edward Bernays, advertising guru Leo Burnett recognized that successful marketing was about creating desire in consumers. Burnett created the Green Giant, Tony the Tiger, and the Marlboro Man, and they were all nearly as successful as Santa Claus.

Selling kids on new imaginary friends was easy: They were, at that time, spending about the same amount of time watching TV as they were sitting in school — around twenty-five hours a week. That number was even higher for preschoolers, and it's higher for all kids now if you substitute the word "screens" for "TV."

What's more, advertising to children was cheap. In 1972, thirty seconds on a Saturday morning cost four thousand dollars. The TV budget of Kellogg's, General Mills, and General Foods was forty-two million dollars, around the same amount, Choate reported, that GM used to advertise cars. The upshot was that many children were watching upwards of twenty thousand commercials a year. Throughout 1977 and '78, the Center for Science in the Public Interest (CSPI), Consumers Union, and Action for Children's Television petitioned the Federal Trade Commission to control marketing to kids. The FTC took up the issue and planned to make new rules for TV advertising to children.

The FTC, led by its heroic deputy director, Tracy Westen, who eventually proposed banning advertising to children under eight, gathered expert testimony to the effect that kid-targeted advertising was devious and deadly effective. One psychologist's description of how a little kid might see a commercial was particularly notable: "Hi, I'm Tony the Tiger, and I love you. I'm your friend, and I want you to eat Sugar Frosted Flakes because I want you to grow up to be big and strong like me."

Meanwhile, the opposition raised thirty million dollars — over half the FTC's entire budget — to counter the campaign, and accused the agency of overstepping its jurisdiction. Big Sugar was at the center of the fray, pushing an amendment through a House Appropriations subcommittee that crippled the FTC. Instead of taking action on advertisements that it could show were "unfair," the House raised the bar and mandated that an advertisement must be proven "false and deceptive" before it could be banned.

Big Sugar's campaign led to the *Washington Post*'s labeling the FTC a "National Nanny." The final blow came in 1981, when Reagan appointed an FTC chairman who helped Congress deliver what the former chairman called a "legislative prefrontal lobotomy." That was that. The FTC has never recovered from this kneecapping.

Of course, marketing to kids has evolved well beyond cereal. The McDonald's Happy Meal is probably the best-known example. Ray Kroc famously said that the original plan for establishing new McDonald's outlets was to fly over communities and look for schools. But Big Food's presence is felt in every medium that addresses kids, in almost every school in the country, where it sponsors everything from sports teams to printed materials to "educational" programing, all of which includes at least logos if not full ads.

In hindsight, Tony the Tiger and Ronald McDonald may seem like risible symbols. But through these beaming mascots, marketers had discovered that they could turn dessert into breakfast—one serving of cereal in many cases contains more sugar than several cookies, or a Twinkie. They could create foods that hit the perfect bliss point, run commercials designed to appeal to children, convince those children (and to a large extent adults as well) to eat virtually anything, and then watch the junk food fly off shelves.

Countering this machine is one of modern nutrition's greatest challenges. If formula, an inferior and often harmful product, can be legally sold as "doctor recommended," where are the limits? If brands insist that sugar-sweetened cereals are a matter of "choice," while kids are being trained by the media to choose products that harm them, how do we build a healthy community? And, as we'll see, now that we're three or four generations into a food system that's killing us, charting a course correction is way more involved than "educating" parents about the right way to eat.

12

The So-Called Green Revolution

THE GREEN REVOLUTION is usually touted as an American gift to the developing world, the introduction of an agricultural system that relieved hunger and increased wealth, especially for farmers. But as we've seen, industrial agriculture was hardly a benefit for most Americans, and its global spread was no less complicated.

The 1949 revolution that created the People's Republic of China struck fear in the West's rulers, who dreaded the prospect of similar revolts elsewhere. And with old-style colonialism dying after World War II, newly self-governed countries faced a choice between East and West.

Most peasants around the world—who, again, described themselves as such, with no negative connotations attached—simply wanted control over the land they worked. But redistribution of land was (and still is) uncommon. Even where Western governments saw it as desirable, there were no accepted democratic mechanisms for the transfer of land from wealthy owners to peasants, especially since those wealthy owners also had a large say in how the "accepted democratic mechanisms" operated.

Exceptionally, and paradoxically, the postwar American occupiers of Japan, led by General Douglas MacArthur, designed and executed a seven-year plan to make sure land was owned by those who tilled it. Similar programs were established in South Korea and Taiwan, and many argued that this U.S.-initiated reform was the economic foundation of the first "Asian Miracle," the period of the smooth, relatively egalitarian industrialization of Japan, South Korea, Hong Kong, Taiwan, and Singapore between the fifties and the nineties.

Another kind of land reform took place in China, where, by 1950, landlords had been eliminated—in a very literal sense. The state parceled land and forced collectivization in the model of Stalin. This wasn't without benefit: Three hundred million Chinese peasants were given land, tools, livestock, and infrastructure and relieved of rent payments. There were aspects of this that had to look appealing elsewhere, until Mao forced millions to migrate to cities while killing millions of others; the most catastrophic famine in human history followed less than a decade later.

It's complicated: For centuries peasants had lived in oppressive conditions, and the argument that everyone deserves enough land to support their family is compelling. In fact, the concept is increasingly accepted as a human right today, commonly referred to as "food sovereignty." It's also important to acknowledge that no system is ideologically pure. Both the West and the East spouted egalitarian rhetoric but supported and quashed democratic movements as was expedient; there was little consistency.

The West wanted to persuade developing governments and their people that, unlike Mao and Stalin, it offered a nonviolent route to prosperity, via industrial-scale agriculture, and no one could argue that the U.S. agriculture system wasn't a modern miracle of human ingenuity, producing gobs of wealth and unparalleled surpluses.

But even when developing nations pushed for aid that would help them reestablish the food-producing autonomy dismantled by colonialism, the United States aggressively hawked machines, chemicals, and seeds, sometimes on favorable terms, sometimes not.

In 1968, William Gaud, the director of the United States Agency for International Development, coined the name for this U.S.-backed spread of industrial agriculture: "These and other developments in the field of agriculture contain the makings of a new revolution. It is not a violent Red Revolution like that of the

Soviets, nor is it a White Revolution like that of the Shah of Iran. I call it the Green Revolution."

Was the Green Revolution a technological miracle, one that showed the way to end world hunger, to liberate poor farmers while increasing yields and promising all the riches and pleasures of the postwar USA? The real answer is not the one its adherents would like you to believe.

The Green Revolution began in the forties (before it was named), when hybrid seed pioneer Henry Wallace, the Rockefeller Foundation, and the Mexican government founded the Mexican Agricultural Program. Joining the effort was the young American agronomist Norman Borlaug, who, while virtually ignoring what was traditionally grown, developed and brought in high-yielding hybrid seeds along with chemical fertilizers and pesticides, with the idea of producing cash crops to sell on the global market.

If you look at one particular set of numbers resulting from this strategy, the Green Revolution indeed appears miraculous. Overall, food production in the developing world doubled — and sometimes more — from the early sixties to the late eighties, growing faster than the population itself. Mexico went from an importer of wheat to an exporter. Higher yields led to a nearly three hundred percent increase in rice production in Indonesia. Latin American corn production increased by a third.

By the nineties, close to seventy-five percent of Asia's rice and half of the wheat in Africa, Latin America, and Asia were grown using new hybrid varieties. The Green Revolution reportedly doubled food supply in Asia in just twenty-five years. That outpaced population growth significantly, and by 2000 world food supplies were twenty percent higher per capita than in 1961. The number of people going hungry decreased by sixteen percent between 1970 and 1990. Green Revolutionaries often point to numbers that show global yields doubling for rice, corn, and potatoes and tripling for wheat.

So successful did the Green Revolution appear to be that Borlaug, its figurehead, won the Nobel Peace Prize in 1970. "To millions of these unfortunates, who have long lived in despair," he said, "the green revolution seems like a miracle that has generated new hope for the future."

Yet the Green Revolution did not end hunger. And even the mainstream analysis has changed, if news headlines are any indicator: "Green Revolution in India Wilts as Subsidies Backfire" (*Wall Street Journal*); "India's Farming 'Revolution' Heading for Collapse" (NPR); "The Toxic Consequences of the Green Revolution" (*U.S. News and World Report*).

That's because increased yields do not necessarily lead to better lives, because more food in the market has never meant fewer people in need, and because there's been immeasurable damage resulting from chemical-, capital-, debt-based agriculture.

The truth is that the Green Revolution was never about "feeding the world." That was, and remains, the public relations spin. Rather, it was a front for selling American agricultural machinery, chemicals, and seeds — sales that were aimed mostly at farmers or investors who had the substantial capital needed for land and equipment.

In fact, increased global yields stemmed from a combination of factors best summed up in a 2019 piece in *The Geographical Journal* by anthropologist Glenn Davis Stone: "The legendary wheat-field triumphs came from financial incentives, irrigation, and the return of the rains, and they came at the expense of more important food crops. Long-term growth trends in food production and food production per capita did not change, [and] the Green Revolution years, when separated out, actually marked a slowdown."

For example, the Green Revolution takes credit for higher yields in India. But there had been several years of drought before the American miracle varieties of wheat and rice were planted, so the baseline was depressed. And while these new crops' yields were on the rise, so were those of traditional crops like barley and chickpeas. Tobacco, jute, cotton, and tea — none of which are Green Revolution crops — also saw better yields from 1967 to '70. In fact, over the long term, grain production in India had been increasing steadily without the new seeds or techniques, which didn't change trends much, if at all. Wheat production increased, but since the wheat often replaced legumes, it was detrimental to both soil and diet. In rice, which fed vastly more people, growth in yield actually declined.

Increased wheat production didn't help most Mexican farmers or eaters either, because the land given over to wheat was taken from subsistence farmers, depriving many people of the corn, squash, and beans that constituted their traditional diets.

What boosted numbers was not so much scientific miracles but massive price subsidies. As Raj Patel points out, in the Philippines, "price supports for rice increased by 50%. In Mexico, the government purchased domestically grown wheat at 33% above world market prices. India and Pakistan paid 100% more for their wheat."

British scientist and former president of the Rockefeller Foundation Gordon Conway elaborates: "By the mid-1980s the subsidies were 68 percent of the world price for pesticides, 40 percent for fertilizers, and nearly 90 percent for water." And historian Kapil Subramanian makes a compelling case that major government investment in private wells across the Indian countryside helped particularly with rice, and that the new seeds themselves made little difference.

The percentage of hungry people around the world has inarguably decreased since the sixties, but hunger fell nowhere as markedly as it did in China, where there was no Green Revolution intervention at all. There, saner land reform, distribution of (domestic) hybrid seeds, investment in irrigation, and more generous price subsidies paid directly to rural peasants brought about an internal agricultural revolution that owed little or nothing to the West.

China allowed individual families to produce their own food and sell it on a semi-open but controlled market, while social policy protected food security and local production. The goal was not only to increase yield but to reduce poverty and enhance well-being. And it worked: Production tripled post-Mao, but, more important, the world's most dramatic decrease in poverty *ever* took place. World Bank statistics from 2016 report that the number of poor people in rural China—defined as those living on less than a dollar a day—fell from around 490 million in 1979 to around 82 million in 2014, from fifty percent of the populace to just over six percent.

If you exclude China, the number of hungry people in the world actually *increased* during the heyday of the Green Revolution, despite increases in yield. In South America, for example, per capita food supplies rose almost eight percent; the number of hungry people went up by nineteen percent. Similarly, in South Asia there was a nine percent increase in food per person by 1990, accompanied by a nine percent increase in hungry people. The fruits of the Green Revolution weren't feeding people *in situ;* they were being sold on the global market.

There were other problems, even in China, which was far from a perfect model. Hybrid seeds were worth anything only if you could afford the pesticides that protected them. In India, for example, pesticide use increased by a factor of *twenty* in the second half of the twentieth century. More generally, it's estimated that a million people a year either die or have their lives shortened as a result of pesticide poisoning.

Green Revolution–style agriculture also required new equipment and larger plots of land, which required credit. This disqualified most peasants and meant that, as in early-twentieth-century America, the new technologies almost exclusively benefited wealthier farmers. Most small stakeholders didn't have the land to participate, nor could they invest in equipment even if they'd wanted to, and many of those who borrowed money to switch to "modern" techniques went bankrupt. Farmer suicides in India and elsewhere spiked as a result. Furthermore, the new-style agriculture also minimized labor. This drove peasants to cities, where unemployment awaited many of them.

Green Revolution advocates saw local, farmer-oriented economies as outmoded, even impossible. In their arrogance and naivete, they believed that nature exists to serve us, and that by properly exploiting it, science could solve problems of fairness and inequality.

These beliefs persisted even though the consequences were stark. Chemical agriculture was poisoning the soil, air, water, and other resources, destroying the livelihoods of millions of people, and altering diets in unforeseen and detrimental ways, all while doing little or nothing to alleviate hunger. Some "Green Revolutionaries" may have been motivated by idealism, however misguided it was. But for most, the impetus was money.

To be clear, poor farmers knew how to do their jobs; the vast majority of the world's food comes from small-time farmers, who have far fewer resources at their disposal than their wealthier counterparts. If the energy, scientific studies, and government subsidies that stimulated industrial agriculture had instead gone into improving peasant agriculture, reducing poverty, and making land use more fair, the progress would have been profound, and far more tangible than the Green Revolution's "We can feed the world" hype.

It's impossible to know how sustainable agricultural strategies would have fared had they been backed by the United States. But stimulating rational land reform and researching ways to support and improve traditional agriculture was never the point. Those methods just didn't have the same profit potential as industrial agriculture.

And the benefits from the Green Revolution's heralded boost in grain yields went not to local farmers but to traders, for whom the system was working fabulously.

By the seventies, Europe had long since recovered from the war, and Brazil, Argentina, China, South Africa, and others had begun to industrialize their agriculture. Throw in OPEC, shifting currency values, and the increasing power of corporations, and the global trading scene became increasingly arcane. Those who understood it best were the usually privately held, vertically and horizontally integrated companies now known as ABCD: Archer Daniels Midland, Bunge, Cargill, and Louis Dreyfus. These controlled the market, operated in secret, and knew more than entire governments about the prices and locations of commodities. This led to a dramatic moment that Martha McNeil Hamilton called the Great Grain Robbery.

Hundreds of millions of tons of grain were being milled, processed, and sold each year. And U.S. export programs ensured that
when traders bought American grain, the USDA subsidized the
difference between low global prices and higher domestic prices.
By manipulating those subsidies, traders were guaranteed profits.

Thus the United States maintained a kind of geopolitical stability by keeping other countries dependent on its food. Much
of this was done through "dumping"—selling the subsidized,
lower-priced goods on the world market, undercutting the sale
of locally produced goods. Dumping was officially prohibited by
the General Agreement on Tariffs and Trade (GATT), but when
it came to agriculture, loopholes abounded, and prohibition was
rarely enforced.

In the summer of 1972, the Soviet Union, anticipating a short-
fall in its grain harvest, contracted with traders for massive purchases that, unbeknownst to the world, amounted to a third of
the American wheat harvest—by far the biggest grain deal in
history. This put the USDA on the hook for around three hundred million dollars in export subsidies while causing grain supplies to plunge. The USDA was notified about the trades in advance and could have adjusted prices or reserves to give farmers a
slice of the deal and/or diminish the effects of the food crisis that
followed, but the agency ignored the warning signs, then lied to
Congress.

By 1974 domestic wheat reserves had fallen by about two-thirds
and prices had nearly tripled. Farmers, almost needless to say, did
not benefit. Cargill's earnings, however, increased by *more than
seven times* within a year.

Less grain meant fewer cattle; beef became relatively scarce
and expensive. This gave Secretary of Agriculture Earl Butz an
excuse to ax conservation programs while he famously instructed
farmers to plant "fencerow to fencerow," with the assumption that
the crops could be bought for cheap and sold at the "new" high
prices, a win for his agribusiness buddies. His line: "Get big or
get out." Later that decade, Jimmy Carter cut off grain shipments
to the USSR after it invaded Afghanistan, and as a result domes-

tic markets were flooded once again. Prices plummeted accordingly, and interest rates peaked at twenty percent, a disaster for farmers and others with new debt. This in turn led to the farm foreclosures of the eighties, perhaps the final blow to the family farm. Nor was the government sympathetic: Appearing before a group of senators from rural America, President Reagan quipped, "I think we should keep the grain and export the farmers."

The jovial Reagan all but guaranteed that his wish would come true by decreasing price supports and eliminating antitrust policies, moves whose generosity might have surprised even the greediest businessmen. A major wave of mergers and acquisitions followed and, despite "free market" rhetoric, corporate power increased and competition decreased.

Most contemporary tellings of the decline in American farming and rural communities start here. But while the eighties farm crisis was a particularly bleak period, it was hardly an anomaly. Those small farms that hadn't been doomed from the start by geography, weather, or innovations like the tractor succumbed to consolidation. Farms were foreclosed, which resulted in slaughterhouses shutting down, followed by grocery and hardware stores, and seed, feed, and equipment dealers. Walmart put whole downtowns out of business, and fast-food joints killed locally owned restaurants. Consolidation displaced a million rural people, and once-thriving communities became ghost towns.

The great American small-farm experiment was effectively over. Big farms, however, still had room to grow. But the usual question remained: Where were all these crops—especially, in this era, corn—going to go? We've seen part of that answer: ethanol and high-fructose corn syrup. Much of the remainder left the country.

Mexico was a prime target for surplus U.S. farm goods, in part because it was already a semi-dependent neighbor and in part because it could serve as a proving ground for the trendy economic theory known as "comparative advantage," which held that if one party could produce a certain good more efficiently than another, it was best for the weaker producer to abandon production of that good, and trade for it instead. In short, every country should grow what they were best at growing, and trade for what they needed.

This *sounds* logical, but for farmers, people in general, the soil, carbon emissions, and a half dozen other factors, it's a terrible idea, and it has failed horribly. We see a stark example of this failure in the corn trade between the United States and Mexico.

Mexico supported its peasant population, including through government purchases of staples from subsistence farmers and the sale of that food at low prices. But, like countries from Brazil to India, it appeared to face a choice: Would it adapt industrial methods to the countryside, produce as much as possible, eliminate the peasantry, and become a food-exporting machine? Or would it empower small-plot landowners to remain the core of a healthy economy?

The choice was likely an illusion, given international pressure and Mexico's wavering and often corrupt government. A loose federation formed by the United States, multinational corporations, members of the Mexican elite, and lending organizations like the World Bank and the International Monetary Fund ushered in a new form of domination that was far more subtle than the Opium Wars, the blatant colonization of Africa, or the overthrow of Central American governments.

Thus was born the North American Free Trade Agreement, which purported to level the playing field by eliminating as many tariffs and regulations as possible, allowing wealth to flow more easily between countries.

A level playing field can't exist, however, if one country is fifteen times more powerful than the other. And in 1994, that was the ratio of the United States' GDP to Mexico's. And wealth did flow more freely, but not back and forth between the two countries. It only flowed north. (Canada is part of NAFTA, but in this case it can be thought of as an economic subset of the United States.)

Nevertheless, NAFTA began the dismantling of protective trade laws and other rules. Once it did away with those regulations, investment by U.S. companies could increase, and subsistence farmers could be moved off their land to become factory laborers.

Until then, Mexico's small-scale farming, which needed few chemicals and little fossil fuel infrastructure, produced a nutritious diet based on corn, squash, beans, and green vegetables. With minuscule transportation costs and a small carbon footprint, it supported people through the growing of crops, raising of livestock, small food markets, millers, and other processors; non-farmers in these rural communities made small crafts and ran businesses. It may not have been perfectly secure, but it wasn't the disaster it has since become.

Under the Green Revolution's paradigm and the dogmas of comparative advantage and free trade, however, it made no sense for Mexicans to grow corn for one another. As Alyshia Gálvez wrote in *Eating NAFTA*, in 2004, "to produce one ton of corn requires 17.8 labor *days* in Mexico, versus 1.2 *hours* in the United States." Since "efficient" economies manufactured what they were best suited to, then met their other needs through international trade — and since no one was better suited to producing corn than the United States — Mexico had to both take some of the U.S. surplus and find a new commodity to contribute to the global market. Since its farmers now had no local market and were fast becoming landless, that "commodity" was their cheap labor.

As one Mexican farmer said, if "the U.S. sends subsidized corn into Mexico, send it in trains with benches to bring back the Mexican farmers who will need jobs." Excluding the benches, that's exactly what happened. Two million farmers were put out of work, unemployment rose, emigration soared, and income stagnated. Mexican imports of American corn, meanwhile, multiplied by six in the twenty years after the implementation of NAFTA. Since then, they've doubled again.

Twenty-five years later, the United States supplies Mexico with forty-two percent of its food. American pork exports to Mexico, for example, have increased ninefold. In place of subsistence production, Mexican industrial farms now produce berries and tomatoes for North Americans, most of whom are ignorant of the human costs of producing them — worker and child abuse, withheld and stolen wages, and generally horrific living and working conditions. Additionally, high-paying manufacturing jobs moved from the States to Mexico, where wages were lower, crippling U.S. labor unions.

NAFTA also brought junk food to Mexico. Imports of high-fructose corn syrup increased by almost *nine hundred* times, and soda consumption nearly doubled. Mexico is now the world's fourth-leading per capita soda consumer. For all the destruction of livelihoods, environmental consequences, and transfer of power (the United States calls this "development"), the health consequences of NAFTA are perhaps most damaging. Mexico now leads the world's populous nations in obesity, and diabetes—almost always caused by a modern Western diet—is among the country's leading killers.

Mexico is a paradigm of much of what has since happened elsewhere, and it's difficult to see a path toward change, given a global economy that allows corporations to run roughshod over national borders. And yet even the countries that have benefited most from a globalized economy—most notably the United States—are in the throes of declining health (largely a result of the surplus-driven diet), rising inequality, and a poisoned environment.

Some of the first hints of that environmental damage emerged even before the Green Revolution took chemical pesticides global.

Pesticides aren't new. (The word includes killers of insects, weeds, fungi, mold, and mildew—anything that targets the intended crop.) The Sumerians used sulfur as an insecticide around forty-five hundred years ago. The ancient Chinese developed the first devoted pesticide, pyrethrum, a derivative of chrysanthemum that's still used as an organic pesticide.

By the same time, or not much later, growers throughout Asia were employing beneficial predatory insects. (In the West, a desperate, bizarre, and presumably less effective practice involved excommunicating cutworms and caterpillars from the Church.) Eventually, outright poisons like arsenic and mercury became popular, and they were still routinely used in the twentieth century. While mercury has since been abandoned as a pesticide, arsenic, though mostly banned from U.S. and European agriculture, is in use elsewhere.

Farmers have every reason to take pests and blights seriously, but biodiverse farms manage to do so without deadly chemicals. Non-harmful controls require more labor, of course, as well as an understanding of what a particular plot of land is best suited to grow. And a variety of species is integral to soil health.

But monoculture works by killing just about everything except the main crop, because you can't keep huge crops of corn healthy without pesticides, especially when they've been bred to be grown with them. The bigger the harvests, the more chemicals are needed.

It's not surprising that most producers of pesticides have experience with other killing agents. Bayer and Monsanto (now one company, the first having bought the second) and DuPont and Dow (which merged) all made wartime killing agents, from nerve gas to Agent Orange. Zyklon B, the gas chamber chemical, was made by a subsidiary of the Nazi-allied IG Farben, which was divided after World War II among several companies, including Bayer; and DuPont was instrumental in the Manhattan Project. (Another big producer, Syngenta—now owned by ChemChina —was originally Swiss, so it's a little different.)

Just as chemical fertilizers developed in tandem with the weapons of World War I, a new breed of pesticides designed to kill insects and weeds came of age during World War II. Chief among them was dichlorodiphenyltrichloroethane: DDT.

DDT was synthesized in 1874 but largely ignored until it was found to be an effective pesticide, in 1939, just in time for the United States to bring it to the Pacific theater, where troops were fighting malaria-carrying mosquitoes as well as enemy soldiers.

Powerful, effective, cheap, and once considered close to harmless—it was used as a straight-onto-the-body delousing powder—DDT eliminated mosquitoes and malaria from large sections of the tropics. By the fifties it was being sprayed with no restrictions and was popular for everything from agriculture (crop-spraying pilots were paid by the gallon) to making suburban evenings more pleasant. If you're of a certain age and spent any time at all in a southeastern summer, you will remember the spray truck driving right down the middle of the street at dusk, trailing its mist and the sweet smell of DDT. From the end of the war until the mid-seventies, more than a billion pounds of the pesticide had been sprayed or dusted—close to seven pounds for every American.

Need I say that there were consequences? Insects became resistant to DDT, which, like other chemical killers, is indiscriminate in its attacks, poisoning beneficial insects and plants and even animals on higher trophic levels, like fish and mammals. When a DDT-sprayed plant is eaten by an animal, the DDT is concentrated in the animal's body. When *that* animal is eaten by a predator, the chemical concentrates even further, in a process known as biomagnification. Up the food chain, this causes thinning of eggshells in birds and birth defects in mammals, including humans.

Rampant use of pesticides did not stop with DDT, nor were they used solely for agriculture and mosquito control. Nearly four million acres of Vietnam and Laos were defoliated during the American incursion into Southeast Asia, through the use of the infamous Agent Orange. Even putting aside the environmental damage, those pesticides have been responsible for countless cancers among the local population and the American soldiers exposed.

These chemicals' job is to kill, and collateral damage is a given: Chemical poisoning is worst for humans with direct exposure (today, that means mostly farmworkers), but rampant pesticide use also contaminates rivers, streams, lakes, groundwater, even bays and oceans. It damages or destroys the soil's microbial populations, making the soil ever more dependent on chemical fertilizers. It even contributes to air pollution and, of course, has an impact on non-targeted animals and plants that come into contact with the chemicals. Notable among those non-targeted animals are human consumers—we all routinely consume pesticides that wind up on and in our food.

That pesticides don't discriminate is important: They're simply poisons, not targeted but shotgun. For the most part, they'll kill or damage what they touch.

One of the great promises of the late twentieth century was to change that, to make pesticides that could target rather than simply kill everything in their path. This led to one of the period's great disappointments: the genetically engineered seed.

First developed in the seventies, genetic engineering involves creating or altering genes, then inserting those genes into organisms to change their characteristics. The process promises plants that are resistant to pests, are tolerant of drought or flood, and grow bigger and faster with boosted nutrition. That fundamental tinkering sounds great, and remains full of potential. But in agriculture, to date, it's done far more harm than good. And certainly, successfully engineering new seeds hasn't been as fast or sensational as was once hoped.

But the results have been profitable. The new, altered seeds boosted features beyond those of already patented hybrids and required that farmers purchase yet more products — like a specific pesticide — to be used in tandem for best results. Monsanto came early to the game and was cunning enough to win some critical patents for genetically engineered seeds. These patents, and the accompanying chemicals that were essential to those seeds' growth, are the keys to profits.

It's a simple system. Genetically engineered seeds are sold with licensing agreements, which state that farmers are licensing the seed's desired traits for one planting season. The next season, they must pay again. Monsanto defends this scheme vigorously, prosecuting farmers for saving seeds and even coming after farmers who didn't destroy windblown seed that took root in their fields.

The first commercially available food from genetically engineered seeds was the 1994 Flavr Savr tomato, which slowed the ripening process so that tomatoes could be picked red rather than green, as is the norm. But Flavr Savrs became mushy just as quickly as traditional tomatoes, and they brought a host of public relations problems. People feared that mixing genes from different varieties—and even different species and genera—would create seeds with undesirable and uncontrollable properties, essentially "Frankenfoods."

The notion that genetically modified organisms are harmful in and of themselves has not (to date) been demonstrated to be true. But even if the seeds or the crops they produce are not harmful, and even if genetically modified organisms (GMOs) are not themselves all that scary, the chemicals that are required to grow those seeds are as destructive as many other pesticides.

On the safety question, the FDA declared "substantial equivalence" between traditionally bred crops and gene-tampered crops (you might think that "substantial equivalence" would void patents, but no) and ruled that pre-market safety testing of GMOs wasn't necessary unless the edited genes in question were *known* to cause allergies or other reactions. (How one learns of these adverse reactions without pre-market testing is beyond anyone's guess.) But the United States has never really prioritized the precautionary principle, the process of determining that a new product or process will cause no harm before releasing it. Europe's approach is different. There, genetically engineered agricultural products can be sold only if they are evaluated first.

Not only are GMOs present in tens or hundreds of thousands of foods, but those foods are not identified. (In this country, if it has corn or soy in it and it isn't certified organic, it's almost certain to contain GMOs.) This is despite poll after poll in which as many as ninety percent of Americans surveyed made it clear that they would prefer to know if the food they are eating is made from genetically modified seed.

Flavr Savr was not the only high-profile example of a failed modification. Recombinant bovine growth hormone (rBGH), a genetically engineered hormone that increases cow's milk production, was largely rejected by milk drinkers, because it was known to make the cows sick. (Monsanto tried and failed to hide the damning evidence.)

None of these strikeouts mattered much once Monsanto followed up with its grand slam. By 2013, reports Jennifer Clapp,

"Monsanto alone accounted for 90 percent of the global genetically engineered seed market." Much of this is thanks to the company's line of "Roundup Ready" seeds, that is, seeds that are impervious to Roundup, the company's "broad-spectrum" herbicide. Roundup's primary ingredient is glyphosate, a chemical that kills pretty much every plant it touches by preventing photosynthesis.

At first, Roundup was useful only insofar as you could spray it accurately. If you missed the poison ivy and hit the azalea—well, bye-bye, azalea. Similarly, if you missed the giant ragweed and hit the corn . . .

But with the development of Roundup Ready seeds, you could spray indiscriminately and kill everything but the crop you wanted to grow, primarily corn and soybeans. Or at least that's the theory.

To large-scale farmers, that sounded ideal. The use of glyphosate in the United States went from fourteen million pounds in 1992 to around three hundred million pounds today; global use has approached two billion pounds annually.

But if it seemed too good to be true, that's because it was. Since Roundup's early years, a variety of plants have developed resistance to glyphosate, leading to a generation of "superweeds" that aren't killed by the chemical. Monsanto's responses have included augmenting glyphosate with other herbicides and funding studies that make glyphosate seem essential and "prove" its safety.

The promises of genetically engineered seeds included decreased pesticide use and increased yield. Monsanto's products have done neither: Pesticide use has *increased*, and there is no scientific consensus that genetically modified seeds—this includes but isn't limited to Roundup Ready seeds—yield bigger harvests than conventional seeds.

In fact, for anyone other than Monsanto, Roundup has had very few actual benefits: It's raised farmers' costs without raising income, created generations of pesticide-tolerant weeds, and appears to have caused cancer in gardeners, farm owners, farmworkers, and even bystanders.

Bayer bought Monsanto in 2016, for a sixty-six-billion-dollar cash payment that the parent company almost certainly now regrets. As of this writing, three lawsuits have found Monsanto

liable for causing cancer. Juries awarded nearly two billion dollars in damages, all told, and in June of 2020, Monsanto settled
with almost 100,000 class-action plaintiffs for ten billion dollars,
a sum that places it "among the largest settlements ever in civil
litigation."

This hasn't been enough to brand genetic engineering in agriculture a failure, because other products have fared better and, at
first glance, are more defensible. These crops harness a bacterium
called *Bacillus thuringiensis* (Bt), and they have become as important in cotton as Roundup Ready seeds are in corn.

When Bt is used responsibly as an insecticide, its effects dissi-
pate after a week. (It's even permitted by organic standards.) But
Bt-embedded crops don't actually replace insecticides — they *produce* the insecticides themselves, emitting a constant mist of the
bacterium. Predictably, the constant presence of Bt increased resistance over time, and another pesticide had to be added to the
rotation. In most cases, the added pesticide is a neonicotinoid, a
class of pesticide that's largely responsible for the massive die-off
of honeybee colonies. Such is the bar for "success" in genetic engineering.

There are other examples (advocates will complain about the
short shrift I'm giving Golden Rice, another agricultural "revolution" that's led to disappointment), but it's safe to say that so far,
the products of genetic engineering in agriculture have done little
but advance industrial methods and compound existing problems
— especially by increasing the sale of chemicals and propping up
monocropping — while creating new ones.

PART III

Change

13

The Resistance

I T'S MOST ACCURATE to think of industrial agriculture as a
form of mining—extracting soil, water, elements, fossil fuel,
and more, rapidly using riches that developed over eons. And,
as such, it's easy to see how it can't last—how, to use contemporary language, it's not sustainable; it can't endure.

Liebig recognized this in the nineteenth century when he
pointed out the "folly" of operating as if "the Earth is inexhaustible in its gifts." And our understanding of nature's limits stretches
back even further. Newton's laws discussed the finite nature of
matter, and the ancient Greek philosopher Epicurus said, "The totality of things was always such as it is now, and always will be."

Yet despite the laws of nature, mainstream economic thought
would have us believe that unlimited economic growth in every
sphere, including agriculture, is synonymous with a healthy society—even if that growth means unmitigated environmental destruction. It would also have us believe that the agri-food complex
(like the fossil fuel industry) has full license to steadfastly avoid
paying for "externalities"—economic jargon for unintended consequences of business, such as environmental damage or disease.

These consequences are both real and dire. Like its resources,
nature's capacity to absorb physical and chemical abuse is limited.
So, of course, is that of the human body.

Until the fifties, development, depression, and war were such
large-scale distractions that industrial farming became dominant without attracting much attention. If it was thought about

at all, it was as a wondrous machine, productive and convenient. And most people had no idea how it worked: My parents' generation was the first in which most Americans didn't know a single farmer.

Nevertheless, by midcentury the indications that industrial farming and food production were damaging were becoming clear.

To be sure, environmental damage from agriculture had always been observable—it began with burning forests, after all. But when populations were smaller, the losses were tolerable. This new kind of farming was quickly degrading the land (Iowa, for example, has lost about seven inches of topsoil since the Europeans took over) and even injecting it with poisons.

Some open-minded thinkers began to realize that cold-blooded reductionist thought—that a farm or a local environment or a food system or a planet can best be understood as simply the sum of its parts—doesn't capture the mystery of the natural world. And when disciplines like ecology emerged, they led to a closer look at the earth's complex systems, where interactions between easily explained forces result in intricate outcomes that are difficult and sometimes impossible to understand.

Scientists called this emergence: the notion that the whole is greater than the sum of its parts, that elements may synergize to create something greater. Life itself was the emergence of a number of interactions among systems, each of which is explainable on its own but, taken together, becomes far more mysterious.

Our "primitive" ancestors knew that humans are a part of nature, not above it. After World War II, this fundamental truth became a philosophical countercurrent to the reigning propaganda of industrial growth. Barry Commoner, originally a biologist, developed the "Four Laws of Ecology." Although they may now appear self-evident, at the time they were radical. Their impact on industry and government is still far from what it should be. Commoner's laws were straightforward:

Everything is connected to everything else. This is a version of Newton's Third Law, which says that each action has an equal and opposite reaction. Commoner, like many nineteenth- and twentieth-century analysts, believed that all social justice causes—from racism to income inequality—are interrelated, and that they're all related to nature.

Everything must go somewhere, the second law, was a restatement of Lavoisier's Law of Conservation of Mass and Energy, which states that mass and energy may change form, but they can't be created or destroyed. Thus, waste, from human to nuclear, cannot be made to disappear and will therefore always have an impact on the environment.

Nature knows best is Commoner's simplest rule. It argues that working with nature is the smartest way to live on this planet.

Last of all, and most foreboding: *There is no such thing as a free lunch*. Here Commoner argues that every "gain" has a cost. The Greek Parmenides said it first: *"Ex nihilo nihil fit"*—Nothing comes from nothing.

Less well known but equally important are the sociologist John Bellamy Foster's Commoner-inspired Four Laws of Capitalism, which demonstrate how opposed the status quo is to sound ecology:

The only lasting connection between things is the cash nexus. Every relationship is about money, including the relationship between humans and nature.

It doesn't matter where something goes, as long as it doesn't reenter the circuit of capital. Producers will always ignore the damages caused by production. For example, industrial farmers ignore the externalities of their operations and products, like pollution and diabetes. Waste can be ignored.

The *self-regulating market knows best* argues that it doesn't matter what you sell—junk food, pesticides, assault rifles—as long as it's profitable.

Finally: *Nature's bounty is a free gift to the property owner*. Foster stated this best: "Nowhere in establishment economic models does one find an adequate accounting of nature's contribution."

Ecologists recognized that resources are finite, and that nature is in charge. That's basic science. Capitalists believe that nature exists to be exploited by humans, a tenet perfectly in tune with Western religion.

It's not a coincidence that there's been a conspicuous correlation between the advances of capitalism and the threats to our species's survival. Capitalists may understand that resources are finite, but they choose to ignore that fact (as they ignore the climate crisis), instead pretending that unending growth is achievable. You might argue that this has served parts of humanity well in the past, but it would be fruitless to argue that it ever served *all* of humanity well, and it's now threatening our existence.

Not surprisingly, the limits of growth began to be recognized in parallel with the Industrial Revolution. The word "ecology" was coined in 1873, a period when visionaries began to talk about alternatives to what was becoming industrial agriculture. Among those visionaries was George Washington Carver, a son of enslaved people.

Carver, who was raised in southwest Missouri in the 1860s, seems to have been a born genius. One of his biographers, Christina Vella, writes, "Before he was ten years old, people around the area . . . were bringing him diseased plants which he would 'treat' by changing the soil or water or amount of sunlight, or by diagnosing some mold or insect attacker."

Carver pursued education diligently and, after a series of typically racism-based hardships, eventually wound up at the Iowa State College of Agriculture and Mechanic Arts, in Ames. There, he found his calling: to help provide Black southerners with the knowledge they needed to improve their agriculture and their diets.

Carver was all about traditional polyculture, with minimal machinery, and mostly chemical-free. His methods and his teachings symbolized what the USDA could have been — what Lincoln, its creator, called the "people's department." Carver did not train farmers as dutiful consumers of the products of agribusiness. He helped them be more independent, sustain their soil, and better feed their families.

When he left school, in 1894, as Iowa State's first Black graduate, he was widely courted. He chose to go to work for the famously charismatic Booker T. Washington, who needed a botanist for his growing Tuskegee Institute, in Alabama. There, Carver led all of Tuskegee's farm programs as well as a USDA experiment station, where he conducted studies designed to help poor farmers. (His legendary *How to Grow the Peanut, and 105 Ways of Preparing It for Human Consumption* remains in print.)

Though overwhelmed by work and requests, Carver unfailingly addressed the concerns of farmers, many of whom traveled long distances to see him. He walked them through his plots, where he used, as Vella writes, "no commercial fertilizer whatever," and where he would "show a profit of seventy-five dollars an acre. To cash-starved tenant farmers, trying to squeeze a subsistence out of fifteen or twenty acres, seventy-five dollars was a fortune."

Meanwhile (more or less), a trio of Europeans were arguing that a return to older traditions was the intelligent path forward. Austrian Rudolf Steiner championed sound uses of waste products as fertilizers and soil enhancers and warned that repeated use of chemical fertilizers would destroy the soil. Biodynamics, as his methods were called, required that all nutrients come from the soil of the home farm, which he called a living organism—not a stretch by any measure. His holistic approach to farming included techniques that drew from spiritual traditions, which, like most traditional practices, were rejected by conventional science as unfounded.

Beginning in 1905, Steiner's rough contemporary Sir Albert Howard spent two decades in India, where he moved to become imperial economic botanist and teach local farmers about "modern" agriculture.

Howard quickly realized that he had more to learn than to teach. (A colleague noted that Howard always said that "he learned more from the *ryot* [peasant] in his fields than he did from text books and the pundits of the class room.") His 1940 book *An Agricultural Testament* introduced "the Law of Return," which argued that *all* organic material, including human waste, should be returned to the farm, and that what was taken out of the soil in one form needed to be returned in another. Life begins in soil, and in death its nutrients are returned. "There is no waste," Howard wrote; "the processes of growth and the processes of decay balance one another."

Howard argued that when organic matter is recycled through composting, "no mineral deficiencies of any kind occur," and that disease and pests are symptoms of flawed practices. "The rule" should be "mixed farming" of "many species of plants and of animals all [living] together." Decades later, all of Howard's ideas have proven to be true.

Pioneering the empirical case for organic agriculture was Lady Eve Balfour, who cofounded the Soil Association in Britain in 1946. She synthesized existing knowledge in her seminal 1943 book *The Living Soil*, conducted the first, three-decades-long experiments to compare organic and conventional agriculture, and focused on the direct connection between soil health and human health. Again, her once radical views are now widely accepted.

Little of the above was news to the billions of farmers in the "developing" world, who still practiced sustainable (or organic or regenerative or traditional) farming, Wisconsin native Franklin Hiram King discussed in his 1911 book *Farmers of Forty Centuries; or, Permanent Agriculture in China, Korea and Japan.* But smallholding farmers of the global South did not proselytize or market or bully.

So, word of this "new" style of sustainable farming—which is, of course, the old style—had to spread by less official means: word of mouth among experimenters or farmers who were traveling overseas, talks with old-timers, and Rodale's *Organic Farming and Gardening* magazine, later renamed *Organic Gardening.* When J. I. Rodale, who ran a publishing house in Emmaus, Pennsylvania, read Albert Howard in the early forties, he was so inspired he immediately bought a farm, began experimenting with organic agriculture, and launched the magazine. Although it was ignored by the USDA and the ag establishment, "organic farming" had arrived or, more accurately, returned.

With it came a variety of forms of pushback against industrial agriculture. In 1957, a group of Long Island neighbors, led by a pair of biodynamic farmers, sued the government for indiscriminate aerial spraying of DDT, which they claimed threatened their crops. One expert testified that what would become known as the Long Island Spray Trial was "about the future of the human race." The plaintiffs lost.

But in January 1958, marine scientist and journalist Rachel Carson received a letter from an old friend, Olga Owens Huckins, a member of the lawsuit team, alerting her that the spraying of DDT had devastated a local wildlife sanctuary. Huckins reported "the ghastly deaths of birds, claws clutched to their breasts and bills agape in agony."

Carson had published *The Sea Around Us* a few years earlier, an uncontroversial tribute to the oceans and their creatures, and she'd long been interested in the effects of pesticides on non-targeted animals. Yet although the dangers of chemicals in farming had been widely discussed by then, the subject was too hot to handle for the generally timid press.

Carson began writing what became *Silent Spring*, exposing the toxic consequences of rampant pesticide use. It was eventually serialized in *The New Yorker* in 1962, just before the book was published.

Carson had the book peer-reviewed, like an academic paper, and her science was unassailable. Yet she was attacked for being anti-science, alarmist, even pro-bug, and accused of threatening the well-being of our food supply, still a common charge levied against those who criticize industrial agriculture. As if he were representing the official reactionary position, Secretary of Agriculture (and industrial farming hawk) Earl Butz said she was "probably a Communist."

Although she didn't argue that pesticides should be banned, Carson did rail against the lack of federal regulation. "If the Bill of Rights contains no guarantee that a citizen shall be secure against lethal poisons . . . it is surely only because our forefathers . . . could conceive of no such problem." And, as she predicted, scientists soon found DDT resistance in insects. The chemical's subsequent ineffectuality, combined with increasing public concern, led manufacturers to beat a strategic retreat. They gradually withdrew DDT from the domestic market while making it clear that they expected no government interference in international sales. DDT was banned outright in America in 1973; it's still used extensively overseas, mostly as a critical tool for malaria control.

Few books of our time have had a greater impact than *Silent*

Spring, and no author of her time was more prescient than Carson, who was among the first contemporary Americans to see and talk about humans as part of nature, not a separate class of animal that stood above the rest. According to biographer Linda Lear, Carson considered this as her book's opening sentence: "This is a book about man's war against nature, and because man is part of nature it is also inevitably a book about man's war against himself." She popularized the wisdom that humans' impact on the environment is often unintentional and unforeseen, but we must still recognize it and act accordingly.

When the 1968 Apollo 8 mission took its iconic photo of Earth from space—the "Earthrise"—the average American's perspective shifted. There was an increased understanding of and sympathy for nature, a recognition of Earth as a collective home. In the realm of food, this new perspective was reflected by Frances Moore Lappé, a twenty-seven-year-old living in Berkeley, who wrote *Diet for a Small Planet*.

Lappé contended that feeding grain to meat animals deprived the world's poor of needed and valuable nutrients. Furthermore, she claimed, the use of that grain to produce junk food for Americans was making us sick while others starved—still the most sensible analysis of the failings of the contemporary food system.

This less-meat-less-hunger argument jibed with a self-sustaining back-to-the-land movement that, while it may now be mocked and recalled as naive, was in fact of special importance for two starkly different groups: African Americans, perhaps best represented by Fannie Lou Hamer, and a number of well-to-do or at least well-educated middle-class white people representing the early days of "the counterculture," best symbolized by Helen and Scott Nearing.

Institutionalized racism had made Black Americans—whose presence in the United States was as long-term and legitimate as that of any other except for Indigenous people—the most landless group in the country. The civil rights movement, which focused on voting rights and desegregation, did little to address economic and land justice for Black people.

Farmers can't get by without support: credit for purchasing equipment and seeds, research and advice for best practices, a seat at the table in policy decisions, emergency assistance, and more. In all of these necessary systems, Black farmers were at a major disadvantage, and never more so than when dealing with the USDA bureaucracy.

There was never a heyday for Black farmers in America, whose prospects seemed to go from bad to worse. The amount of Black-owned acreage peaked in 1910 but declined steadily after 1920. Black farmers went from more than fourteen percent of all farmers at that peak to fewer than two percent today. (African Americans make up at least twelve percent of the U.S. population.) Black people farm less than half of one percent of the land, account for a quarter of a percent of the market value of all products sold, and earn, on average, eight percent of the net cash income of the average U.S. farm.

But the relationship between African Americans and farming is more complicated than those numbers suggest. The first Black farmers in the United States were indeed enslaved, but they were also dedicated, skilled, and ingenious practitioners without whose expertise the old South would not have thrived. And, as Monica White writes in "Freedom's Seeds: Reflections of Food, Race, and Community Development," "Slavery, sharecropping, and tenant farming do not tell the whole story."

After the Civil War, Black farmers were never given a fair chance, yet when White examined the history of cooperative land-ownership and farming among Black Americans and interviewed contemporary Black farmers, she heard about "the autonomy and the freedom to take a stand that agriculture conferred . . . that agricultural cooperatives made it possible for Black farmers to find communal success."

White also documents many African Americans' ongoing attempts to reverse the midcentury northern migration and return to the South. By 1970, more Blacks were moving south than north, staking their well-deserved claim.

The best known of the freedom farmers, as they came to be called, was Fannie Lou Hamer, an early voting rights activist who in the sixties came to define freedom as the ability to have "a pig and a garden." With those, Hamer "might be harassed and physically harmed but at least she would not starve to death." Her quest for land and self-sufficiency was consistent with that of the former slaves who'd met with General Sherman almost exactly a hundred years earlier.

Today we'd call Hamer's ideology food sovereignty. It wasn't news to Blacks that landownership and access to food meant freedom: "Land is the key," said Hamer. "It's tied to voter registration."

In 1967 Hamer formed the Freedom Farm Cooperative in Sunflower County, Mississippi, to organize southern farmworkers. Along with several other cooperatives formed by Blacks in the South, it changed the lives of thousands of families by creating communities around local economies and political structures. To that end, they farmed and shared food collaboratively, built schools and banks, and established an affordable healthcare system.

At the other end of the back-to-the-land spectrum was Scott Nearing, a socialist, pacifist, and anti-war activist who was born in 1883, left New York for Vermont with his second wife, Helen, and wound up in Maine in the fifties. There, the Nearings wrote books with titles like *Living the Good Life*, ate raw oats with wooden spoons, and "[did] what we could" to build a resistance to the "plutocratic military oligarchy" and try to salvage "what was still usable from the wreckage of the decaying social order" while "formulating the principles and practices of an alternative social system" and showing how to live "sanely in a troubled world."

It's strident, sure. But if you think it's naive or quaint, think about global warming, ongoing inequality and hunger, and forced migration. The Nearings were trying to find a path to break the system while establishing a way of life that was fair to fellow humans and to the earth. That they relied on their privilege (they mostly lived on inheritances) doesn't discount the truth of their analyses. Like Hamer and many others, they saw that the problems underlying hunger and social justice were not to be minimized or easily solved.

Although they were white and wealthy, the Nearings were still harassed by the pre-FBI Justice Department, and later by the

FBI. Predictably, however, the people and organizations attempting to establish a communal Black agrarian culture in the South were far more vigorously challenged by local and national agencies, including the FBI, which worked to minimize the reach and impact of the freedom farmers.

Black activists had sounded the alarm about USDA racism and land justice for decades, and, even though other government agencies backed up their discrimination claims, the department granted only token or toothless concessions. President Reagan's response to repeated U.S. Commission on Civil Rights reports that uncovered examples of the USDA's racism was to close the USDA's Office of Civil Rights. By the time President Clinton reopened the office, thirteen years later, the Black farm population had further declined. By then even the USDA's internal investigations were uncovering the department's racism, which was historic and inexcusable.

In 1997, a North Carolina corn and soybean farmer named Timothy Pigford filed a lawsuit against the USDA. Pigford's own story was bad enough: He'd received operating loans from the USDA, which repeatedly refused to loan him the money he needed to buy his own farm, crippling his ability to make a living. After filing a discrimination complaint—over which the USDA dithered—he was unable to pay back the original loan, and lost his house.

Pigford knew he wasn't alone. He filed a class action suit for discrimination on behalf of thousands of Black farmers, claiming that they had been denied loans over a sixteen-year period, that agency offices outright ignored farmers' legitimate requests, and that claims had been left unprocessed. In 1999 the department was ordered to pay a settlement of more than a billion dollars, the largest civil rights payment in history. Individual farmers received up to fifty thousand dollars, and they were forgiven those few loans that the Agriculture Department had granted. In "willful obstruction of justice by the USDA," the agency spent a fortune fighting the claims, even as a second settlement during the Obama administration expanded claimants to include women and Latinx farmers.

Still, the USDA was the one federal agency that had long been charged with helping people eat. In 1936, Public Law 320 gave the agency discretionary funds to "encourage the domestic consumption of certain agricultural commodities (usually those in surplus supply) by diverting them from the normal channels of trade and commerce."

Translation: The USDA could buy food from producers and give it away. Thus, seven years into the Depression, needy families and school lunch programs began receiving donations of surplus food, guaranteeing processors yet another way to sell their goods with government support and once again dodging the larger question of how the food system could be improved rather than propped up.

Before the existence of food stamps, goods like "government cheese," as it was and still is sometimes called, were distributed off the backs of trucks, a practice later replaced by food banks. When John Kennedy took office, in 1961, he was determined to expand the "program of food distribution for needy families."

Connecticut food economist Isabelle Kelley, the force behind the revolutionary National School Lunch Program, led a task force to design and pilot a more wide-ranging assistance program. The model they developed, in which the USDA gives qualified applicants credit to spend at grocery stores, remains to this day. It became the Food Stamp Act of 1964, part of Lyndon Johnson's larger War on Poverty.

The prosperity of the postwar era largely benefited the white population, and racism led words like "poor" and "hungry" to become synonymous with "Black" in the press and among many if not most white people. But in truth, fewer than a third of those people categorized as "poor" in the sixties were African American.

In 1968, the CBS documentary "Hunger in America" argued that it was not race but class that caused hunger. (Perhaps it was a revelation for some that people without money don't eat well.) The piece looked at Mexican Americans in San Antonio; white tenant farmers in Loudoun County, Virginia; Black Alabama families squeezed out of cotton jobs by mechanical harvesters; and

Navajo trying to coax a nourishing diet out of the desolate high desert of Arizona.

Although it's undeniably melodramatic, the documentary remains powerful, with footage of doctors poking at infants and children while describing the damage lack of nutrition does to cognition and general health. The visuals of dead-eyed toddlers and parents describing their inability to feed their families were new and shocking to many of their fellow Americans.

An Alabama woman flatly declares that although food stamps save money, she doesn't have the cash to buy them. It wasn't seen as odd that the system took money from people who couldn't afford food, creating a budget surplus that allowed the USDA to claim that assistance programs were well funded. (Today, food stamps are a direct credit to recipients, and using them requires no cash outlay.)

"Hunger in America" exposed USDA practices, saying that "foods that farmers cannot sell and nobody else wants" were becoming poor people's main nutrition source, "an inadequate dole" resulting from a policy of "dumping excess rather than providing essentials," and that "the Department of Agriculture protects farmers, not consumers, especially not destitute consumers." It declared that "in this country, the most basic human need must become a human right." (Reading this now, I'm struck by how little has changed and how sound the segment's arguments remain.)

Food stamp enrollment multiplied by almost five times in the next four years. But even after the school lunch program expanded to breakfast and summer in 1968, and even after the 1972 addition of the Special Supplemental Nutrition Program for Women, Infants, and Children (known as WIC), which provided increased benefits for pregnant women and preschool children, there were still hungry Americans.

In a way, the most effective anti-hunger group was not the USDA, but one that rose from a West Coast political movement best known for fighting racial injustice. They called themselves the Black Panthers.

The Black Panther Party for Self-Defense, formed in 1966, was in many ways successful despite persecution by the FBI and other renegade law enforcement agencies. The party's free breakfast program, begun in an Oakland church in January 1969, served eleven children the first day. By that April it served twelve hundred children at nine locations, as far east as Chicago. Six months later, twenty-three cities had Panther-led free breakfast programs. The USDA had never moved this quickly.

By providing free breakfasts and bags of food to as many people as possible, the Panthers were doing what CBS had insisted was crucial: treating food as a human right. And despite trying to undermine the Panthers at every turn, the federal government couldn't deny the impact of these programs. In response, the government amended the Child Nutrition Act to give greater access to free breakfasts and lunches, and permanently funded the School Breakfast Program in 1975.

That it took a self-described revolutionary group to prod the USDA to do its job showed not only how unresponsive the agency could be to people's needs but how little power it had over how the industry grew, marketed, and even defined food. The seventies cast that powerlessness into even sharper relief.

Despite the food industry's muddy rhetoric, the general uneasiness among Americans — mostly viewed through the lens of the civil rights and anti-war movements, the burgeoning women's movement, and the so-called counterculture (which included a small but significant trend toward vegetarianism and organic food) — was accompanied by an increasing concern about both the quality of food and the relationship between diet and disease. That, along with the uproar that followed "Hunger in America," prompted the U.S. Senate, in 1968, to form the Senate Select Committee on Nutrition and Human Needs.

Chaired by future presidential candidate George McGovern, the committee supported the expansion of food stamps and school lunch programs, and the establishment of WIC. Industry had no problem with any of these, as they were just novel ways of selling food. If the government wanted to subsidize poor people's purchases of their products — well, that simply meant greater profits.

But the problems surrounding food clearly went beyond hunger, and industry began to be concerned in 1976, when the committee began hearings on "Diet Related to Killer Diseases."

At their foundation, the "Killer" hearings assumed that diet could encourage or tame chronic disease, and that the dietary components most responsible for illness were, in the words of one senator, "super-rich, fat-loaded, addictive and sugar-filled" foods.

Committee adviser Mark Hegsted—who worked with the Sugar Research Foundation and also created the "Hegsted formula," linking cholesterol and heart disease—told the press that the typical American diet was "a happenstance related to our affluence, the productivity of our farmers and the activities of our food industry." McGovern hoped that the report would "perform a function similar to that of the Surgeon General's Report on Smoking." Industry wished and worked for a radically different outcome.

Unwittingly, the committee set about its work with a flawed outlook. Like almost everyone in the nutrition movement at that time—whether out of ignorance, habit, naivete, reliance on reductionist science, susceptibility to industry pressure, or all of these—it sought a single culprit: What nutrient, what food, was causing heart disease? We'd figured out what caused scurvy, and we'd figured out what caused polio. Why couldn't this be the same?

There's an answer to that question: Food isn't a single substance, and eating can't be separated from life.

You either smoke or you don't. But everyone eats a wide variety of foods. And while the types of diets that were best at combatting (or best at causing) chronic disease were clear, the specific attributes of the foods they featured were not. The closest thing to a smoking gun we have in linking eating to disease is ultra-processed foods. But you can't ethically put people on an exclusive diet of junk for twenty or fifty years in order to find out what befalls them, especially since the assumption is that it won't be good.

One could reasonably ask: So what if we don't know the exact process or cause? We don't fully understand gravity, either, nor do most us know how our phones work, but we rely on them all the same. Similarly, carrots are good for us, and although it's hard to say exactly why, that shouldn't affect our willingness to eat

them. Ultra-processed foods are not good for us; again, we don't
know the extent to which that's true, or precisely why, avoidance
is the best course.

The committee could not see then what we see now: that traditional diets of real food are better for us than diets of foods that
were literally invented in the twentieth century. What they could
see was evidence condemning saturated fat, and there was little or
no risk in advising Americans to reduce the amount of it—and of
sugar—in their diets.

The lack of absolute proof, however, gave the industry an opening to cloud that conclusion and call it into doubt. Industry recruited "impartial" scientists to its defense; those scientists insisted that adequate proof of sugar and fat's dangers did not exist.
This allowed industry representatives to call real scientific progress into question and say things like "They have not gained majority expert opinion." (See "global warming.")

So in January 1977, when the committee—informed by hundreds of hours of testimony and scientific consensus—issued its
Dietary Goals for the United States, recommending a reduction
of fat *and* cholesterol *and* sugar *and* salt, and that we should "decrease consumption of meat," apoplectic industry representatives
went into action and used political pressure to force a revision of
the goals.

The "reduce meat" language was replaced by "choose meats,
poultry, and fish which will reduce saturated fat intake," which
likely made the chicken industry jump for joy while beef producers issued a sigh of relief. And as the meat and poultry lobbies became more powerful, their influence over government messaging
steadily grew: The last official federal publication to explicitly ad-
vise people to "eat less red meat" was published in 1979.

But government intervention had brought a bit of progress, as
Marion Nestle notes in *Soda Politics:* "The revised goals, which
appeared in December 1977, called for a startling 45 percent reduction in intake to bring sugars down to 10 percent or less of calories. How?" As the report itself notes, "In reviewing ways of cutting the consumption of refined and processed sugars, the most
obvious item for general reduction is soft drinks. Total elimina-

tion of soft drinks from the diet, for many people, would bring at least half the recommended reduction of consumption of such sugars." Soft drinks at that point were the largest source of added sugars in American diets.

But here's the rub: To a great extent, producers determine what people eat. And while the committee and a variety of diverse movements all moved the needle on food, agriculture, and environmental protection, multinational corporations' counterattack was far more powerful. Between then and now, under pressure from food companies, the advice of federal agencies about sugars and fats has grown increasingly complex and convoluted.

The straightforward "avoid . . ." became "choose and prepare . . ." or "reduce the intake of . . ." The simplest advice would have been to "eat real food in moderate amounts," but reductionist thinking wouldn't allow for something so holistic. As one edition of the guidelines followed another (they're revised every five years), each failed to make clear statements about the dangers of added sugars. By 2010 sugars had disappeared as a separate guideline altogether and were folded in with "solid fats" — butter and other animal fats, along with trans fats — under the obfuscating abbreviation SoFAS: solid fats and added sugars.

The industry hadn't just survived this attack from the nutrition community. It had routed its opponents and won the battle. People were not instructed to eat more fruits, vegetables, and whole grains. Rather, they were encouraged to eat more "bread, cereal, rice, and pasta." Wonder Bread? Froot Loops? Rice-A-Roni? Chef Boyardee? Why not? As long as you were cutting back on "fat," you could eat whatever you wanted, in whatever quantity.

With the USDA suggesting that high-carb, low-fat foods were the key to good health, the "SnackWell's phenomenon" — a proliferation of "heart-healthy" low-fat, high-sugar UPFs — made national weight gain inevitable.

In the decades to come, the industry would continue to follow the leads of the USDA, the FDA, and nutrition research in general: Whatever the agencies said was "good for you," industry would pile into processed foods; if the agencies said it was "bad for you," the opposite would happen. Antioxidants, oat bran, fiber,

a variety of vitamins and minerals ("more calcium!"), protein—
all went in in their turn, while fat, "carbs," cholesterol, and more
were removed. Every one of the "new and improved" products
was a food manufacturer's dream and a move away from actual
food.

In general, ultra-processed foods contain far more calories than
are justified by their nutrient levels, calories largely derived from
corn, in the form of high-fructose corn syrup; soy, in the form of
extracted protein or oil; and wheat, in the form of white flour.
Common sense tells us that this stuff couldn't possibly be healthy,
but the industry did its work.

Still, with each passing decade there has been growing awareness that most foods invented in the twentieth century were not,
to say the least, whole or nutritious, and the public began to demand more transparency. Through the sixties, the defining regulation of food labeling was still the antiquated 1938 Food, Drug,
and Cosmetic Act, whose strictest prohibition was that marketers
couldn't claim that a product's ingredients would prevent or cure
a disease or symptom—a pretty low bar to meet.

In 1973, the Food and Drug Administration took a cautious
step (whether forward or backward is debatable) by allowing labels to make health claims as long as they were backed up with accurate, transparent nutrition facts.

An avalanche of health claims about heart disease and cancer
followed. Since many of these were unjustifiable, the FDA was
forced to respond, in 1990, with a new and mandatory label for
most foods. Fruits and vegetables were excused: Obviously, the
one "ingredient" in an apple is apple, and unless a label were to
list how it was grown—What pesticides were used? How were
workers treated?—it would be superfluous. Industry pressure
forced the agency to exempt meat as well, although ingredients
beyond meat were common.

The new label provided real information, like quantities of protein, carbohydrates, sugars, and vitamins. But in treating a food's
nutritional value as the sum of its individual parts, the FDA at
least indirectly supported the absurd reasoning that a chemical-

laced engineered food could be nutritionally equivalent, or even superior, to real food.

Based on a nutrition label alone, for example, you might reasonably conclude that there's not much difference between a banana and a "serving" of Oreos, at least as far as sugar is concerned. And if the Oreos have added fiber or vitamin C, they might even appear to be "better."

To the label, it's not the quality of food that matters, or how it was produced, or its actual impact on the body. All that matters is its composition, which flies in the face of both common sense and well-established science. Yet the country's largest agencies responsible for public health seem unable to counter industry's narrative that "a calorie is a calorie" and that if only we exercise enough we can drink as much soda as we like.

In 2009, the label underwent commendable revisions, including a line for added sugars and a percentage daily value for total sugars, a line for trans fats (which have since been banned), one each for saturated and unsaturated fats, and more prominent calorie counts. Labeling now recommends that sugar make up "less than" ten percent of daily calories, which in a two-thousand-calorie diet is under fifty grams, about the amount in most twelve-ounce sugar-sweetened beverages. The average American consumes at least double that, and by some estimates triple.

Yet, as in 1906, as in the seventies, this new label provided marketing opportunities. With government-validated nutrition standards, it was open season for advertisers. Nutrition claims developed rapidly over the coming decades: pomegranate juice that prevents prostate cancer, breakfast cereal that cures ADHD, yogurt that boosts immunity, and the endless array of fat killers, heart attack and cancer preventers, weight losers, cholesterol blockers, and other miracle cures.

A very few of these claims were contested by the FDA. Dannon, for example, paid thirty-five million dollars for bragging, incredibly, that its Activia yogurt was "clinically proven to help regulate your digestive system in two weeks." But most were legitimized by the nutrition facts on their labels. To this day, the industry weaponizes labels to catch the attention of permanently confused eaters, while real food remains lost in the shuffle.

Part of the problem is that there has never been a sane, authoritative, trusted voice speaking loud and clear enough to convince the public that a diet of natural foods is the only sane path forward. Even the word "natural" had long since been co-opted and rendered nearly meaningless.

As unrest over pesticides grew stronger and demand grew for verifiably chemical-free packaged foods, many eaters — on their own, and reasonably — began to turn to organic food. In the years after Earl Butz said that organic farming "would condemn hundreds of millions of people to a lingering death by malnutrition and starvation" (a moronic argument that is still made today), a more moderate USDA was forced to recognize the science behind organic farming and even begin to half-heartedly endorse it.

The USDA saw nothing wrong with large-scale organic farming. And, just as eaters in the early twentieth century needed to know that "milk" was milk, those in the nineties needed to know that "organic" was organic; if the product was to demand a premium, as it must, it had to be legitimized. So the 1990 Farm Bill included the Organic Foods Production Act, the National Organic Standards Board, and a new "USDA Organic" label. Organic codes were also being established globally, including an EU-wide program that began in 1991 and a series of UN-led agreements thereafter.

USDA Organic identifies foods that are grown without synthetic fertilizers or pesticides (there are some exceptions), without GMOs, and without radiation, a rarely used food safety technique. Organic animals are raised on organic food, and no antibiotics or growth hormones can be used in rearing them. They're also supposed to be kept "in living conditions accommodating their natural behavior," which in practice means giving them a bit more room and perhaps some access to the outdoors. To be labeled organic, processed food must contain no "artificial" ingredients, though that rule has been loosened. And there are levels of organic, too. "Made with Organic" means the product contains at least seventy percent organic ingredients; the remaining thirty percent can contain no prohibited ingredients, such as food grown with synthetic fertilizers or GMOs.

These labels all but ignore the history, spirit, and potential of organic farming as identified by Howard, Balfour, and others and practiced by thousands of dedicated and principled small farmers all across the country and the world. The agency codified "organic" in the narrowest possible way, even though it "was always more than merely an approach to farming," as Brian Obach writes in *Organic Struggle*. "It was a philosophy tied to broader understandings of how the world works and the rightful place of humans within it."

The industrial hybrid is designed for Big Food to employ "organic" as a marketing tool. "Organic cane sugar" is sugar, and "organic grass-fed beef" may well be raised in near-total confinement and fed hay from thousands of miles away. Once marketers realized the possibilities of "organic" in junk food, health food, off-season grapes from Chile, milk from tortured cows, and much more — shampoo and clothing, for example — the industrial vision of organic boomed.

Traditional organic farmers suffered. The approval process for organic labeling requires extensive record-keeping and expensive applications. Many smaller farmers can't afford the time or expense required for certification. And since those farmers who actually tend their soil might grow forty crops in rotation, they must do unimaginably more paperwork than those who monocrop. It's nearly impossible for such farmers to compete in the mass market.

That "USDA Organic" doesn't mean "no monocropping" is a huge determinant. Almost all of the problems I've described in industrial agriculture are present in certified organic agriculture. The significant exceptions are that workers in organic fields are not exposed to as many dangerous chemicals, that the foods contain fewer chemical residues, and that organic farming does not support the products of genetic engineering. That's all good.

But there is no requirement that organic food be of good quality, or even real at all; as Marion Nestle famously said, "organic junk food is still junk food." It may have a massive carbon footprint, be grown and harvested by near slaves, or processed from tortured animals and still be "organic."

It may not even be that: Imported food with the USDA Organic label is required to meet the same standards as that raised domestically. But the inspection process has always been inadequate (it may have gotten worse during the coronavirus pandemic), so there's no guarantee that certification is genuine. None of these caveats has any impact on how these foods are marketed to consumers.

Nevertheless, many people who can afford the premium price have "gone organic," believing that the food in every store can be broken down into "good" (organic) and "bad" (conventional). This simplistic attitude encourages the production of commodity-based, mass-produced organic UPFs, whose market ballooned from one billion dollars in 1990 to fifteen billion by 2005. It's now around fifty billion dollars a year.

In the decade after the standards discussion began, Big Food absorbed sixty-six of the eighty-one existing organic processors, from Stonyfield Farms (now owned by the French firm Lactalis) to Cascadian Farms, Muir Glen, and Annie's (all General Mills) to Honest Tea (Coca-Cola), and so on. If there was any promise of integrity in the mass-produced organic sector, it was destroyed. Most organic food is now part of the larger system, one that still fails to ask the key question: What do we grow food for? If we ask that question earnestly, and answer it thoughtfully, we can begin to make some much needed changes.

14

Where We're At

S UFFICE IT TO say, the world of food is rife with formidable problems, some of which are the consequences of turning an essential source of nourishment into a major global profit center.

You will hear, "The food system is broken." But the truth is that it works almost perfectly for Big Food. It also works well enough for around a third of the world's people, who have the money to demand and have at a moment's notice virtually any food in the world.

But it doesn't work well enough to nourish most of humanity, and it doesn't work well enough to husband our resources so that it can endure. Indeed, the system has created a public health crisis (one whose effects have, in turn, exacerbated the deadly effects of COVID-19), and, perhaps even more crucially, it's a chief contributor to the foremost threat to our species: the climate crisis. The way we produce food threatens everyone, even the wealthiest and cleverest.

Although it's immoral and cruel, and overseen by mostly immoral and cruel people—only a few of whom were sadistic masterminds—the system is largely the result of incremental decisions, some made as far back as ten thousand years ago, others recently. Whether those decisions could have been made differently is speculation, but one thing is certain: The future isn't set. There is time to change how we grow and what we eat.

The stakes are high.

You may be sick of hearing about climate change, but if the planet becomes inhospitable to agriculture, it'll be too late to reduce our cheeseburger consumption—we simply won't live long enough for it to matter. And, as with COVID-19, there can be no truce with climate: You either deal with it or you don't. We have not.

As of early 2020, to meet the modest goals of the Paris agreement, the world would need to reduce carbon emissions by almost ten percent a year—each year for the next ten. The longer we wait to start, the more drastic those cuts will have to be. That kind of change can happen only if even bigger change happens first: an agreement among the world's industrialized countries to mandate it. Says Bill McKibben, our leading climate journalist and voice of sanity, "in seventy-five years the world will probably run on sun and wind because they are so cheap, but if we wait for economics alone to do the job, it will be a broken world."

Big Ag has a huge role in greenhouse gas emissions, even rivaling those of the oil and gas companies. The top five meat and dairy companies combine to produce more emissions than ExxonMobil, and the top twenty have a combined carbon footprint the size of Germany. Tyson Foods, the second-largest meat company in the world, produces twice as much greenhouse gas as all of Ireland.

It's impossible to determine the exact percentage of greenhouse gas emissions that comes from agriculture as opposed to fossil fuels. Does petrol-driven farm machinery count as an agricultural source or a fossil fuel source? Actually, both—you can't do industrial agriculture without fossil fuel to run machinery, transport food, and produce fertilizers and pesticides.

Cutting fossil fuel use would change agriculture dramatically. And reforming the agriculture industry would cut fossil fuel use.

The (as of this writing, July 2020) climate-change-denying Environmental Protection Agency claims that agriculture contributes as little as ten percent to total greenhouse gas emissions. Worldwatch, on the other hand, estimates that it's more than fifty percent. What matters is not the exact percentage—it's hardly a competition—but that food production is a major emissions contributor, throughout every facet of the industry.

The industrial production of animals leads the way. Methane, a way more potent greenhouse gas than carbon dioxide, is released when cows, sheep, and goats burp. Producers raise nearly seventy billion livestock worldwide, using a quarter of all ice-free land, and they're likely responsible for the majority of all agricultural emissions — up to fifteen percent of total global emissions.

Under the right conditions, grazing ruminants can be beneficial to landscapes, keeping carbon, topsoil, and water in the ground while adding nutrients. But by confining these animals, by feeding them grain, we not only wreck their health but increase the amount of land used for monoculture of corn and soy, contributing to erosion and runoff problems, soil oxidation, and the release of carbon. Taken together, this may double the contribution of industrial animal production to greenhouse gas emissions.

Since we began to break the plains in the mid-nineteenth century, as much as seventy percent of the carbon in the soil has been sent airborne. Currently, deforestation for growing animal feed and grazing accounts for around eight percent of greenhouse gas, because it releases stored carbon from the soil and destroys carbon-absorbing habitats. The rapidly disappearing Amazon rainforest is close to the point where it will fail to produce enough rain to sustain itself and degrade into a drier savanna, depriving us of one of our biggest carbon sinks.

We usually think of "waste" as willfully throwing food out or allowing it to spoil; some rots in fields or is lost in transport, never making it to market. For reasons that vary from one culture to the next, at least thirty percent of the food we produce goes uneaten.

But there's more to waste: In the United States, great swaths of the landscape (twenty-three million acres in Iowa alone) are used to grow crops that have a negative impact on the food supply: corn for ethanol, and corn and soy for confined animals and junk food. For that reason, the percentage of greenhouse gases attributed to "waste" is vastly underestimated. As we saw during the early days of the coronavirus disruptions, the global supply chain's bottlenecks are prone to waste, creating situations where milk must be dumped, acres of produce tilled under, and animals exterminated and buried because markets are disrupted.

Making bananas, tomatoes, and every other "fresh" food available every day of the year, anywhere in the world that people can pay for it, also has environmental costs. Trucking and shipping food in climate-controlled vehicles accounts for something like ten percent of agriculture's greenhouse gas emissions.

I'm obligated to mention that rice cultivation produces methane, and its contribution to greenhouse gases might be as much as three percent of the global total. But rice, the world's most widely grown grain, also supports billions of people who had little or no role in causing the climate crisis. So although growing rice could be done more sustainably (and is, in some places), focusing on rice blames plant eaters for a problem largely caused by meat eaters. Though they had the smallest role in causing it, small-scale farmers are already bearing the most acute consequences of climate change. In every facet of the climate crisis, who we blame for the mess, and who we make clean it up, matters.

That's agriculture's impact on climate; what does the climate crisis mean for agriculture?

What used to be really hot is now normal. The recent spike in heat (eight of the ten warmest years on record occurred in the past decade or so) has already created more dramatic droughts, floods, wildfires, and pest invasions.

Warmer clouds hold more water, so when it rains, it rains more: From July 2018 to June 2019, the United States experienced the highest annual rainfall ever recorded.

All the same, we're running out of water: The UN predicts that around two billion people will live with the possibility of water shortages by 2025, and perhaps five billion by 2050. And this isn't because people drink or bathe too much: Roughly eighty percent of all freshwater is used for agriculture. The Ogallala Aquifer (the "cure" for the water shortages of the Dust Bowl) is a typical case: Ninety-four percent of the water drawn from it is used for crop irrigation; even in years of record rainfall, it cannot be replenished. In Texas and elsewhere, so much water is being pumped out of aquifers that the land is sinking. Conflicts over water bring war, as in Syria, or less dramatic but still serious results, as in California, whose chronic water issues may be resolved only by literally reducing the land used for intensive agriculture by half.

It's not just water: Yields of important crops have begun to decline, and that trend will increase. "Carbon's abundance stimulates photosynthesis," says Lewis Ziska, a professor at Columbia Mailman School of Public Health, "but shifts the balance between carbon and other nutrients, making plants carbon rich, but potentially nutrient poor." Erosion, biodiversity loss, pests that thrive in warmth, and heat stress on land and animals (including water dwellers) all have the potential to hamstring crop yields. Industrial agriculture's response will be to try to maintain yields by burning more forests and using more chemicals, further compounding the problem. The UN's Food and Agriculture Organization (FAO) says the number of hungry people could triple by midcentury.

I could go on. The upshot is that, although we may be able to significantly reduce carbon emissions without changing agriculture, and we may find better ways to sequester some of the carbon we've already released, neither of these measures will keep the food system intact. At some point it will become too hot for farmers to be outside, for animals to live, for crops to thrive, for the very landscape to survive. Dust bowls will spring up, and harvests will fail. That means famine for perhaps billions of people, maybe before 2050 and almost certainly by the end of the century. As David Wallace-Wells says, "It is worse, much worse, than you think."

There are no people with money going hungry. The most glaring failure of our food system is not hunger, a failure of our economic system, but disease-causing diets. Big food has created a world in which, to use the title of Raj Patel's groundbreaking book, people are both "stuffed and starved." Junk made it possible to encourage people to—really, to make it difficult for them *not* to—eat too much non-nourishing food over a prolonged period.

The system delivers a nearly uninterruptible stream of food, regardless of season. It produces roughly 2,800 calories for every

person in the world, plenty even for the projected 2050 population of ten billion.

Junk was born in America, but it's spread worldwide, and everywhere the American diet goes, disease follows. People who
switch from traditional diets and the traditional agriculture that
supports them to food invented in the twentieth century develop
more chronic diseases. Generally, I've tried to avoid statistics, but
here is a boatload of them, and they all point in the same direction:
Two-thirds of the world's population lives in countries where more
people die from diseases linked to being overweight than ones
linked to being underweight. The global number of people living
with diabetes has quadrupled since 1980, and since 1990 deaths
from diabetes-caused chronic kidney disease have doubled. Both
global sugar consumption and obesity have nearly tripled in the
past half century. Half of the Mediterranean's adult population
has abandoned the traditional (and beneficial) Mediterranean diet,
and almost no children adhere to it. American fast-food chains
increased their international sales by thirty percent from 2011 to
2016; those sales now account for fifty percent of those chains' profits, and many young people in other countries eat more fast food
than Americans. The international fast-food market is expected
to approach seven hundred billion dollars by 2022 — if it were a
country, it would rank in economic value among the top twenty.
These figures are expected to double again in the coming decade.

By definition, food provides nourishment, and nourishment promotes health. And yet, in our perverse reality, so much of what we
eat is promoting health's opposite. Ultra-processed foods, more
akin to poison than actual food, are making us sick as surely as if
we were vitamin deficient.

Forty-two countries have a higher life expectancy than the
United States. Even accounting for COVID-19, chronic disease is
our country's and the world's leading killer, taking over from the
infectious diseases, like measles, smallpox, and polio, with which
we've mostly dealt with successfully. In the United States, the *majority* of people have at least one chronic disease (nearly half have
two), and these diseases are responsible for about seventy percent

of all deaths—1.8 million per year; they also markedly increase the risk of serious complications resulting from COVID. So it's safe to say that diet-related diseases are the leading killers in the United States.

Within years, deaths from COVID will likely be reduced to flu-like numbers. The same cannot be said about diabetes.

A 2013 study of 175 countries found that, independent of obesity rates, a 150-calorie increase in the availability of sugar resulted in a one percent increase in rates of Type 2 diabetes: You can be slender and still have metabolic syndrome (itself a group of unhealthy conditions), high blood pressure, Type 2 diabetes, heart disease, and any of a dozen diet-related cancers; you can be overweight and have none. Our obsession with obesity as the problem to be solved is influenced by our cultural aversion to it, along with our propensity to assign blame to individuals rather than examining less obvious causes experienced by all of us.

We don't know exactly how or why being overweight increases the risk of diabetes and other premature causes of death. Nor do we fully understand the mechanisms and relationships between calorie intake, exercise, fat accumulation, insulin resistance, and other factors that influence diet-related diseases. We do know that a better diet fixes many things, and we know enough to give good nutrition advice.

But sound advice isn't enough; the reigning, destructive Western diet isn't the result of a lack of understanding or education about which foods harm or benefit us, or even a lack of trying to make things right: Most people know what a "good" diet is.

For reference, here's an attempt at the world's shortest serious discussion of the optimum human diet—*diets*, really, because they can take many forms. You can choose the Mediterranean diet or the Okinawan or Paleo, or whatever you like. You can even figure out your own, according to your own tastes and preferences. The key is to remember that all good diets have a host of beneficial elements in common, a few more that are optional, and some that should be avoided as much as possible.

Desirable: Rely on to whatever extent possible	Optional: Eat in limited quantities	Undesirable: Stay away from as much as possible
Vegetables, including roots and tubers	Fats extracted from vegetables, nuts, seeds, fruits	Ultra-processed foods (UPFs), including chemically extracted oils, sugars, flours, etc.
Fruits	Meat	Industrially produced animal products
Whole grains, including (true) whole-grain flour	Dairy	"Junk" food, "sweets," etc.
Legumes	Seafood	Sugar-sweetened beverages
Nuts	Eggs	
Seeds	Coffee, tea, alcohol (debatable)	
Water		

This is all well-documented by nutrition research and virtually inarguable. Nor will it change much: There may be some tinkering around the margins, but much of that will be splitting hairs —like saying exercise is important and then debating whether swimming is better than running.

No food stands alone. There are no superfoods, and, even in the case of junk, the dose makes the poison. Your craving for a Whopper or a handful of M&M's is not going to kill you if the rest of your diet is balanced.

In short, the diet that allows us to thrive has been "solved." We don't understand every detail of it, but we know how to eat for health and well-being, and it's simple. Yet our diets have been turned against us, and it's wrong to chalk that up to personal choice. The blame lies with what's grown and sold.

The food advertising budget in the United States is around $14 billion. (The total budget for "chronic disease prevention and health promotion" is $1 billion.) That money is spent convincing us to eat too much, and too much of the wrong things: Americans eat a third more calories than we did in the fifties, and around sixty percent of our total calories are from ultra-processed foods. And people of color and the economically vulnerable generally suffer most acutely.

We've evolved to eat our fill whenever food is abundant. That's now dangerous: One study drew a strong correlation between economic insecurity and overeating. It makes sense, then, that where poverty prevails, so do diabetes and related hazards. Black Americans, for example, have a seventy-seven percent higher rate of diabetes than whites.

In general, health-producing foods are pushed on wealthier people, while poorer whites and especially people of color are targeted with unhealthy foods. There are nine fast-food restaurants for every supermarket in the United States, and they're found more in poor areas than in wealthy ones.

"Food deserts" are about a lack of money, not a fluke of location. It's money that brings supermarkets and good food options to a neighborhood. Supermarkets are profit chasers, and the minute they smell money in a neighborhood, they flock to it. Similarly, bringing a grocery store to a lower-income neighborhood, if people's incomes remain low, doesn't improve things much.

Public health advocates commonly say we have to "make the good choice the easy choice," and there's truth to that logic. But as it stands, the easy choice is often the unhealthy one and, for twenty percent or more of our population, the better ones may be inaccessible for reasons of time, geography, or income.

It's not obvious at first, but all of these issues stem from industrial agriculture's marriage to high-yield monoculture, which in every way runs counter to the way nature establishes things.

Look at a forest or a meadow: You will see thousands of inter-dependent species. There is balance and stability in these unfet-tered habitats that allows them to thrive *for millennia*. Nature likes diversity, even chaos.

Now consider a modern cornfield. There is one species, and ev-erything else, even symbiotic organisms, is chased away or killed. At best, it can survive a month without attention. It's the embodi-ment of the nineteenth-century belief that humans could finally, once and for all, conquer nature.

We've seen the folly of that notion. Five percent of farms sell seventy-five percent of the United States' agricultural products, and sixty percent of U.S. farmland is controlled by farms that op-erate on two thousand acres or more. (That's three square miles of crops. It would take you all day to walk those rows, let alone work them.)

"Conventional" farms spend about eleven billion dollars a year on chemicals, and thirteen billion on fertilizer; the use of each has risen sixtyfold since the end of World War II. Six billion pounds of pesticides are used worldwide each year, about a pound for each human. Much less than one percent of sprayed pesticides actually reaches the target species, but these chemicals contaminate land, water, and living creatures all over the planet and are found in around eighty-five percent of all foods.

And because weeds and bugs build resistance, the effectiveness of chemicals decreases over time, leading to a scary cycle in which even more powerful and dangerous substances become succes-sors. Exactly that scenario has led Bayer (which absorbed Mon-santo) to market seeds that are resistant to multiple pesticides at once—at press time, it proposed a variety that could withstand five chemicals.

Neonicotinoids ("neonics"), now the world's most popular in-secticides, have caused mass deaths in hordes of beneficial insects, including ladybugs and honeybees. Germany spent thirty years counting insects and found a more than seventy-five percent pop-ulation decline across sixty-three of the country's nature pre-serves. (Neonics have been all but banned in the EU.)

Although eaters can at least partially avoid pesticides by eschewing UPFs and focusing on organic food, when contamination is universal, you can stop eating altogether and still be poisoned. Beyond pesticides, there are thousands of human-made poisons in our environment, and we are bombarded by them constantly. (Worldwide, about a quarter as many people die from these poisons as from chronic disease — more than twelve million per year total.) These chemicals are found in foods, as well as in packaging, cleansers, furniture, clothing, and more. Many are endocrine-disrupting chemicals (EDCs), shown to play a role in hormone-related cancers (especially breast, uterine, ovarian, prostate, and thyroid), neurodevelopment problems in children (like ADHD), early puberty, undescended testicles, low sperm count, and metabolic interference that promotes weight gain and diabetes onset; others upset the bacteria that keep our digestive system healthy.

Research on toxins and public health is underfunded, ignored, suppressed, or covered up; testing has been mostly voluntary and ineffectual, conducted by industry. The Food and Drug Administration could conduct safety testing, but generally it has not.

The low crop prices of the seventies became the keystone of a brilliant and terrible idea that now dominates livestock production: the concentrated animal feeding operation (CAFO), one of the most egregious offshoots of monoculture.

The chicken industry led the way in establishing protocol. Production was centered in a few under-regulated states like Iowa — now ground zero for CAFOs — and the biggest operators hired subcontractors who were paid meager wages to maintain the cavernous animal-filled barns.

Following the successful streamlining of chicken and egg production — by weight, three-fourths of the bird biomass on this planet is farm-raised chickens — hogs and cattle were the logical next step. Like chickens, these animals were crammed into large barns and fattened with formulaic food, mostly soybeans. Previously, there had been practical limitations to this kind of cruel "efficiency," but the CAFO addresses these problems with routine doses of prophylactic antibiotics.

It remains economical to keep young beef cattle on pasture,

but for the last six months of their lives, they're moved to feed-lots and fed grain. Soybeans become the animals' main protein source, and that's especially hard for cattle, whose complex digestive systems are adapted to grazing. ("Grazing" and "grass" have the same root.) This new diet makes them sick, further increasing the need for drugs.

It's even worse for most of America's nine million or so dairy cows. Milked twice a day, they spend much of their lives in stalls and muddy feedlots. They're artificially inseminated, to remain in a perpetual state of lactation, and promptly separated from their offspring after giving birth. Once tended by a patchwork of small dairies throughout the country, the dairy industry is now dominated by CAFOs, which run below the cost of production of those small dairies and have steadily worked toward eliminating them altogether.

Layers and broilers, hogs (which rarely see daylight and are restricted in their movement), and beef and dairy cattle are by far our most significant sources of meat and other animal products. We process around ten billion animals a year—around twenty-six for every person living in the United States. And, as you'd expect, the industry is concentrated: Just seventeen percent of hog producers sell ninety-six percent of pork, all raised in CAFOs of two thousand or more animals each. Feedlots housing a thousand or more cattle represent fewer than five percent of feeding operations but nearly ninety percent of the market; almost half of all feedlots hold thirty thousand cattle or more.

Each hog CAFO generates, on average, waste equivalent to that of a town of around ten thousand people. (To produce as much waste as Iowa's confined animals would take 168 million humans; that amounts to more than four Californias, or fifty-three Iowas.) This manure is stored in massive "lagoons," which occasionally flood, poisoning the surrounding land and water; sludge from the lagoons is routinely pumped into the air, producing a disease-causing chemical fog for miles around.

The mega-barns also use huge fans to propel accumulated ammonia, methane, and hydrogen sulfide outside in order to avoid poisoning their animals. This creates a poisonous fog locally, irritating eyes and respiratory systems and increasing the risk of cancer and asthma. But "right-to-farm" statutes allow CAFO operators to ignore the health and well-being of their human neighbors.

Predictably, poor communities and those dominated by minority populations suffer the worst of it. People of color in North Carolina, for example, are fifty percent more likely to live within smelling distance of a CAFO than average, and more likely to suffer from a variety of diseases and incur premature death.

Were it not for the tight security and secrecy around CAFOs—few people will ever see the inside of one—public opinion would brand this arm of industrial agriculture cruel and unusual punishment, which it is. (The philosopher Peter Singer likens CAFOs to concentration camps.) Indeed, in the eighties, when industrial animal production was just getting started, the public reacted vehemently to the confinement of veal calves, and a national boycott cut consumption by more than eighty percent.

The federal government hasn't moved forward in protecting animals since . . . ever. Each state sets its own laws and standards, known as Common Farming Exemptions. This mostly means that virtually any practice is legal as long as it's common. "In other words," as Jonathan Safran Foer once wrote me, "the industry has the power to define cruelty." Grinding hundreds of millions of male chicks, an unfortunate by-product of the egg industry: that's legal. Castrating sixty-five million calves and piglets a year, usually without any anesthetic: legal. Allowing sick animals to die without individual veterinary care, imprisoning animals in cages so small they cannot turn around, and skinning live animals: all legal. (What's illegal? Kicking your pet dog.) The occasional viral video that shows the rule breakers abusing animals in exceptional ways distracts from the real story—that the everyday practices we take for granted are equally horrifying.

CAFOs have led to more "efficient" slaughterhouses as well. Smaller ones, which processed in a year what new operations do in an hour, nearly disappeared. Workers—primarily people of color, often immigrants—are forced to work faster, often at their own peril. Some operations moved overseas, further decreasing domestic wages. By 2017, the majority of cattle and hogs were processed by the dozen largest slaughterhouses, among the most dangerous workplaces in the country. Some of the precariousness and violence of these conditions drew attention when slaughter-houses became deadly hot spots for the coronavirus pandemic, but no substantial reforms were enacted.

Owners have successfully quashed any attempts to limit or reg-ulate confinement, and CAFOs have grown: A big dairy operation might have tens of thousands of cows, and a chicken CAFO may contain hundreds of thousands of birds. No one actually knows how big these operations may be, because no government agency tracks them accurately. Even the existing lax regulations go un-enforced. Only a third of the nation's CAFOs even have permits, and the EPA doesn't know how many of them there are; a recent report found more than five thousand of them unaccounted for in Iowa alone. (I flew in a helicopter over central Iowa a few years ago and saw way more of the distinctive-looking metal CAFO barns than I could count.)

In fact, the EPA has gone out of its way to avoid regulating the industry. In 2004, the agency struck a deal with livestock produc-ers who, in exchange for helping to fund an EPA study that would form the basis of new regulation, would be exempt from EPA law-suits over the course of the study. The majority of the country's biggest livestock farmers wisely purchased that immunity. Fifteen years later, the study remains ongoing. (Not surprisingly, Presi-dent Trump worsened the situation.)

This system needs the support of millions of acres devoted to growing animal feed. Since ninety-nine percent of that is done in-dustrially, the excess nitrates from fertilizer runoff alone pose a huge problem; Des Moines, for example, was forced to build the biggest municipal water treatment plant in the world so its citi-zens could drink safe tap water. In addition to the impact of the animals' waste, there are also spills of growth hormones that may wind up in our meat and drinking water in alarming quantities.

As do antibiotics: Eighty percent of all antibiotics are fed to farm animals, and that's allowed generations of germs to mutate and develop immunity. The result is antibiotic-resistant strains of bacteria, and, every year, 700,000 people die around the world from infections previously curable with standard drugs. There are drug-resistant forms of bacteria, particularly salmonella, present in mass-produced meat. Where antibiotic use in meat production is highest (the United States, China, and India), so is the prevalence of antibiotic-resistant bacteria. Where it's been curbed, as in the EU, resistance is much lower. Experts agree that, if left unchecked for a generation, resistance to antibiotics will saddle routine medical procedures with mortal risk.

Finally, industrial animal production is at least in part responsible for our vulnerability to novel diseases like COVID-19. Deforestation and habitat destruction create fertile ground for transmission of dangerous diseases between wild animals and humans as forests disappear and farmers are forced to push deeper into the wild. And once a virus of any kind is introduced into a herd or flock of confined animals, it spreads without resistance. Many of the novel infectious diseases in recent decades — not only coronavirus but the avian flu, SARS, and others — have followed this path.

In short, industrial animal production is an ecological and moral mess, nearly as degrading to human souls as it is to animal life. CAFOs have turned meat into a dangerous ultra-processed food and mark a fittingly horrific end point for an industry with an endless tolerance for cruelty.

Fish is a critical source of protein for more than a billion people and accounts for about a third of the world's animal consumption. And nearly every mistake made with land and air animals has been or is being made with sea dwellers. Just as buffalo were wiped from the Plains and passenger pigeons from the sky, a variety of species are being taken from the seas using methods that make a baited hook seem merciful. Fish are now literally vacuumed out of the water, or caught in nets that stretch for miles. To date, most "solutions" to these methods involve environmentally damaging fish farms that rely on wild fish for feed.

A third of all fish are caught at unsustainable levels, and large species like tuna and swordfish are at ten percent of their pre-industrial populations, leading some credible experts to say that by 2050 the major fishing industries will have collapsed. Others maintain that with more sustainable management practices, "only" half of the world's edible seafood species will be threatened by midcentury.

Many factors are to blame, but they boil down to greed and power. Illegal fishing operations are rampant, mostly carried out by fleets based in China, Spain, Taiwan, Japan, and South Korea. Lack of government oversight is also a culprit. U.S. regulations are among the world's strongest, but they mostly have impact on local waters.

Industrial fishing is egregiously wasteful, indiscriminate, and inefficient. As much as a quarter of the total wild catch is discarded as "bycatch" and destined to die. Add to that coastal building and development that contaminates and disturbs small fisheries, the use of wild fish to feed farmed fish, and the well-documented use of forced labor, child labor, and outright slavery in the global seafood supply chain, and the industry is rotten to its core.

And, of course, climate change is profoundly disrupting the ocean environment. Warming is permanently altering migration patterns and habitats, scrambling ecosystems into chaos. In addition, ocean acidification resulting from climate change hinders the growth of fish and even kills them. Many worry that there soon won't be any fish left in the tropics at all.

Once, almost all fish that were caught fed humans. That's no longer the case. In addition to the quarter of fish lost to bycatch, another third of harvested fish are now made into fertilizer and food for farmed fish and other animals, and put to a variety of other industrial uses. What's especially distressing is that most of these are smaller fish like anchovies, mackerel, and herring — important to many traditional diets but increasingly unavailable to poor fishers and their families and neighbors. Those same fish, often labeled "sustainable" in wealthy countries, are increasingly being pushed as better choices than farmed salmon. Which they are. Except, again, if fish that were once caught in sustainable quantities by local fishers for local eaters are now being harvested by factory vessels and shipped worldwide to be eaten by wealthy people, local food security is disrupted. Once again, people living in systems that favor small-scale subsistence farming or fishing are forced into the global cash economy.

What's sometimes called the Blue Revolution — aquaculture, or fish farming — is now producing about half the world's fish. That could be considered progress, but aquaculture uses around half of the world's fish meal and nearly ninety percent of its fish oil.

Nor is this use efficient: It takes a pound and a half of wild anchovies to produce one pound of farmed salmon. Even worse, it takes twenty-eight pounds of wild fish to produce one pound of farmed tuna, a conversion ratio worse than that of beef. Although conversion ratios for fish are generally better than those for land animals, it's fair to say that all forms of livestock agriculture use far more energy, including calories of food, than they produce. That's a prime argument for an increasingly plant-based diet in those parts of the world relying heavily on animals for food.

Current aquaculture techniques also degrade both land and water. Shrimp farming destroys mangroves, for example, a key protector from typhoons, and 200,000 fish on a salmon farm release about as much excrement as 60,000 people. Aquaculture also imperils those wild populations that come into contact with farmed salmon.

Finally, aquaculture uses a large but seemingly indeterminable amount of antibiotics, in pretty much the same style as in other agriculture. About eighty percent of those drugs are ultimately released into the environment, through urine, feces, and unconsumed food, predictably contributing to the resistance crisis discussed above.

The myth is that aquaculture reduces pressure on wild populations. In truth, it increases it, because small fish — once not worth catching except to feed local subsistence populations — are now being harvested to feed bigger fish in farms. And those bigger fish feed relatively rich people.

From a practical perspective, the farmland we have now is all that's available. With this finite amount of acreage, we must grow all the food that feeds the world. Yet another consequence of sweeping monoculture is an all-out war on existing small-scale farmers. In the industrialized West, there is almost no land for new ones to get started.

Whereas land had once been valuable only for its use, when banks began to sell agricultural derivatives, it became like gold — valuable simply because it was finite and therefore tradeable. It could be used to grow tulips or weed for all the financial markets care.

This is true for food itself as well: As a financial product, its price is tied to the dynamics of the global money market, rather than outdated ideas of supply and demand. Prices are twisted by the betting and counter-betting on the size of the global harvest and the timing of weather patterns and geopolitical indicators like oil prices.

In the past couple of generations, the value of good farmland has outperformed just about every other investment. As a result, at least thirty percent of American farmland has been bought up by non-operators who lease it to large-scale farmers. And as the remaining individual American farmers age, land is passing to investors at higher-than-ever prices. That's great if your only goal is to sell acres. But speculation has turned stewardship into an almost laughable concept, and poor and new-entry farmers simply can't afford land.

Then there's the land grab, which is most common in South America and Africa, but it happens in the United States, too, where holdings equivalent to the size of Ohio are foreign-owned. From 2008 to 2016, more than seventy-four million acres were sold to foreign investors for food production, and the process is accelerating as the climate worsens and yields decline.

Land grabbing is most often practiced by farmland-poor but cash-rich countries — the Gulf States, China, India, South Korea, and even some EU countries — that see direct landownership as more secure than trading indefinitely. Trade can be unreliable, prices fluctuate, and there are taxes and embargoes, but land is a constant.

Rarely aboveboard and usually exploitative, these land grabs stamp out subsistence farming and further the growth of the crops-for-cash economy. Meanwhile, consolidation continues to swallow small farms. There is little room in this world for competition, especially from the small stakeholders.

So: fewer crops, fewer farms, fewer companies. The dream come true, for Big Food, would be fewer workers.

Since the first enslaved people grew and processed sugar on Madeira, Western food has relied on brutal labor practices. It still does. From industrial agriculture's perspective, labor is a necessary evil—a nuisance.

Small and biodiverse farms are still labor-intensive. But large farms minimize labor in every way possible, relying instead on chemicals, seeds, and machines.

Yet food always comes back to labor. Without workers, none of us would eat. And just about every hand that helps bring food to our tables belongs to a person who may well be worried about putting food on their own. Eight of the ten worst-paying jobs in the United States involve food. Of the twenty million food system jobs that constitute the largest private labor force in our economy, almost all earn wages that hover around the poverty line. At least a third of farmworkers earn *less* than official poverty wage, which is twenty thousand dollars per year per family. That's just about enough to pay for a minimally nutritious diet for a family of four, leaving approximately zero for every other expense other than an unrealistically low rent.

Many of these jobs are repetitive, demeaning, and dangerous. Workers are denied basic rights like regular bathroom breaks; a reliable schedule; freedom from abuse, harassment, and wage theft; and the right to organize and bargain collectively.

That's how the system was designed to work. New Deal laws like the Fair Labor Standards Act and the National Labor Relations Act intentionally excluded agricultural and domestic workers, many of whom were former slaves or their children. Similarly, a sub-minimum-wage standard was established for tipped workers, back then largely railroad porters but now mostly restaurant servers. The Department of Labor is supposed to ensure that pay plus tips meets or exceeds the minimum wage, but an estimated eighty-five percent of restaurants violate those laws.

The restaurant industry employs more minimum-wage workers than any other. Around six million live with the uncertainty of the tipped wage system, and millions of young women begin their work lives enduring grabs, comments, and worse for the sake of tips. In fast food, at least forty percent of women experience harassment.

Automated scheduling—an outcome of computerized management, which determines the minimum amount of labor necessary at any time—means that workers are subject to arbitrary schedules, often determined at the last minute. Double shifts, split shifts, and long stretches without work are added burdens.

Farmwork is probably the worst of all. Mostly done by immigrants or citizens originally from the Global South, it's seasonal, part-time, without benefits, and pays as little as employers can get away with. The work itself can be brutal. Think of spraying carcinogenic pesticides from a fifty-pound tank strapped to your back, or picking tomatoes in 105-degree heat, running with full baskets to the collection truck because you're being paid by the pound. Imagine sorting lettuce leaves into clamshell packages while standing for eight hours a day in an enclosed truck. Weak child labor laws allow twelve-year-olds to work in fields, even though agriculture is the deadliest industry for children in America.

Apologists have argued for centuries that, as people are thrown off their land, jobs open up in cities, but real opportunities are limited. Fewer than ten percent of new jobs created in the past ten years are in traditional full-time work. In food, this might mean hauling product across lonesome highways through six states in a day, or stocking frozen food in a crowded grocery aisle, or following orders barked through a headset during the drive-through rush, or preparing hundreds of cups of coffee a day. It might mean biking through crowded cities to deliver meals and groceries, or plating trays in a school lunch line or prison mess hall, or working in a slaughterhouse at a frenetic pace in forty-five-degree temperatures, risking injuries like repetitive motion syndrome and accidental amputation, all while wearing a diaper because bathroom breaks are so infrequent.

This is the reality food laborers face.

When laws force anything approaching fair treatment for farm and food workers, employers look elsewhere for labor that can be more efficiently exploited. For all the fearmongering about open borders in the United States, that's exactly what multinational corporations enjoy—the ability to look for cheap labor anywhere it's practical to move operations. It's the workers who can't easily cross borders or plan for stability if they find jobs in a new country.

To a large extent, the immigration "crisis" is a food and labor crisis. Spurred by changes in climate, land grabs, and the lack of support for subsistence farming, farmers leave home to look for work. This supplies cheap labor for destination countries, which allow "guest" workers only when they're needed. In the United States, undocumented Mexican workers make up eighty percent of the farmworker population, and they're literally irreplaceable: United Farm Workers reached out to four million American citizens to solicit farmwork during a period of historic unemployment in 2010. Twelve thousand people applied. Twelve showed up for work. None lasted a single day.

Denied income and security, food workers use food stamps at more than one and a half times the rate of the rest of the U.S. workforce. Thus, we're effectively subsidizing the food industry's lousy labor practices, using our collective tax dollars to cover the difference between a living wage and what millions of Americans actually earn. Walmart, the country's highest-grossing grocery store (and famously among the most "efficient" at cutting labor costs, mostly through low wages and part-time workers), reaps four percent of its total sales from SNAP dollars.

Addressing what's broken in our food system means taking a long and hard look at every facet of it—from its chemical-laced and profit-crazed agriculture practices to its central role in our ever cooking climate to its labor practices that reinforce income and wealth disparities in the United States and abroad. It's all interconnected.

But it doesn't have to be this way. To paraphrase Vandana Shiva, just as monoculture destroys the conditions needed for diversity in agriculture, a sort of "monoculture of the mind" stamps out the will to change. Dominant culture would have us believe that a healthier, more just food system—and one that can still feed the world—is a pipe dream. In truth, the delusion is believing that our current system has any hope of success. To survive, we have to reinvent it.

15

The Way Forward

I REALIZE THAT MUCH of this book has been, let's say, not exactly uplifting. And because the United States is the bastion of agricultural innovation, it's likely to be among the last countries to alter course and create a more just system.

But there is reason for hope. Although readers of this book may not see many examples of better food systems in their daily lives, they do exist. Much distribution remains decentralized, and subsistence and small-scale farming thrive and even dominate in most of the world; many people grow food sustainably, with judgment, experience, and wisdom, along with an understanding that agriculture can't be reduced to a formula.

This matters, as do significant changes and efforts to create better food in the West. And so this chapter is about the positive change coming to our food system, change that's widespread, change that's rekindling and enhancing people- and earth-friendly traditions of food production.

The word "agroecology" was first used about a hundred years ago, and it remains the best descriptor for the movements that are rebuilding our relationship with food. The word and practices have been advanced by the global peasant organization La Via Campesina ("the Peasant Way") for decades, and that—along with the fact that, moving forward, agroecology is the most sensible approach for agriculture—has led to its use and at least partial endorsement by the governments of France, Cuba, and others, and by the UN's Food and Agriculture Organization, which included agroecology as a key component of its 2030 Sustainable Development Goals.

For those reasons—and because "producing food in harmony with the planet and its inhabitants" is a mouthful—"agroecology" is the word I'm sticking with. It's a clunky term, but perhaps its unsexiness is an advantage: It's not likely to be co-opted as quickly as "natural" and "organic" were; it's hard to imagine "agroecological" power bars or potato chips, though stranger things have happened.

As you can guess, agroecology is a set of practices that integrates ecological principles into agriculture. As a scientific approach to farming that works with all of nature's power and gifts, rather than seeing nature as something to be conquered, it stands in opposition to industrial agriculture. It is more serious and comprehensive than "organic," and not constrained by USDA definitions.

But agroecology is more than just a series of techniques—it's a philosophy and a broad commitment to improve society. Adherents define it as "an autonomous, pluralist, multicultural movement, political in its demand for social justice." That's key.

Farmers worldwide are struggling to maintain or regain control of their food supply while rejecting the global norms of "development" and "underdevelopment"—norms that mandate urbanization, industrialization, "efficiency," and large scale. La Via Campesina, which is a loose coalition of two hundred million farmers and activists, organizes for food sovereignty: Its goals are to get land to the landless and to enable farmers to control what they produce while making a living and stewarding the earth.

One of agroecology's best Western advocates is former University of California–Santa Cruz professor Steve Gliessman. In the tradition of Albert Howard, Franklin Hiram King, and Rudolf Steiner, Gliessman traveled the world and saw how the strength and good sense of peasant agriculture contrasted with the fragility and recklessness of industrial agriculture.

Gliessman argues that developing an agroecological system would ultimately transform the global food system by first cutting back on the toxic techniques innate to industrial agriculture, starting with chemical fertilizer and pesticides.

Next comes replacing those materials and their associated techniques with alternative practices, such as the use of compost, cover crops, crop rotation, and multicropping; the encouragement of beneficial animal and plant interactions; and the complete elimination of chemicals. To this point, what we're really talking about is organic farming, but this is where farmers will begin to rebuild the system, using from-the-farm fertilizer, intercropping—planting a number of crops together—to reduce pests and unwanted plants, encouraging pollinators, and generally, in Gliessman's words, functioning "on the basis of a new set of ecological processes." The next step involves shortening the food supply chain, reducing the distance between growers and eaters, and establishing new ways of getting food to people.

Finally—and this can't happen without widespread societal change in all arenas, including the economy—the global food system must become sustainable and equitable for all.

No question: a tall order. The alternative is catastrophic.

"Eating is an agricultural act," says Wendell Berry, which is to say, food does not come from nowhere; it comes from land and people. In turn, agriculture is a political act: The policies and investments we decide on as a society determine what agriculture we practice.

How we relate to land and the food we grow has everything to do with how we live on the earth, and who benefits and suffers from that treatment. Thus, agroecology is about not only sane agricultural methods but the empowerment of women and groups of long-exploited people, such as BIPOC, land reform, fair distribution of resources and treatment of labor, affordable food, nutrition and diet, and animal welfare.

Agroecology aims to right social wrongs. The movements for global justice and truly sustainable growing techniques are interwoven, and agroecological change can't simply stop at the first or second steps outlined above. The other yardsticks include how well food nourishes people, protects the environment, and helps farmers lead good lives. Agroecology regenerates the ecology of the soil instead of depleting it, reduces carbon emissions, and sustains local food cultures, businesses, farms, jobs, seeds, and people instead of diminishing or destroying them.

To date, agroecology has received little government research support, maybe five percent of that given to industrial agriculture. Yet agroecology has repeatedly demonstrated that focusing on growing in harmony with nature can be profitable, productive, and enduring. Even within the framework of industrial agriculture, reducing the use of chemicals and patented seeds cuts costs significantly, and yields remain stable or even rise as soil health improves.

Agroecology supports farming as a dignified way to live, creating grounding, family-oriented, life-giving work. We can call that "rural employment" or "revitalization" or "green jobs." With the best ideas and methods of industrial agriculture integrated into a more sensible and equitable system, farming need not involve the drudgery so many millions want to escape.

Thankfully, progressive governments everywhere, from the City of Philadelphia to the Pacific nation of Vanuatu and scores of others in between, have recognized the destructive nature of industrially produced food and begun to act accordingly. The progress is, to many, almost invisible. But it exists. Whether it's enough remains to be seen, but agroecology is hands-down our best bet for changing agriculture's role from a driver of the greatest problems afflicting humankind to a solution.

Some of these may at first sound minor and extremely incremental; and they *are* incremental, but they are decidedly not minor, because they are among the steps outlined by agroecology, and include the beginning of the end of monoculture, more thoughtfulness and fairness in the food system, a more rational way of production. Acknowledging that industrial agriculture is not likely to go away anytime soon means accepting the value of steps that can be taken to mitigate its harshest effects while recognizing those steps that showcase real alternatives and progress. That's what follows.

It starts and ends with land and people. The mistakes of the past cannot be changed, but they can be remedied; this requires a shift in power. Power is at the nexus of all the interlocking issues that define the food system, and an ethical restructuring of food systems must right the historical wrongs of land and wealth distribution and empower the world's most vulnerable people. You can call these changes evolution or revolution, but they will mean the true self-determination of the world's majority of people, which is only right.

Food is central to this, as it is to most things, and food is produced by people. Improving the food system does not mean less involvement by people but more. Treating the land right—reducing monoculture and its ills—is a laborious job.

More labor will indeed threaten industry profits (which are unjustifiably high) and raise consumer prices (which are artificially low). These economic failures are in part due to the industry's ability to ignore "externalities," such as the costs of environmental damage, declining public health, and even food stamps for underpaid workers—all costs that the industry has historically skirted to boost profit margins.

As corporations are held more responsible for these costs, the basic truths about whom the food system serves will be laid more bare. What happens next is anyone's guess, but low wages are the last bulwark of the industrial food system—indeed, of the economic system itself.

Addressing mistreated workers in our food system will require a cascade of changes to the status quo, which makes it a good place to start. And awareness of food-chain labor has accelerated in recent years. It's no coincidence that the "Fight for $15"—the movement to institute a minimum hourly wage of fifteen dollars in place of the current federal minimum of $7.25—began at KFC, McDonald's, and Burger King. In 2012, about two hundred New York City fast-food workers risked their jobs (and, for many, their immigration status) to demand the still-meager wage of fifteen dollars per hour.

As of this writing, estimates put the gains made by the Fight for $15 at more than seventy billion dollars for more than twenty million workers. Many states have raised minimum wages, with a handful establishing the fifteen-dollar standard. Others have done away with the exploitative tipped wage. (California has done both.) It's likely that the next time Democrats have a president in the White House and a majority in Congress, the national minimum wage will be bumped to fifteen dollars per hour, and we'll see tipped wages phased out nationally.

Farmworkers, too, have made progress. The best known example of this is in Florida, which has long provided most of the country's winter tomatoes. For decades, South Florida farm bosses underpaid, mistreated, and sometimes literally imprisoned workers, the majority of whom are immigrants. In 1993, the Coalition of Immokalee Workers, named after the town where it's based, a tomato-growing center, set out to change that.

Demonizing growers was the most obvious way to curb abuse and raise wages, but organizers recognized that the real power lay not with the relatively small farm owners, who were themselves burdened with low margins and an otherwise tricky business, but with their customers—the buyers for supermarkets and fast-food chains, who demanded ever-decreasing prices. So, beginning in 2001, the organization targeted the big boys.

After a four-year battle involving coalitions of students, labor activists, and others, Taco Bell agreed to pay a penny more per pound for tomatoes and to buy only from farms committed to CIW's Fair Food Code of Conduct. Since then, thirteen more major foods brands have signed on, and the penny-per-pound increase has translated into nearly thirty-five million dollars in added wages. By signing the code, employers guarantee that their workers will "not be the victims of forced labor, child labor, or violence . . . go to work without being sexually harassed or verbally abused . . . have shade, clean drinking water, and bathrooms in the fields . . . be permitted to leave the fields when there is lightning, pesticide spraying, or other dangerous conditions," and be entitled to a handful of other protections.

Today, participating buyers in the Fair Food Program include many supermarkets and fast-food chains, most notably Walmart.

Ninety percent of tomato producers in Florida and six other eastern states have signed on to the Fair Food Code of Conduct, and farms that don't meet the code's terms are expelled from the program and thus unable to sell to big buyers who've committed to it. Improved working conditions have brought about a more stable workforce that includes about 35,000 decently treated laborers.

And the model is spreading. There is now a Milk with Dignity Standards Council, with its own code of conduct, working to improve rights for dairy-chain workers.

Nevertheless, most farmworkers—many of whom are undocumented and consequently live in fear of deportation—still lack organizing rights, limits on workweek length, codes for sanitary housing, disability insurance, family leave, or eligibility for unemployment or overtime pay. These protections are guaranteed to most other workers, but not to those who do the work no one else wants to do—producing the food we eat.

Progress was made on this front in New York in 2019, when the Farm Laborers Fair Labor Practices Act was signed into law, righting a wrong that excluded agricultural laborers from the 1938 Fair Labor Standards Act. This made New York a safer, more dignified, and union-friendly place for nearly 100,000 farm laborers. The law includes provisions for collective bargaining, time-and-a-half pay after sixty hours worked in a week, an option for a full day of rest each week, and other long-overdue provisions.

California also made improvements in laws protecting farmworkers, including provisions for overtime pay, and as of this writing, Washington State's supreme court is hearing a case that would decide whether it's constitutional to exclude farmworkers from overtime guarantees. The decision could have implications for a future federal ruling and hopefully pave the way for lasting change.

Change happens in small but important ways. Urban gardens and farms can't compare in scale, appearance, or yield to large rural farms, but by supplying populations with real food and bringing power and understanding of food systems to urban eaters, they become important pieces of the puzzle. This isn't about techy vertical farms providing microgreens to overpriced restaurants but about outdoor plots farmed by urban residents, often people of color, feeding the communities in which they live.

Will Allen, the founder of Milwaukee's Growing Power, once the country's most successful urban farm, said it best: "We're not just growing food, we're growing community." Making good food available to all—or at least showing that local production of nutritious and affordable food is possible—combats systemic inequality and is a tangible partner of wider progress, which is why many urban food activists now talk about battling food apartheid. Food is, or should be, a universal right; lack of access is not a "tragedy" but a crime. And urban farming is about people providing for themselves despite the racism and more general unfairness of the agricultural system.

The best example is in Detroit, where the Detroit Black Community Food Security Network (DBCFSN) is involved in D-Town Farm, the Detroit Food Policy Council, the national-profile Food Summit, and the People's Grocery project. The DBCFSN was convened in 2006 by a few dozen people, including Malik Yakini, a school founder and principal. "Together," writes Monica White in *Freedom Farmers*, "they established DBCFSN and laid out its goals: education, food access, and collective buying. They saw these as critical strategies to ensure that Black Detroiters had what they needed not only to survive but to thrive."

"The idea," Yakini told me on a tour of D-Town, "is to help Black people stand up, to demonstrate that creating reality is not the exclusive domain of white people. . . . The farm can empower, drive the economy, reduce our carbon footprint, and give us better food," he said. "And we're influencing young white people too, because they can see that."

Detroit now has more than a thousand community gardens and farms, supported by the Detroit Food Policy Council, an alliance, typical of those found in many cities, of school and hospital food service directors, food bank CEOs, farmers, distributors, grocers, advocacy groups, and eaters.

Generally, local and regional food networks are growing. Between 1997 and 2015, farm-to-eater sales skyrocketed from $500 million to about $3 billion in commerce. Farmers' markets almost tripled in number, Farm to School programs increased by more than four hundred percent, and the number of CSAs more than doubled, to twelve thousand and rising. (CSA stands for community-supported agriculture, a program in which local eaters prepay to receive a box of a local farm's produce on a set schedule, usually weekly in season.)

For millions of people in the United States, the most visible and important program is the USDA's Supplemental Nutrition Assistance Program (SNAP), usually referred to as "food stamps." The program helps to feed around ten percent of American households whose incomes are too low to buy adequate food, and—although it doesn't address, or pretend to address, a nutritious diet for all—it's the closest this country has come to acknowledging the universal right to food.

The program does address hunger, but because it's not funded adequately or run appropriately, millions of American families still cannot afford to buy wholesome food (and sometimes not even enough of any kind of food), and the lack of access to real food rather than UPFs has contributed to the devastating cycle of stress, poverty, and poor health I've outlined elsewhere.

However, some USDA programs do facilitate the purchase of real food, especially fruits and vegetables, and, in a few small but significant ways, the agency has moved food stamps in a positive direction.

Double Up, piloted in Detroit in 2009, is one such program. It doubles the value of food stamps at farmers' markets, which benefits both shoppers and farmers. Double Up has since gone nationwide, funded by the USDA and by Wholesome Wave and other nonprofits. With more than nine hundred sites in twenty-eight states, and 200,000 families participating, the program has led to fifteen million SNAP dollars spent at farmers' markets on fruits and vegetables. The USDA has also pledged fifty million dollars annually for the Food Insecurity Nutrition Incentive (FINI) program, including a pilot program at Glynwood Center for Regional Food and Farming (run by my partner, Kathleen Finlay) that allows SNAP participants to use their benefits to join a CSA.

These are not insignificant measures. But again, there has never been a full-scale attempt to ensure good food for all in the United States. And although measures on that scale are the most difficult to achieve, positive government action to change agricultural and nutrition policies ultimately is the most effective way to change the way we grow and eat food. To see this, we can look both home and abroad, to find the dozens of reforms, programs, and models that have moved us toward better food. The most common (and, admittedly, a relatively easy one for industry to stomach) is providing information to citizens about the food they're eating, guiding them away from UPFs and toward making informed choices in food. Labeling is the most critical of these.

By taking the relatively uncontroversial step of pointing out that UPFs are less desirable than whole foods, governments can at least steer people in the right direction, and thus influence what's grown and sold. Currently, more than fifty countries mandate food labeling, and another dozen or so have state-defined nonbinding guidelines. The encouraging trends are that we are seeing more labeling, not less, and that labeling is becoming more meaningful as the easy-to-understand "traffic light" system — green means "eat as much as you want," yellow means "eat sparingly," and red means "eat as little as possible" — becomes more popular.

But nudging consumers away from UPFs isn't enough. Only by encouraging the production of real food can the market do a good job; in a market flooded with UPFs, it can be difficult for many people to buy anything but junk, and recommendations to make healthy choices are often drowned out by the noise of Big Food's advertising. In food, supply is more powerful than demand, and the industry's marketers prefer that it stay that way. Kneecapping Big Food's powerhouse marketing machines and changing how and what food is produced are the big steps needed to revolutionize the food landscape.

A dozen or more countries have already passed regulations limiting junk-food marketing to children: Uruguay, France, Turkey, Malaysia, Latvia, Peru, South Korea, Brazil, Taiwan, Mexico, and others. And we know this works: The Canadian province of Quebec banned "commercial advertising directed at persons under thirteen years of age" around forty years ago, and studies have found, unsurprisingly, that Quebec residents buy less junk food than other North Americans and that fewer of their children are overweight.

Others have followed suit. In 2012, Chile, where half of all six-year-olds are overweight or obese, passed a Law of Food Labeling and Advertising, the world's strongest combination of taxes, marketing restrictions, and bans to date. It took effect in 2016 and features the now iconic stop-sign-shaped "black label" for UPFs that are high in calories, sodium, sugar, or saturated fat.

Black-labeled food can't be advertised to kids under fourteen, include toys in its packaging, or be sold in schools. Thus, there are no potato chips in Chilean schools, and Tony the Tiger has effectively vanished. Almost instantly, Chilean children went from seeing 8,500 junk-food advertisements a year to seeing next to none.

But despite their impact, these marketing restrictions are just one piece of the puzzle. To truly revolutionize the food landscape, governments must intercede on behalf of eaters and discourage the production and sale of UPFs.

Chile's done that by instituting an eighteen percent tax on sugar-sweetened beverages, as well as a junk-food tax. Studies have shown that seventy percent of shoppers have changed their buying habits and that soda purchases have declined by nearly twenty-five percent as a result.

Less dramatic but still impressive efforts are under way in Mexico, which as recently as ten years ago led the world in both soda consumption and obesity. (UPFs supply nearly three-fifths of the calories eaten in Mexico.) Soda had long been a standard drink in Mexico, whose citizens have historically had limited access to clean tap water and would have to pay more for bottled water than Coke. In 2014, the country instituted a tax on soda *and* junk food — junk is anything considered "nonessential," with more than 275 calories per hundred grams — in tandem with a program to make clean water universally available. Soda consumption has since fallen by twelve percent.

Projections determined that over ten years, the decrease in purchases owing to a modest soda tax would prevent almost 200,000 people from getting Type 2 diabetes. Others estimate that there would be over twenty thousand fewer strokes and heart attacks, and that the obesity rate in the country could fall by three percent. That alone would transform the lives of millions of people. Although the industry repeatedly attempts to repeal the tax, support has only grown.

Most of the United States has only voluntary (read: useless) restrictions on junk-food marketing, allowing companies to do pretty much whatever they want. However, soda taxes, first enacted in Berkeley in 2015, are now in place in Philadelphia, Seattle, Boulder, Oakland, San Francisco, and Albany (California), and initial studies show that, even at their currently low levels, they can reduce consumption by twenty percent.

Most unbiased public health advocates believe that a larger soda tax—two percent rather than the more common one percent—would be more effective. In 2015, the Navajo Nation (situated in the Four Corners area of Arizona, New Mexico, and Utah) instituted a two percent tax on all junk foods. Anything that had "little to no nutritional value" was fair game. Additionally, they waived the sales tax on fruits and vegetables and spent the added junk-food revenue on community health projects, including exercise classes, farming, and vegetable garden initiatives.

The best, broadest, and most powerful example of a food system moving in the right direction happened in Belo Horizonte, Brazil's third-largest metro area.

In 1993, Brazil's government, responding to twenty years of mass movements asserting the notion that no citizen should go hungry, established a food security council. A year later it convened two thousand leaders for the nation's first food security conference. At the same time, Belo Horizonte's mayor helped establish a municipal department whose stated goal was to improve all citizens' access "to sufficient, healthy and nutritious food." Among other programs, the department launched the Restaurantes Populares (People's Restaurants), which serve high-quality lunches with tiered prices, to make them affordable to all. The program went national, and at its peak close to 100 People's Restaurants were serving well over 100,000 meals daily.

The government also bankrolled cooked-from-scratch daily meals for each of the city's 150,000 schoolchildren, emphasizing more vegetables and fewer processed foods, which helped reduce hunger levels from fifteen percent in 1990 to less than two percent now. By 2010, a similar program was feeding forty-five million students daily nationwide.

Both programs strove to source local ingredients, giving priority to organic farmers and small stakeholders. Ultimately, thirty percent or more of school food was sourced from 120,000 family farms.

Next, the government stepped in to regulate supply to food markets themselves. Staples were sold at reduced prices that were guaranteed to be fair to farmers, and much of the food came from the surrounding countryside, where small-scale producers could sell directly to consumers at public markets. A state agency also bought food from farmers and gave it to food-insecure city dwellers.

Meanwhile, the government funded urban agriculture in the form of school gardens, community plots, container growing, and more. And it promoted food and nutrition education, including online resources, a policy knowledge center, and professional food courses for adult students.

Not only has hunger in B.H. been nearly eliminated, but child mortality, malnutrition, and poverty in children has declined dramatically, while fruit and vegetable consumption (including organics) and farmer income have risen.

Success in B.H. led to the national Zero Hunger program of 2004, the 2006 National Food and Nutritional Security Framework Law (LOSAN), a law declaring the universal right to food and codifying the right to food in the Brazilian constitution in 2010, which helped shape economic policy. In parallel, a land reform initiative distributed 126 million acres—more than the size of California—to small farmers. This represented as much land as had been made available for reform in all of Brazil's previous

history. The country now has four million family farms, which together produce the vast majority of its food, and a crop insurance
program that guarantees prices for small farmers. (It's also a haven for agribusiness, and the Amazon and its defenders are under
violent siege, but in this chapter we're focusing on the positive.)
By 2014, these programs had lifted ten percent of the population
—around thirty million people—out of poverty. It took half of
one percent of the country's GNP to accomplish all of this.

There are broader lessons to be learned from B.H.'s success, beyond the obvious. It illustrates how progressive local policy can
grow into a national initiative, especially when leaders are pushed
by their constituents. It shows that organizing can bring about
significant change. And it cautions that when popular movements
lag, change like this is difficult to sustain: In 2019, President Jair
Bolsonaro dissolved the institutions responsible for the Zero
Hunger policies.

Still, state-supported initiatives remain among the most important mechanisms for improving the food supply. Nowhere is
this better illustrated right now than in the South Indian state
of Andhra Pradesh (A.P.), home to fifty million people. The state
is investing more than two billion dollars to help farmers adopt
Zero Budget Natural Farming (ZBNF), a series of agroecological
practices that use from-the-farm nutrients based on cow waste in
place of the chemical fertilizers and pesticides that have pushed
many farmers into debt.

In addition to natural fertilizer, ZBNF focuses on green cover
crops, biodiversity, soil health, and intercropping. Two fundamental principles are "to promote climate resilient farming in harmony with nature" and "to reduce the cost of cultivation to make
farming a viable and sustainable livelihood."

Unlike chemical farming, ZBNF can become self-sustaining.
Costs are reduced by around two-thirds, and, according to most
farmers (I've spoken to a few, but program directors are in touch
with thousands), overall yields increase. Because ZBNF involves
intercropping, even if main-crop yield doesn't increase, overall
production does, while irrigation needs are reduced.

More than 280,000 farmers have switched to ZBNF, and it's estimated that 500,000 farmers in three thousand villages will have done so by the end of 2019. A hundred and sixty thousand landless poor have become home gardeners, and the government plans to expand natural farming to all six million farmers in A.P. before 2030. This would mean the state's entire cultivable area—twenty million acres, which is close to all the farmland in Iowa—would be farmed using ZBNF.

In 2018, I met with farmers in Andhra Pradesh, including young people who'd moved from the home farm to the city, taken jobs in the software industry, and returned to join the ZBNF movement. "This is simply the better life," one said to me.

Since my visit, the North Indian states of Madhya Pradesh and Gujarat have begun to support state programs, and there is talk of taking ZBNF national. The FAO, which supports the A.P. program, is working with similar initiatives in Senegal and in Mexico, where there is a national plan to transition to agro-ecology.

Strong agricultural programs like ZBNF are most feasible in countries with strong institutions and government. But even without those conditions, there can be progress. In Haiti, food and farmer-led, education-focused peasant associations are thriving with little money or government support. The Partnership for Local Development program (PDL), for example—which now reaches more than twenty thousand farmers—needs only $152 per farmer to provide five years of training in agroecology.

And even in the industrialized West, there is progress. Generally, EU countries, and even the Union as a whole, are more progressive than the United States. Neonics are banned for outdoor use, and glyphosate is restricted or forbidden in twenty-one countries and in almost countless smaller political units.

Denmark, among the world's leading exporters of pork, in 2000 stopped antibiotic use for farm animals for any reason other than treatment of disease. Antibiotic use has been reduced by fifty percent since then. (In case you're concerned, the country's pork industry is thriving.) All of this convinced the EU to ban the use of antibiotics for growth promotion in 2006, and it committed to banning the use of the drugs as preventive measures entirely.

And there's EU and individual government support for agroecology, most notably in France, where the rallying cry "Produisons autrement"— "Let's produce differently" —accompanied the 2014 "Law on the Future of Agriculture, Food and Forestry," whose goal is to implement agroecological practices on nearly half of all farms by the end of this decade.

France is Europe's paramount farming country, producing one-fifth of the EU's agricultural output. So it matters when France prioritizes agriculture that places environment over yield, phases out chemical pesticides and routine antibiotic use, provides incentives and educational resources for ecological methods, makes land available to new farmers, and acknowledges that environmental and social ills are intertwined.

The birthplace of industrial agriculture—and still firmly in its grip—the United States has been among the most difficult places to change. That it's *known* that pesticides are carcinogenic and that their regulation nevertheless remains minimal means that we're likely to see this cycle repeated: Chemical companies will introduce new pesticides and claim they're safe. Time will show that they are not as animals (including humans) fall ill and die. Lawsuits will stop that particular pesticide's use, and a new one will take its place. This you cannot blame on Donald Trump—it predates him and, sadly, is likely to postdate him as well—but on a system that values industry's "innovation" and corporate right to profits more than people's health. Antibiotic use in the animal industry is similar: There's been precious little reform in the United States.

But dozens, if not hundreds, of local, provincial, and state governments have taken action to curb the use of both glyphosate and neonicotinoids. When pesticide use is inadequately restricted at the federal level, there are two main courses of action. The first is through local authorities, like the Los Angeles County Board of Supervisors, which enacted a full and formal ban on Roundup. (Miami has acted similarly.) The second is individual and group legal action: There are around forty-two thousand court suits pending involving damages caused by toxic chemicals.

Government is also important in helping individuals make the *right* choices in food, especially when the vast majority of our options are "wrong." Meatless Mondays are great, and so are the part-time vegan movements, but imagine if the production of meat and junk were actually reined in.

That's not happening anytime soon, and, given that supply overwhelms real choice, it's important to teach children what real food means. The sooner we begin to raise children who recognize that Coke and Snickers don't bring happiness, and the sooner we teach children how and by whom food is produced, the sooner we'll stop producing generations of adults who struggle with diet.

Everyone reading these words knows how difficult it is to change the eating habits with which we grew up. This makes school lunchrooms an important battleground. And although it should go without saying, schools must serve real food. The National School Lunch Program could do this, in theory, but it's spent half a century moving in the wrong direction. Thus, change must come from independent actors. And it is.

Start with the Good Food Purchasing Program, begun in Los Angeles in 2012. Along the lines of Leadership in Energy and Environmental Design (LEED) certification, GFPP sets standards in five areas: benefit for local economies, environmental sustainability, treatment of workforce, animal welfare, and nutrition. The program provides incentives for vendors to improve practices in order to earn or retain contracts with institutions, and gives purchasing agents real guidelines.

For example, when the Los Angeles Unified School District (LAUSD), the country's second-largest public school district, signed on to GFPP, its main distributor, Gold Star Foods, reached out to wheat farms whose crops could meet GFPP standards. Among those was Shepherd's Grain, in Portland, Oregon, whose contract with LAUSD resulted in the expansion of its network of wheat farms and the addition of sixty-five full-time living-wage jobs. LAUSD's local fruit and vegetable purchases skyrocketed from nine percent to seventy-five percent of the total in just two years, while spending on meat decreased by fifteen percent.

To date, GFPP standards have been adopted in Cincinnati, San Francisco, Oakland, Boston, Austin, Washington, D.C., Chicago, and the Twin Cities. By the time you read this, New York City will likely have joined in. All told, they've made over a billion dollars a year in food purchases, all of which has encouraged fair pay for workers and higher-quality food for eaters.

There are, of course, limits to purchasing power. To provide better food, institutional kitchens—which have shrunk thanks to heat-and-eat meals—must increase their space, upgrade their cooking equipment, and hire more workers. This means budgets must grow. It's yet another way that getting good food into the mouths of eaters gets complicated. Yet what's more important than feeding children well?

That's the attitude of Berkeley restaurateur Alice Waters, who founded Edible Schoolyard, the most ambitious school lunch program in the United States. Waters's big idea was to create a "kitchen classroom" that would put food at the core of curriculum. Waters argues that, by doing this, a widespread introduction of the Edible Schoolyard would transform diet, education, and even farming.

Edible Schoolyard has become a paradigm. There are hundreds of schools participating, and thousands more have been influenced by its core philosophy. Were it a national, fully funded program, it would look something like what's existed in Japan since the nineties. There, *shokuiku* (food education) teaches Japanese elementary school children not only how to eat but where their food comes from.

Lunch is set in the classroom, with food and nutrition education integrated into meals prepared from scratch. Thirty percent of ingredients are sourced locally and seasonally, nutritional guidelines are strict, and meals are mostly traditional. Students are taught to understand the culture of their own food and that of others, and to take responsibility for serving meals to their peers and cleaning up afterwards. It's night and day compared with the assembly-line mode of lunch service in most U.S. schools.

And Japan isn't alone. Most countries with generally progressive national policies have good school food programs, and vice versa. For example, Finland began universal free lunch in 1948. Vegetables take up half the plate; grain and meat, fish, or beans the remainder. Beverages are water or milk, and dessert is fruit. There's no ultra-processed food.

Sweden also provides free lunch, usually a stew, salad, and cooked vegetables, along with bread, milk or water, and fruit. France spends three times as much per student on lunch as the United States. Rome serves its schoolchildren mostly made-from-scratch meals, using seventy percent organic ingredients, mostly fresh and minimally handled.

In 2007 the City of Copenhagen vowed to use ninety percent organic ingredients in its eighty thousand daily meals served across nine hundred kitchens, from medical centers to schools and employee cafeterias. The new system reduces waste, serves seasonal food and less meat, employs more people, and cooks from scratch.

Back in the United States, some states and an assortment of school districts mandate local sourcing and responsibly produced food. They establish programs like Meatless Mondays (as Brooklyn has done), work with programs like GFPP, take advantage of the USDA's Farm to School program, and support school gardens. Minneapolis Public Schools made a one-hundred-million-dollar commitment to food infrastructure, prioritizing from-scratch cooking, establishing "Minnesota Thursdays," featuring local ingredients, improving benefits and hours for cafeteria workers, and eliminating the "harmful seven": trans fats, high-fructose corn syrup, hormones and antibiotics, artificial preservatives, artificial colors and flavors, bleached flour, and artificial sweeteners.

Food in colleges is also ripe for improvement, and students are increasingly pressuring institutions to reform or eliminate partnerships with Compass, Sodexo, Aramark, and other huge food service companies. Coalitions like Real Food Challenge have won meaningful shifts toward local, ecologically sound, fair, and humane farms and food businesses.

Institutional food goes beyond public schools, of course. It includes prisons, hospitals, and more, and to move beyond heat-and-serve processed foods requires a reimagining and revitalization of how large kitchens operate. An organization called Health Care Without Harm works with hundreds of hospitals to make hospital food healthier (an ironic but very real issue) while encouraging the purchase of local, healthy food through farmers' markets, community gardens, and more. Within its network, which includes about a third of American hospitals, Health Care Without Harm has reduced total meat consumption at two-thirds of their partners' facilities; of the remainder, most is antibiotic-free. The group has nearly doubled sustainable and local food purchases and instituted prescription programs for fruits and vegetables—doctors can literally prescribe food as medicine.

You have to look hard to find progress in American agriculture, but it exists. Sometimes it's corralled into the "alternative" agriculture category, implying that it's impractical and unrealistic. Yet if you allow that seventy percent of the world's agriculture remains nonindustrial, it's closer to mainstream.

Still, when the system of price supports allows farmers to practice monoculture even when soil is so poor, operating costs so high, and prices so low that the crop itself loses money, it's hard for farmers to break out. But what if fallowing some of that land didn't reduce farmers' income or even yield—without subsidies? That's the concept behind prairie strips, which make marked improvements on monocultural farms, mitigating the worst of their impact without reducing farmers' income.

Led by Matt Liebman, researchers at Iowa State University have demonstrated that large-scale farmers can retire the least productive ten percent of their acreage, to reduce phosphorus and nitrogen runoff as well as overall soil loss by eighty-five percent or more, and at the same time *increase* overall yield and profit. The fallowed land becomes an area of "diverse, native perennial vegetation"—more commonly called a "prairie strip" for the way it streaks through planted farmland. Iowa State University has recruited sixty farmers to build the movement and continue the research.

More radical and difficult-to-implement approaches seek to return way more than ten percent of farmland to the prairie. Wes Jackson, who founded the Land Institute in Salina, Kansas, has been working on one such approach for forty-five years. Jackson's vision was to change what's planted in the Plains by developing a perennial form of wheat called Kernza. Kernza has deep roots —like the original, native buffalo grass—and leaves soil undisturbed from year to year, which means building instead of destroying it, and sequestering carbon rather than emitting it.

Enough Kernza is now being grown that it's available to bakeries, breweries, and chefs. The Land Institute hopes that by 2030 it will have an even more productive variety of seed that will eventually supplant commonly grown wheat. That would be a game changer, eliminating huge areas of industrial monoculture.

Alternatives to industrial agriculture don't stop on land. Many efforts are being made, worldwide, to improve aquaculture. Among the most encouraging is the 3D Ocean Farming system developed by New Haven's Bren Smith, in which seaweed (specifically, kelp), mussels, scallops, and oysters are all grown symbiotically in a regenerative ocean farm that produces as much food per acre as a potato field yet uses no pesticides or fertilizers and requires little initial investment. The system reduces both nitrogen and phosphorus levels in the ocean while boosting the sustainable production of food and fertilizer.

In all of these cases, the true obstacle isn't necessarily discovering a sustainable farming method that mitigates the damage of industrial agriculture, but making the efforts more widespread so they become viable alternatives. People talk about "scaling up," but that really isn't the answer; it's more about scaling *out*, replicating small- and medium-scale sustainable systems in millions of places worldwide. In this way we can begin to transform and replace the industrial agricultural system.

There are even a few models for the farm of the future. The one I know best is Full Belly Farm, founded in 1985 in California's Capay Valley. On its four hundred acres—the perfect "medium" size for a farm—Full Belly focuses on biodiversity and soil fertility through crop rotation, cover cropping, composting, and livestock husbandry. It sells dozens of crops wholesale to stores and restaurants, at farmers' markets, and to an eleven-hundred-family CSA. The farm was founded by four partners, and it's since been joined by a second generation and eighty employees, for whom it provides year-round employment with benefits.

It's a beautiful landscape: The farm has fifty independently managed fields that showcase the diversity of nature. Native flowers attract pollinators of all kinds, livestock act as "mowers and fertilizers," and composting plays a major and effective role: In an area where the average amount of organic matter in the soil is 0.7 percent, Full Belly's is three percent, which makes injections of synthetic and fossil-fueled nutrients unnecessary. Water management, always important in California, includes hyper-efficient underground drip.

The entire setup offers a stark contrast to monoculture's miles of uniformity. The farm has achieved long-term sustainability, and it is now as close to an agricultural paradise as one could imagine.

As an exercise, I once did a back-of-the-envelope calculation of how many farms like Full Belly it would take to truly influence the American food system. (At the moment, there may be a dozen of its size and stability.) I'd guess that five thousand farms of Full Belly's caliber could feed perhaps five million people, more than the population of Alabama, and on just 400,000 acres of farmland, less than five percent of all the farmland in that state. Most counties in Iowa plant more than that in unsustainably grown corn and soybeans—which, as we've seen, do almost no one any good.

Isolated instances of near paradise are inspiring, but to make that the norm requires work and organizing: Progress for the many rather than the few begins with the power of grassroots movements. In 1969, when the Black Panthers supported the UFW's boycott on table grapes, it pointed the way to a multiracial, status-quo-challenging coalition. That's the model for the HEAL (Health, Environment, Agriculture, Labor) Food Alliance, a group of fifty organizations with the overall mission of building collective power to create a better food system.

Many of the organizations that are part of HEAL are discussed in these pages. Some others include the I-Collective, a group of Indigenous chefs, artists, seed keepers, and activists rallying around food sovereignty; Soul Fire Farm, an eighty-acre site in Petersburg, New York, that runs a one-hundred-family CSA and is known for hosting trainings in food justice activism among BIPOC farmers and nonfarmers; Family Farm Action, which rallies Midwestern livestock farmers and ranchers around antitrust reform and rural policy; and Justicia Migrante (Migrant Justice), led by farmworkers in Vermont's dairy barns, which in 2015 won a Milk with Dignity agreement—modeled on CIW's Fair Food Agreement—with Unilever, the owner of Ben & Jerry's.

And there are, of course, non-HEAL organizations doing similar work all over the country. Nuestras Raíces (Our Roots), for example, uses thirty acres of Massachusetts farmland to give young, mostly Puerto Rican farmers a way to develop their own businesses to grow and produce foods for the community. Agriculture and Land-Based Training Association (ALBA), in California's Central Valley, provides land and financial assistance and training to help farmworkers establish their own farms. And, after fighting for and winning a union for their Driscoll's working crew in Washington State, four Mexican farmworkers started Cooperativa Tierra y Libertad to fill the demand for fruit grown and harvested with fair labor.

There are dozens, if not hundreds, of such examples, most with a common goal of developing a policy platform and a movement "For Real Food," as HEAL puts it.

In a world in which food is a political tool and power is built through coalitions, HEAL and other movements like it are our best hope for bringing near-future change to the food system. What's clear is that it will take group effort and organizing to move toward obtaining food justice—land for those who want to work it, a country filled with farms serving their communities, healthy food for all, and so on—for more than a few smart and lucky people.

Every solution in the realm of food is interconnected. Like the other great battles we have yet to win—those for racial and economic justice, an end to gender discrimination, the existential struggle to mitigate climate change—they all circle back to the wealth of nature, and how we humans protect and share it.

Conclusion

We Are All Eaters

THERE IS NO end to this story, or none that anyone alive will ever see. We do know that we cannot continue to eat or live without a sensible food system. We don't know exactly what that might that look like (and anyone who pretends that they do is likely wrong), and yet we can see the beginnings of the roads that will transport us; there are many, most discussed in the last chapter.

What is a system? A set of things or principles working together. A car is a system, a collection of parts that work together to a predictable end. It's a simple system: We know when a Camry is working and when it isn't. Five Toyota mechanics would agree on how to fix it, and they'd do so in prescribed, tried-and-true ways.

A reductionist worldview sees every system like this. But some systems are more complicated. In these — the global economy, animal bodies, weather — interactions are unpredictable and hard to quantify. These form a whole that's different from the sum of its parts. And when these complex systems develop problems, they're difficult to diagnose, let alone solve.

The food system is complicated. Its components are myriad and their interactions multifaceted. And it's in rough shape: It's developed into a profit machine that ignores the way its components interact and depend on one another. It's not fair, resilient, or sustainable. It doesn't even do a good job at what should be its primary purpose: providing nourishment. (In reality, the current food system's primary purpose is to profit its owners.)

The food system needs work, and there's no user manual.

Determining the way forward is a team effort, one that must be guided by those whose voices have been discounted: women, people of color, and the formerly colonized, among others. This is true of not just food. A survivable society must be cooperative, with goals of equality, justice, and judicious treatment of the earth.

Bold vision is critical, because changing complicated systems requires constant adjustment. You can't go from broken to fixed in a day, as you can with a car's brakes. You have to progress without knowing what the journey will look like. "We want a fair and sustainable food system" is a fine statement to make, and quite likely one with which most people would agree, just as most agree that people should have equal access to necessities and opportunity for lives without undue suffering. But charting a single path to that end is impossible: It will happen in small steps.

And there will be setbacks, each of which will require adjustment and reinvention. Yet we have to start now. The climate and COVID-19 crises demonstrate that we should have started at least twenty years ago.

Unchecked, the rulers of all big industries will extract wealth, at great cost to nature and to most humans. To the best of their abilities, they will fight for the "right" to ignore these costs, usually by buying politicians, fighting corrective policies, paying little or no heed to those that do exist, and absorbing any costs that their behavior does create, as long as that behavior remains profitable.

Capitalism depends on everlasting economic growth, which is impossible according to both science and common sense. That growth is measured by GDP, which includes all money spent on goods and services. By these standards, war is an asset, because it stimulates production; clear-cutting a forest for farmland creates jobs and goods; growing corn and soy to produce sellable junk, and even the healthcare costs resulting from that—all represent "growth." The costs of this growth are then charged against the health and well-being of the majority of humans, and of the planet itself. Thus "growth" and GDP are terrible measures of well-being.

Agriculture is a subset. Its current masters want "growth," and to get that, they'd like us to worry over the need to "feed ten billion" — the presumed population of the earth in 2050. They want to keep us focused on higher yields at any cost, but this is nothing more than a magician's misdirection ("Look over here!") when the real action is elsewhere.

There is already enough food (and enough of virtually every other crucial resource) for all humans to live well, and without ravaging the planet. To let desperation and myths of scarcity guide our vision is to fall into industry's hands. Better to prioritize food security for all and intelligently use the abundance that already exists. Our greatest challenges are to do so with less harm to people and to the environment, to ensure that riches and power and privilege are distributed equitably, and to be guided by morality.

It's corny to say the earth will provide, but it's true. What might be called the peasant food system feeds seventy percent of the world's population with just twenty-five percent of its agricultural resources. Industrial agriculture uses the other seventy-five percent to produce food that reaches fewer than a third of the world's people, in part because half of what's produced by Big Ag isn't even meant to feed humans.

Ignored by state-funded research, fought by global finance, discouraged by most rulers, peasant farming remains more efficient than industrial farming. Were it given the kind of support that's been lent to industry-backed farming — research, subsidies, cheap or free land, and such — it could become better still. Instead, those resources are siphoned away from the people who could build a real food system and instead used to ensure profits for industrial agriculture.

Some insist that technological innovation will pave the path, that tweaking and improving the current system will save it. And undoubtedly innovation will be useful in building a sustainable system: creating meat without animals, or biofuels without corn or other living plant matter, increasing plants' photosynthesis, even using genetic engineering wisely, to increase crops' nutrition or ability to fix nitrogen, or employing various forms of "precision agriculture" that minimize water and chemicals.

But technology won't fix the fundamentally flawed relationship between food, people, and planet. It won't give more people control over their own food, and in almost every case it is legally bound to put profit before true progress, regardless of costs. Because despite the "disruption" rhetoric, most technocrats believe that the system is fundamentally sound; even those who claim to be working for sustainability are usually greenwashing. And remember: Technological innovations in agriculture are a part of what got us into this mess in the first place.

Technology is agnostic. Like science in general, when it's used in the interests of a broad community, it can work wonders. When it's used as a profit machine, it can have side effects that are both good and bad. When a pesticide is shown to be harmful, for example, the technocrat's solution is not to figure out how to farm without chemicals but to create a "better" pesticide.

The current version of the fake meat "solution" is another example. Although vegan burgers laudably offer an alternative to meat, one that's produced without animal suffering, they are still an ultra-processed food, and as such they fail to address monoculture, chemicals, extraction, and exploitation. Nor will they "replace" industrially produced meat (whose sales have not fallen at all since fake meat became popular) but rather simply wedge themselves into supermarket space. (They'll more likely replace Tofurky.) True progress means addressing those underlying issues.

Similarly, when soda is reverse-engineered to make it less harmful, when candy bars or similarly un-nutritious "granola" bars are pumped up with fiber or other nutrients, when corn is grown to produce "sustainable" energy, these do little to benefit eaters or farmers.

Industry's favorite "solution" puts the onus on eaters to change our behaviors. Admonitions to "get up and move" or even to "eat a wide variety of foods" aren't *wrong*, but unless they're accompanied by changes in supply and policy, they'll do little to challenge the status quo.

It's obvious that a sensible and nutritious diet is essential, as is exercise. But stacked against the ubiquity and dominance of UPFs, the battle is lost before it begins, and adding a dose of guilt to toxic diets doesn't help. "Change what you eat and farming will follow" also falls short of the truth. Of course eating well is important, but the ability to do so is far from universal.

It's often true that production determines consumption, and nowhere is this more obvious than in food: Produce whole-grain bread instead of Wonder Bread, offer rice and beans instead of Lunchables, and eaters will be healthier and medical costs go down.

Food production has long been subsidized. In the Western Hemisphere, it began with Europeans' violent seizure of land from its original inhabitants and the granting of that land to white males. Today, government subsidizes a destructive form of production that produces a harmful form of food and forces it into markets everywhere.

It may well be that food is always subsidized, and that's okay. Food—even more than highways, healthcare, the military, railroads, airlines, banks, the electrical grid—is a critical need. We can spend our common money to support destructive industrial agriculture or to establish more farms run by people who want to grow real food that will then dominate production and distribution. This is what society is "for."

When behavior change is driven by sound and ethical policy, we see progress. We've normalized seat-belt use and reduced smoking, for example, we've sparked behavior change with taxes and regulation and education, we've crippled the marketing campaigns of some things that harm people, *and* we've made more available the things that heal them. As described in the last chapter, if you tax soda and make free water available everywhere, people drink less soda and more water. Health will improve, and the initiatives will pay for themselves. This is a simple beginning.

Innovation from industry is not going to fix food and diet, and neither is "buying right." Both are patches on a tire with no tread. The system itself needs to be changed, its values and goals challenged and reimagined. We need legislation to support agriculture that stewards the land. We need food processing whose goal is to nourish. And we need an economy that supports people who want to grow and cook food for their communities. Those will come about when citizens organize and force government to do its job. A good diet will follow.

Change is inevitable, and may be sudden, even catastrophic. COVID-19, the Great Recession of 2008 and after, and the tsunami of 2004 are all recent and notable examples. Each has been an opportunity for humans to enact our own forms of change. As Naomi Klein revealed in *The Shock Doctrine*, corporations and allied governments often use disasters as opportunities to consolidate power and profits. But Klein also talks, as does Rebecca Solnit, about solidarity and generosity among people, even when policies don't change for the better. These moments offer chances to positively transform society.

COVID-19 demonstrated that austerity budgets are a convenient mask and scare tactic to perpetuate greed, and easily disregarded; a two-trillion-dollar aid package was swiftly enacted with bipartisan support, and more aid followed. Two trillion dollars is more than three times the military budget, which is already enough to establish and nurture, for example, ten million new farmers—around enough to supply all Americans with real food.

Flawed as the initial COVID bailout was, it showed that when circumstances necessitate action, we can achieve what once seemed impossible. Reforms years and even decades in the making unexpectedly became "sensible" within a month of the pandemic, and without much fanfare. And for some who needed it, there was free food, free childcare, free housing, free transit, mortgage and debt relief, a freeze on utility shutoffs. There were more bike lanes and pedestrian areas, fewer arrests and prosecutions, freedom for prisoners, a crude form of guaranteed minimum income, and even a slight "suspension of capitalism," the likes of which had not been seen since World War II. Little of this was official national policy, none of it was heralded as lasting change, and, as always, many of the people who needed help most were ignored—so let's not get carried away. But even with Donald Trump, an uncooperative (to say the least!) "leader," many people recognized for the first time that there was a common good, and that no one should have their well-being tethered to producing profit for someone else. (Surveys in 2020 found that a majority of people favored prioritizing health and well-being over "the economy.")

There is a difference, though, between a new form of anarchy and a good new set of rules. Alternatives are clear, but hardly guaranteed. They were clear in 2008 also, and business as usual returned quickly. Though I suppose one could always say this, we may be at a tipping point. Let's hope so.

It shouldn't take a crisis to spark needed change, but since that's often the way things happen, perhaps we should revisit the term "crisis." In the words of teenage climate activist Greta Thunberg, "We cannot solve an emergency without treating it like an emergency."

COVID-19 showed once again that human action to cope with a crisis can be swift. But more often, intentional change is steady and incremental. Each step forward determines the next. The civil rights struggles of the fifties and sixties led to Black Power and the Black Lives Matter movement. "Don't ask, don't tell" was a step on the path to ending same-sex restrictions on marriage. Organizing to recognize the horrible impact of AIDS spurred treatment. The voting rights struggle began in the nineteenth century.

Ecology teaches us that everything is interconnected, and that as each part improves, so does the whole. Even our bodies are complex systems of trillions of microbes and cells, which do best when they interact with one another and the world at large. Yes, humans are special. So, as we are discovering with each passing study on the subject, are other animals, and it's increasingly uninformed and unacceptable to consider other animals inferior:

they're simply different. When we realize that we are less individual and more a part of air, water, tree, universe, life, in communication with other living things, we can become healthier participants in our environment.

We are not entirely driven by instinct, like other animals; we risk failure and make our own decisions, and cooperation, equality, and altruism are parts of our true selves. Like bees, we can each act as a unit for our common benefit.

Fair treatment for those who've historically been exploited or brutalized is a case of a rising tide actually lifting all boats. Martin Luther King Jr. understood this when he said, "The black revolution is much more than a struggle for the rights of Negroes. It is, rather, forcing America to face all its interrelated flaws: racism, poverty, militarism, and materialism."

Dominant culture would have us believe that a better system is impossible to achieve. But, to paraphrase Ursula Le Guin, the divine right of kings was once considered permanent. To say, as Margaret Thatcher famously did, that "there is no alternative" to unbridled corporatism is to say that the only way to sustain humanity is to destroy it.

The delusion is not that change is possible, but that it's avoidable. The choice is not to change our way of life or simply muddle along as we always have. The choice is to change the system or suffer catastrophe.

As individuals, we have little power. But as a collective, only nature is stronger. We are now in the Anthropocene: the era in which humans have changed the face of the earth and will determine its future. It's up to us to use that control for good, and ignorance is no longer an excuse: We know our strength, and we know the consequences of using it unwisely.

We may create leaders with the vision needed to stand with communities behind significant, positive change. But change doesn't start with a savior's rise to power; it starts with the strength of people uniting around common goals. Barack Obama was elected because most people wanted change and justice, but as a change agent he was ineffectual, because he was not pushed by a movement. The source of change is the people who organize locally, nationally, and internationally through protesting, voting, door-to-door outreach, "speechifying," and coalition building.

We must create pressure on the defenders of the status quo. In food, this means picketing and boycotting fast-food chains that refuse to adopt fair labor standards or protections against sexual harassment, and supporting meatpacking workers hoping to unionize, and joining class action lawsuits to protect the environment from CAFOs, and boosting student strikes to divest universities from Big Food, and working for the universal right to good food.

What incremental change can we make this week, month, or year to move us in the direction of a just food system? And what would a move in the right direction even look like? The answers are nuanced and complex, because it's all interconnected and every action has consequences. Paying farmworkers fairly, for example, would raise the price of real food, which would reverberate through the food system, the healthcare system, the international economy, and the environment.

That's not, of course, a reason not to pay farmworkers fairly. It's a reason to see necessary change as comprehensive, to examine change and see what flaws it exposes that must be addressed quickly.

Lasting change to our food system requires a two-pronged approach. Personal-level change is important wherever possible, for our own health and sanity, to support others doing good work, and even as an example. That may mean joining a CSA that supports small-scale, agroecological farming, or changing our eating habits, or joining or forming a community garden, or supporting initiatives that improve the wages, working conditions, and rights of food and farm workers. These can be done by many of us today and, given the privilege that allows some of us to do them, might be viewed as obligations.

At the same time, we need change on the macro level, change that starts by recognizing that access to healthy food is a basic and universal human right, and that the planet's well-being takes precedence over corporate profits. Thinking hard about these things, embracing radical ideas we'd never considered, begins to change culture. One change will lead to another.

You may ask, "What can I do now?" In addition to the ideas above, I'd recommend supporting the Green New Deal.

Few of us were alive during the Roosevelt-era New Deal, but we all live with its impact. Despite shortcomings, its achievements were notable: increased employment, support for unionizing, benefits for workers and even the unemployed, social security, environmental defense and repair, and public works, including bringing electricity to rural areas and building hundreds of airports, tens of thousands of bridges, and hundreds of thousands of miles of roads.

The Green New Deal could have even greater impact. With carbon neutrality as a starting goal, it would necessarily support renewable energy generation and sustainable agriculture. It could also include guaranteed employment for those who can work and guaranteed income for everyone; an end to homelessness; universal healthcare; access to land for new farmers, especially those of color; the rewilding and rehabilitating of natural areas; and more.

Ideally, the Green New Deal would be global and equitable, with rich countries paying more and investing in poorer ones while guaranteeing their autonomy. Now is the time to put to rest the myth of American exceptionalism, to convert global competition to global cooperation.

Only by changing the entire power and economic structure (see Naomi Klein's *This Changes Everything*) can we stop poisoning the environment. Similarly, instituting fairness in race and gender means in part undoing land theft, racial and gender-based violence, and centuries of wealth accumulation by mostly European and European American males, wealth accumulation that is still being compounded. This means land reform, this means affordable nutritious food regardless of the ability to pay . . . this means wholesale change.

It's our job to push the government to deal with threats to our collective well-being, from corporate immoralism to climate change to chronic disease. But just when we need it most, government has been largely dismantled. And what's left is impotent at best, malicious at worst.

To quote the philosopher Max Roser: "Three things are true at the same time. The world is much better; the world is awful; and the world can be much better." There is plenty of good work to do.

We must choose how to respond to crisis. We can choose denial ("There is no crisis . . .") or hopelessness ("There's no way to stop it . . ."). Or we can choose the best reaction: action. Redeeming this disaster of a global food system will be a challenging and painstaking journey, but doing it gives us the opportunity to remake our society in an image that comes closer to its rhetoric.

Thankfully, we don't need to know how to get to the end of this road to embark on it. We can be thoughtful and thorough, and choose reason and justice over greed and fear. We can build stronger, saner systems that benefit the many, not the few, and communities all players have a part in building. We can consistently choose peace and cooperation over strife. Changing all of this is within our control and power.

We are all eaters. Providing the food we need to sustain ourselves and flourish is the single most fundamental and important human occupation. How we do it defines our present and determines our future.

Afterword

I PUT THE FINISHING touches on *Animal, Vegetable, Junk* in the fall of 2020—not all that long ago. Food-wise, little has changed. Nor has any of the history, my understanding of that history, the present, or what I believe should happen in the future.

What's changed is that after well over a year of talking publicly about little other than *Animal Vegetable Junk* (I'm calling it *AVJ* from here on), I can present its core message succinctly. It centers around a broad definition of food, and in particular *good* food. Perhaps, even after reading this book—which I hope you have, or will—you'll find these few paragraphs of interest.

We all think about food all the time, yet it's something most of us never think about seriously—and that's a problem. Because there are three things about food that need to be considered carefully:

The first is that our food system has either spurred or contributed to a dreadful state of affairs in public health, the environment, labor, the state of the land, and more. It should be easy to convince people of that, and yet—like climate change—it's the kind of slow-moving emergency that is easy for politicians to ignore, especially when those who benefit from it (fossil fuel companies, Big Pharma, Big Ag, and so on) work so hard to maintain the status quo.

The second is that we need to examine the term "good food" and define it so that it actually means something. It's not sufficient to define good food as "that which tastes good" or even "that which is nutritious." There is more to it than that, and if we attended to a meaningful definition, the first and third items on this list would be better addressed.

Here's my definition:

> Good food should benefit everyone who produces it, everyone who works with it, and everyone who eats it. It must be fair and just in the areas of farming, labor, and the environment; it must be nutritious; and everyone should be able to find and afford it.

The third thing about food to consider is how to guarantee that good food is available to everyone? That's one of the great earth- and people-saving challenges of the twenty-first century, and if we meet it, we will create a healthier and more just world. Nothing — *nothing* — is more important. Changing our food system changes everything.

Some caveats: In a country and a world that seems incapable of dealing with its biggest problems — climate change comes to mind immediately — it's difficult to be optimistic; it can even be difficult to avoid despair. But we *can* be hopeful and do the exciting, hard work that will result in visible progress, which will in turn generate optimism. We need action; we must work.

You might say — as some people do — that if each of us simply begins to eat differently, the food system will change. There is truth in that. And of course our individual diet matters, although mostly to us individually. But some people have more control over their diet than others, so this is a limited menu for change.

The bigger truth is that the entire food system must change in order for all of us to eat differently. The food supply — the way food is planned, grown, processed, distributed, and offered to us — is *the* great determinant of what we eat. Individual choices can only get us so far; the best way to enable all of us to eat better is to make changes to the system.

These are among the core mandates of *AVJ*: I want to convince you that the food system is a problem, define what good food is, and propose a way to get that good food to more people.

Most food is not "good." More than half the calories consumed in the United States come from ultra-processed food, and that junk goes a long way toward explaining our skyrocketing rates of chronic disease and shortening lifespans. Food should be something that nourishes. But the majority of calories we eat are closer to what the dictionary calls poison—something that causes harm or ill health—than they are to food. Our diet also plays a large role in the climate crisis and other environmental damage, like deforestation and carcinogenic landscapes.

If it's odd to think of food as a destructive force, imagine a scenario like this: Alien invaders (from another planet or another country) turn our food into a disease-causing vehicle, tripling our rates of chronic disease and shortening our lifespans. Imagine them stripping our land of nutrients and wasting our valuable farmland by growing things that are unnecessary, even damaging. Imagine them spraying and spewing cancer-causing chemicals into the air and water; torturing our land animals and vacuuming the fish right out of the sea; ruthlessly exploiting our most vulnerable workers; and manipulating our children into craving foods that are actually anti-nutritious. Through all of this, they kill more than a million people a year, far more than COVID-19, but much more quietly.

We would attack that situation as fast and hard as we could, even if it meant declaring war.

Yet here in the real world we allow this assault, because it's developed so slowly and insidiously that we've become acclimated, and because not only have we been trained to worship at the altar of high yields, but also because most of us can buy a tomato or a cheeseburger within five minutes of where we're sitting. For this convenience, we tolerate illness, cruelty, unfairness, and environmental destruction.

We ignore the true costs of this food system, which is not set up—as you imagine it should be—to nourish the maximum number of people it can as well as it can.

By my definition, good food has four pillars.

1. It starts with farming. American farm policy subsidizes the production of food that's destructive—monocultures of

commodity crops — rather than health-giving. Eliminating these subsidies and using them instead to support truly
sustainable farming that produces real food would be a profound change. Responsible subsidies would encourage farmers to care for the land, steward it for future generations,
and grow food that will nourish more people.

2. The second pillar is labor. Many if not most of the worst-
paying jobs in the United States are food related. Food
workers include the farmworkers you see stooped in fields
as you whiz by, the overworked and bathroom-deprived
slaughterhouse workers, the masked people on bikes bringing delicious food to your door in miserable weather, the obviously unhappy fast-food worker, the harried server at your
local restaurant. These people are often immigrants, people
of color, and/or women — the all-too-commonly disempow-
ered.

These are the people who make it possible for us to eat.
To treat them right, we must make the minimum wage a living wage, and make sure that these most valuable workers
have access to health care, childcare, and higher education as
well.

3. Nutrition is the third pillar. The connection between ultra-
processed foods and illness is well established: We should
all strive to eat little or no junk food (which is best thought
of as the tobacco of the twenty-first century), to reduce our
consumption of animal products (for environmental and ethical as well as health reasons), and to eat as many plants as
possible in as close to their natural form as possible.

Yet we continue to allow our children to be targeted by
marketers of junk, purveyors of poison. The first steps to
remedy this are to improve school lunches, constrain the
ability of marketers to sell junk to four-year-olds, and teach
our own children the truth about food.

4. Some people can afford to change their diets (and their kids')
to eat food that meets the three requirements above — some
cannot. And that brings us to the fourth pillar of good food:
access and affordability. The U.S. food system makes un-

healthy calories ubiquitous and cheap, while healthier foods
are less common and more expensive.

Thus the nation's poorest people have the most difficulty
changing their diets for the better, and they suffer the consequences; most people who don't eat well have no other
choice. Fixing that means making access to good food universal, shifting federal dollars from supporting the production of sugar and beef to foods that support health. I will
repeat: We have been subsidizing unhealthy, destructive, exploitative, extractive food and farming since the nineteenth
century; we can re-create the system so that it subsidizes
what I'm defining as good food. We need good farming to
support good diets; it's all tied together.

In short, good food prioritizes human well-being over agricultural yield and corporate profit. You can't have good food without
having fairness and justice baked in.

And all of this makes it clear that good food is, if not rare, then
hardly the default.

Why is this? Why wouldn't we want to protect the land and
distribute it fairly, feed ourselves well, and reward the people who
enable us to do that?

The answer is as clear as it is under-discussed: Although it's
possible to meet all these requirements, it's *im*possible to do so
profitably within the current system. And since that system — we
can call it capitalism — prioritizes profit, businesses survive by
systematically shortchanging producers, the environment, workers, even customers.

To make good food as I've defined it available to all, we must insist that long-term well-being for *all* of us is more important than
riches for a very few. Long-term well-being is more practical and
more sustainable not only for the planet but for our species and
even for our individual selves.

Achieving this may sound like a pipe dream, but change is inevitable. Our job, as humans, as citizens, is to try to guide that
change in the right direction. Rather than taking a rotten food
system as a given, we must fight for one that works for all of us.

Aside from the measures I've already mentioned, there are some specific and achievable first steps: Eliminating the routine use of antibiotics in factory farms; making animal production transparent and ethical; regulating pesticides so they don't poison humans or other nontargeted species; limiting the marketing of junk food to kids; and putting land into the hands of people who have been previously shut out but who will farm it well. There are many other steps we can take, but these few would make a fine start. (All of this is presented in detail in the last part of *AVJ*, of course.)

Much of this will require government involvement, the thought of which causes some people to bristle. But food — even more than roads and airlines, the military, education, banks, or the electrical grid — is a critical need, so it's likely the government will *always* be involved in one way or another. We spend our common money on those things to make them work for us, and we must spend it to support the production and distribution of good food as I've defined it. This is what society is for.

Some will scoff, and say that a system that supports good food, health, well-being, and the environment, is impossible to achieve. But remember this: Once, the divine right of kings was considered permanent. Once, the British and others believed they had a right to dominate the rest of the world. Once, resources were thought to be inexhaustible. Once, individual gas-powered vehicles for all was a great idea.

We've changed those things and our thinking about them, and now we must change the system — the food system as well as the bigger system that contains it — or suffer catastrophe.

Creating a just and fair global food system will give us the opportunity to remake our society in an image that comes closer to its rhetoric. We can build stronger, saner systems that benefit the many, not the few, and communities that all players have a part in building. It's within our power.

One more thing: Since I wrote *AVJ*, it's become more clear than ever that the leaders of this movement, the people who understand these solutions best, are not — not to put too fine a point on it — old white men. As an old white man myself, it's hard for me to say something as facile as "these are the enemy." But the world created by previous generations—by white, mostly European, mostly men—is a world that needs to change, and the leaders in this change are women, people of color, and non-Europeans. This is true in every aspect of the movement for good food and indeed the movements for a better world.

We are all eaters. Providing the food we need to sustain ourselves and flourish is the most basic and important human occupation. How we do it defines our present and determines our future.

Please join me on markbittman.com, bittmanproject.com, and my podcast, *Food with Mark Bittman*, to be a part of this discussion as it evolves.

Peace and justice,

PHILIPSTOWN, NEW YORK
NOVEMBER 2021

Acknowledgments

In 1983, my late friend Gene Cooney said to me, "At some point you just gotta put a '30' on it," a "30" being old-style journalism talk for the end of a story. *Animal, Vegetable, Junk* is evolving, but the deadline is here. This means both relief and frustration for me, because, not for the first time, I'm recognizing how quickly things change, and how a story like this one is no more than an attempt to catch a moment in time, to define the past and the present, as "the present" becomes the past. So it goes.

My awareness of "justice" began in 1960, with a recognition of the cruelty of capital punishment, and continued with an introduction to the civil rights movement and its heroes and, later, the anti-war, Black Power, and women's movements. I came to environmental justice late, and didn't really understand the role of food and agriculture until even later.

Still, this book is a landmark in a long journey, with many people to thank. On the personal side, there are Jim Cohen, Mitch Orfuss, Mark Roth, Ken Heisler, Fred Zolna, Etta Milbauer Rosen, David Vogelstein, Madeleine Julie Meacham, Karen Baar, Ellen Furstenberg, Bruce Cohn, J. W. Bancroft, David Paskin, Pamela Hort, Allan Gummerson, John Willoughby, Trish Hall, Andrea Graziosi, Bob Spitz, Alisa X. Smith, Charlie Pinsky, Serene Jones, John Lanchester, Kelly Doe, Josh Horwitz, and Sinan Antoon. The late Roy Sweetgall, Charles Richard Christopher Fitzgerald III, Felix Berenberg, Sherry Slade, Phil Maniaci, Jill Goldstein, and Josh Lipton. Alive or dead, all of these people helped me begin to learn how to think.

In my journalism career (many of these people are friends as well): Andy Houlding, John Schwing, Louise Kennedy, Linda Giuca, Chris Kimball, Pam Hoenig, Rick Berke, Bill Keller, Sam Sifton, Rick Flaste, Andy Rosenthal, Chris Conway, George Kalogerakis, Sewell Chan, Nick Kristof, Charles Blow, Gail Collins, Gerry Marzorati, Hugo Lindgren, and a slew of other editors and colleagues at various newspapers and magazines, some of whom I've no doubt forgotten. I'll use this sentence to remember Michael Hawley, a special and supremely supportive friend.

Dozens of people answered my requests for help with this book, including, especially, Steve Brescia, Vijay Thallam, Jahi Chappell, Malik Yakini, Leah Penniman, Navina Khanna, and Chellie Pingree. Some supported me professionally in other ways in recent years, especially Julie Kornfeld, Michael Sparer, Linda Fried, Ann Thrupp, Mirella Blum, and Nina Ichikawa. Eric Schlosser, Michael Pollan, Alice Waters, Marion Nestle, Raj Patel, and David Katz I'm happy to count as both inspirations and friends; without their work, I'd be lost. Thanks, too, to those who've been and are there for me — I'm thinking of Kerri Conan, Daniel Meyer, Angela Miller, Danielle Svetcov, and Melissa McCart.

Five institutions nourished me during this phase. Both the Mesa Refuge and the Bellagio Center provided me with solitude and like-minded companionship when I needed it most. The Union of Concerned Scientists gave me reason and inspiration to take this subject seriously. Columbia Mailman School of Public Health offered me a home and both freedom and responsibility, which contributed mightily to my ability to finish this book. And, of course, my longtime publisher Houghton Mifflin Harcourt demonstrated early on that they believed in it, and me; thank you, Bruce Nichols, Stephanie Fletcher, and Deb Brody.

About Ricardo Salvador, my brother from another family and the should-be secretary of agriculture, not enough can be said; he's forgotten more than I know, unfortunately for both of us. Charlie Mitchell, who began helping me with *Animal, Vegetable,*

Junk when he was still in college, has been invaluable in ways only he and I know, and has a bright and wonderful future of which I hope to be a part.

My daughters, Kate and Emma, have been and will be a big part of the work of this book and, more important, have never stopped loving me and allowing me to love them. Nick and Jeffrey, too, know how much I care about them.

And to my partner, Kathleen, all I can say is "Onward, together!"

Notes

1. The Food-Brain Feedback Loop

5 *We're hardwired to eat:* Andrew D. Higginson, John M. McNamara, and Alasdair I. Houston, "Fatness and Fitness: Exposing the Logic of Evolutionary Explanations for Obesity," *Proceedings of the Royal Society of Biology*, January 13, 2016, https://doi.org/10.1098/rspb.2015.2443.

7 *1.8 million years ago:* Richard Wrangham, *Catching Fire: How Cooking Made Us Human* (New York: Basic Books, 2009).

8 *"challenged by the Agta":* Colin G. Scanes, "Hunter-Gatherers," in *Animals and Human Society*, ed. Colin G. Scanes and Samia R. Toukhsati (Cambridge: Academic Press, 2018), 65–82.

"Ice Age females": Linda R. Owen, *Distorting the Past: Gender and the Division of Labor in the European Upper Paleolithic* (Tübingen, Germany: Kerns Verlag, 2005).

12 *"all departments of human life":* V Gordon Childe, *Man Makes Himself* (London: Watts & Co., 1936).

17 *"the worst mistake":* Jared Diamond, "The Worst Mistake in the History of the Human Race," *Discover*, May 1987.

"history's biggest fraud": Yuval Noah Harari, *Sapiens: A Brief History of Humankind* (New York: Harper, 2011).

2. Soil and Civilization

21 *"partnership of land and farmer":* Walter Clay Lowdermilk, *Conquest of the Land Through Seven Thousand Years* (Washington, DC: Natural Resource Conservation Service, 1953).

22 *writes David Montgomery:* David R. Montgomery, *Dirt: The Erosion of Civilizations* (Berkeley: University of California Press, 2007).

25 *"The Farmer's Instructions":* "The Farmer's Instructions: Translation," Electronic Text Corpus of Sumerian Literature, last modified July 9, 2001, http://etcsl.orinst.ox.ac.uk/section5/tr563.htm.

29 *"strong, patient, persevering, thoughtful":* Franklin Hiram King, *Farmers of Forty Centuries* (Madison, WI: Mrs. F. H. King, 1911), https://ia800202.us.archive.org/30/items/farmersoffortyce00king _0/farmersoffortyce00king_0.pdf.

32 *"Mayan civilization unraveled":* Montgomery, *Dirt.*

33 *"Should one call the arrival":* Fernand Braudel, *Memory and the Mediterranean,* trans. Siân Reynolds (New York; Vintage, 2001).
economist Ester Boserup: Ester Boserup, *The Conditions of Agricultural Growth: The Economics of Agrarian Change Under Population Pressure* (Venice, Italy: Aldine Press, 1965).

34 *more time inside:* Ester Boserup, *Woman's Role in Economic Development* (London: George Allen and Unwin, 1970).
"patriarchal norms and beliefs": Casper Worm Hansen et al., "Modern Gender Roles and Agricultural History: The Neolithic Inheritance," *Journal of Economic Growth,* August 2015.

3. Agriculture Goes Global

38 *"a privileged country":* Fernand Braudel, *The Structures of Everyday Life,* trans. Siân Reynolds (London and New York: Collins and Harper & Row, 1981).

39 *entire budgets on food:* Carlo M. Cipolla, *Before the Industrial Revolution: European Society and Economy, 1000–1700,* 3rd ed. (New York: Norton, 1994).
"more peasant autonomy": Raj Patel and Jason W. Moore, *A History of the World in Seven Cheap Things: A Guide to Capitalism, Nature, and the Future of the Planet* (Berkeley: University of California Press, 2017).

40 *closure of the commons:* Ellen Meiksins Wood, *The Origin of Capitalism* (New York: Monthly Review Press, 1999).

41 *"whole villages were wiped out":* Slicher van Bath, *The Agrarian History of Western Europe, A.D. 500–1850,* trans. Olive Cornish (New York: St. Martin's Press, 1963).
"devours the soil": Fernand Braudel, *The Structures of Everyday*

Life, trans. Siân Reynolds (London and New York: Collins and Harper & Row, 1981).

42 *kept goods costly:* Patel and Moore, *Seven Cheap Things.*

43 *"slave labor was increasingly used":* J. H. Galloway, *The Sugar Cane Industry: An Historical Geography from Its Origins to 1914* (Cambridge: Cambridge University Press, 1987).
   beginning of industrialization: Patel and Moore, *Seven Cheap Things.*

44 *"wing of the state":* Sidney Mintz, *Sweetness and Power: The Place of Sugar in Modern History* (New York: Viking Press, 1985).

49 *white male supremacy:* Patel and Moore, *Seven Cheap Things.*
   "corrosive separation": Naomi Klein, *This Changes Everything: Capitalism vs. the Climate* (New York: Simon and Schuster, 2015).

4. Creating Famine

53 *impoverished Irish sharecroppers:* Christine Kinealy, *The Great Irish Famine: Impact, Ideology, and Rebellion* (London: MacMillan Education UK, 2001), 105.

57 *public works programs:* Kathryn Edgarton-Tarpley, "Tough Choices: Grappling with Famine in Qing China, the British Empire, and Beyond," *Journal of World History* 24, no. 1 (2013).
   paid for piecework: Nick Wilson, "Political Ecology and the Potato Famine: A Critical Response to Mike Davis' *Late Victorian Holocausts*," *Janus*, accessed June 22, 2020, http://www.janus.umd.edu/completed2002/Nicks/01.html.

58 *"'wise and all-merciful Providence'":* James Vernon, *Hunger: A Modern History* (Cambridge, MA: Harvard University Press, 2007).
   soup kitchens: Mike Davis, *Late Victorian Holocausts: El Niño Famines and the Making of the Third World* (New York: Verso, 2002).
   a million more had emigrated: Davis, *Late Victorian Holocausts.*
   twenty percent of the global GDP: Davis, *Late Victorian Holocausts.*
   China and India had halved: Davis, *Late Victorian Holocausts.*

59 *to those in need "ungrudgingly":* Davis, *Late Victorian Holocausts.*
   global manufacturing market: Davis, *Late Victorian Holocausts,* 294.
   higher standards of living: Davis, *Late Victorian Holocausts,* 292.
   three percent by 1880: Davis, *Late Victorian Holocausts,* 294.
   thirty per century: Davis, *Late Victorian Holocausts,* 287.

60 *second-largest producer of raw cotton:* D. B. Grigg, *Agricultural Systems of the World: An Evolutionary Approach* (Cambridge: Cambridge University Press, 1974).

Britain resumed purchasing: Frenise A. Logan, "India's Loss of the British Cotton Market after 1865," *Southern History* 31, no. 1 (February 1965), https://www.jstor.org/stable/2205009.

more than five million: Davis, *Late Victorian Holocausts*, 7.

61 *"'the fault of the weapon'":* Kathryn Edgarton-Tarpley, "From 'Nourish the People' to 'Sacrifice for the Nation': Changing Responses to Disaster in Late Imperial and Modern China," *Journal of Asian Studies* 73, no. 2 (May 2014), 447–69.

"slippery slope of imperial decline": David Arnold, *Famine: Social Crisis and Historical Change* (Oxford and New York: Blackwell, 1988).

62 *Chinese grain reserves:* Edgarton-Tarpley, "Tough Choices."

"shift grain massively": Davis, *Late Victorian Holocausts*.

63 *no shortage of food:* Andrew C. Revkin, "Study Finds Pattern of Severe Droughts in Africa," *New York Times*, April 16, 2009, https://www.nytimes.com/2009/04/17/science/earth/17drought.html.

more and more peanuts: Arnold, *Famine*.

"'idleness', 'apathy,' and 'fatalism'": Arnold, *Famine*.

64 *"bleak faces of malnutrition":* Evaggelos Vallianatos, "Why Is Africa Falling Apart?" *Truthout*, November 9, 2011, https://truthout.org/articles/why-is-africa-falling-apart/.

65 *thirty million bison:* Maureen Ogle, *In Meat We Trust: An Unexpected History of Carnivore America* (Boston: Houghton Mifflin Harcourt, 2013).

just over a thousand: William T. Hornaday, "The Extermination of the American Bison," Project Gutenberg, February 10, 2006, 525, https://www.gutenberg.org/files/17748/17748-h/17748-h.htm.

billions of passenger pigeons: Joseph Stromberg, "100 Years Ago, the Very Last Passenger Pigeon Died," *Vox*, September 1, 2014, https://www.vox.com/2014/9/1/6079675/passenger-pigeon-extinction.

5. The American Way of Farming

70 *green manure and crop rotation:* Marcel Mazoyer and Laurence Roudart, *A History of World Agriculture: From the Neolithic Age to the Current Crisis* (New York: Monthly Review Press, 2006.)

71 *logic of reductionism:* Raj Patel and Jason W. Moore, *A History*

of the World in Seven Cheap Things: A Guide to Capitalism, Nature, and the Future of the Planet (Berkeley: University of California Press, 2017).

but not consciousness: Rupert Shortt, "Idle Components: An Argument Against Richard Dawkins," *Times Literary Supplement,* December 13, 2019, https://www.the-tls.co.uk/articles/idle-components/.

72 *remains of soldiers:* Charles C. Mann, *1493: Uncovering the New World Columbus Created* (New York: Knopf, 2011).

ground bones of bison: William T. Hornaday, "The Extermination of the American Bison," Project Gutenberg, February 10, 2006, 525, https://www.gutenberg.org/files/17748/17748-h/17748-h.htm.

"a quarter of a mile away": Mann, *1493.*

burn plants' roots: Mann, *1493.*

Each household: Cara Giaimo, "When the Western World Ran on Guano," *Atlas Obscura,* October 14, 2015, https://www.atlasobscura .com/articles/when-the-western-world-ran-on-guano.

73 *British imports of guano:* Dave Hollett, *More Precious than Gold: The Story of the Peruvian Guano Trade* (Madison, NJ: Fairleigh Dickinson University Press, 2008), 109.

74 *"inexhaustible in its gifts":* John Bellamy Foster and Brett Clark, "The Robbery of Nature: Capitalism and the Metabolic Rift," *Monthly Review,* July 1, 2018.

"system of exhaustion": Foster and Clark, "Robbery of Nature."

76 *a pound of meat:* A Well-Fed World, "Feed-to-Meat-Conversion Inefficiency Ratios," October 25, 2015, https://awellfedworld.org/ feed-ratios/.

one animal to another: Vaclav Smil, *Feeding the World: A Challenge for the 21st Century* (Cambridge, MA: MIT Press, 2000), 149.

77 *produced more pork:* Maureen Ogle, *In Meat We Trust: An Unexpected History of Carnivore America* (Boston: Houghton Mifflin Harcourt, 2013).

animals roamed the streets: Liz Gray, "Porkopolis: Cincinnati's Pork-Producing Past," *Great American Country,* https://www.greatameri cancountry.com/places/local-life/porkopolis-cincinnatis -pork-producing-past.

78 *three million hogs and cattle a year:* Louise Carroll Wade, "Meatpacking," *Encyclopedia of Chicago,* http://www.encyclopedia .chicagohistory.org/pages/804.html.

New York's population: Ogle, *In Meat We Trust.*

"Hog Butcher for the World": Carroll Wade, "Meatpacking."

79 *Enslaved Africans were the foundation:* Edward E. Baptist, *The Half Has Never Been Told: Slavery and the Making of American Capitalism* (New York: Basic Books, 2014).

nakedly evil economic system: Matthew Desmond, "Capitalism," *New York Times Magazine,* August 14, 2019.

"It would revolt": Walter Johnson, *River of Dark Dreams: Slavery and Empire in the Cotton Kingdom* (Cambridge, MA: Harvard University Press, 2013), 13.

80 *"laws of nature":* Albert J. Beveridge, "Cuba and Congress," *North American Review* 172, no. 533 (April 1901), https://www.jstor.org/stable/25105151?seq=1#metadata_info_tab_contents.

take it by force: Maria Montoya, Laura A. Belmonte, Carl J. Guarneri, Steven Hackel, and Ellen Hartigan-O'Connor, *Global Americans: A History of the United States* (Boston: Cengage Learning, 2017), 348.

81 *Special Field Order No. 15:* "Newspaper Account of a Meeting Between Black Religious Leaders and Union Military Authorities," February 13, 1865, Freedmen and Southern Society Project, http://www.freedmen.umd.edu/savmtg.htm.

82 *resettlement by African Americans:* "General William T. Sherman's Special Field Order No. 15," *Blackpast,* https://www.blackpast.org/african-american-history/special-field-orders-no-15/.

years to get over: "Newspaper Account," Freedmen and Southern Society Project.

Johnson promptly overturned: Henry Louis Gates Jr., "The Truth Behind '40 Acres and a Mule,'" PBS, https://www.pbs.org/wnet/african-americans-many-rivers-to-cross/history/the-truth-behind-40-acres-and-a-mule/.

83 *self-named Exodusters:* Todd Arrington, "Exodusters," *National Park Service,* https://www.nps.gov/home/learn/historyculture/exodusters.htm.

84 *"To increase this surplus":* Isaac Newton, *Report of the Commissioner of Agriculture for the Year 1862* (Washington, DC: Government Printing Office, 1863).

"greatest market for food": Dan Morgan, *Merchants of Grain* (New York: Penguin, 1980), 73.

85 *exports more than tripled:* Brad Baurerly, *The Agrarian Seeds of Empire: The Political Economy of Agriculture in US State Building* (Chicago: Haymarket Books, 2018).

doubled, to 4.5 million: John Ikerd, "Corporatization of American

Agriculture," *Small Farm Today*, 2010, http://web.missouri.edu/~ik erdj/papers/SFT-Corporatization%20of%20Am%20Ag%20(7-10) .htm.

"invaders of our own country": Wendell Berry, *The Unsettling of America* (San Francisco: Sierra Club Books, 1977), 168.

6. The Farm as Factory

91 *there are five characteristics*: Deborah Fitzgerald, *Every Farm a Factory: The Industrial Ideal in American Agriculture* (New Haven, CT: Yale University Press, 2003).

92 *four hundred competitors*: Hiram M. Drache, "The Impact of John Deere's Plow," Illinois Periodicals Online, https://www.lib.niu.edu/ 2001/iht810102.html.

93 *a hundred bushels of corn*: "Power," Living History Farms, https:// www.lhf.org/learning-fields/power/.

as little as fifteen hours: "Historical Timeline—1930," Growing a Nation: The Story of American Agriculture, https://www .agclassroom.org/ganarchive/timeline/1930.htm.

287 million by the century's end: Bruce Kraig, *A Rich and Fertile Land: A History of Food in America* (London and Islington: Reaktion, 2017).

prone to starting fires: Diotima Booraem, "Steaming into the Future," *Smithsonian Magazine*, September 1998, https://www .smithsonianmag.com/science-nature/steaming-into-the-future -157045311/.

37,000 tractors: Reynold M. Wik, "Henry Ford's Tractors and American Agriculture," *Agricultural History* 38, no. 2 (April 1964).

Ford himself was convinced: Reynold Wik, *Henry Ford and Grass-roots America* (Ann Arbor: University of Michigan Regional Press, 1973).

"plow up the Australian Bush": Wik, *Henry Ford and Grass-roots America*.

tractor population: Willard Cochrane, *The Development of American Agriculture: A Historical Analysis* (Minneapolis: University of Minnesota Press, 1993).

94 *4.7 million tractors*: Cochrane, *Development of American Agriculture*.

"tractor power for animal power": Willard Cochrane, "Farm Prices: Myth and Reality," in *The Curse of American Agricultural Abundance: A Sustainable Solution* (Lincoln: University of Nebraska Press, 2003).

97 *University of Kansas scientists: The Dust Bowl*, directed by Ken Burns, aired 2012 on PBS.

98 *"Great Wheat Speech"*: William Crookes, "Address of the President Before the British Association for the Advancement of Science, Bristol, 1898," *Science*, October 28, 1898, 561–75.

99 *"supremely important munition"*: Crookes, "Address of the President."

100 *Haber's own family were killed*: Robin McKie, "From Fertiliser to Zyklon B: 100 Years of the Scientific Discovery That Brought Life and Death," *The Guardian*, November 2, 2013, https://www.theguardian.com/science/2013/nov/03/fritz-haber -fertiliser-ammonia-centenary.

101 *nineteen percent of the calories*: Avner Offer, *The First World War: An Agrarian Interpretation* (Oxford: Oxford University Press, 1991).

102 *total blockade on all international shipping*: Offer, *First World War*.
   half as much grain per capita: M. Hindhede, "The Effect of Food Restriction During War on Mortality in Copenhagen," *Journal of the American Medical Association*, February 7, 1920.
   "the last requirement": Hindhede, "Effect of Food Restriction."
   Denmark's mortality rate became the lowest ever: Ina Zweiniger-Bargielowska, Dr. Rachel Duffett, and Professor Alain Drouard, *Food and War in Twentieth Century Europe* (Burlington, VT, and London: Ashgate, 2011).
   "Year of Butter": Zweiniger-Bargielowska et al., *Food and War*.

103 *U.S. Food Administration*: Ogle, *In Meat We Trust*.
   fill up on eggs and cheese: Ogle, *In Meat We Trust*.
   Three million previously uncultivated lots: Rose Hayden-Smith, *Sowing the Seeds of Victory: American Gardening Programs of World War I* (Jefferson, NC: McFarland & Co., 2014).
   meat exports tripled: Helen Zoe Veit, "'We Were a Soft People': Asceticism, Self-Discipline and American Food Conservation in the First World War," *Food, Culture & Society* 10, no. 2 (April 29, 2015).
   meat exports quintupled: Veit, "'We Were a Soft People.'"

104 *one-third of American exports*: "Exports from the United States Before and After the Outbreak of the War," Federal Reserve Bulletin, Federal Reserve Bank of St. Louis, October 1, 1919, https:// fraser.stlouisfed.org/files/docs/publications/FRB/pages/1915-1919/ 24528_1915-1919.pdf.
   "same principles of mass production": Fitzgerald, *Every Farm a Factory*.

rewarded with 100,000 acres: Fitzgerald, *Every Farm a Factory.*

105 *"Mr. Average Farmer":* Cochrane, *Curse of American Agricultural Abundance.*

   "Agriculture Treadmill": Cochrane, *Curse of American Agricultural Abundance.*

106 *"administrators never considered":* Charles Rosenberg, "Rational-ization and Reality in the Shaping of American Agricultural Re-search, 1875–1914," *Social Studies of Science* 7, no. 4 (November 1977).

   "colleges of agriculture": Wendell Berry, *The Unsettling of America: Culture & Agriculture* (San Francisco: Sierra Club Books, 1977).

107 *debt or taxes:* Wenonah Hauter, *Foodopoly: The Battle Over the Fu-ture of Food and Farming in America* (New York: New Press, 2012).

   extended lenient credit: "John Deere's General Purpose Wide-Tread Tractor Gets Its Due," *John Deere Journal,* Novem-ber 5, 2018, https://johndeerejournal.com/2018/11/john-deeres -general-purpose-wide-tread-tractor-gets-its-due/.

   Drache, "John Deere's Plow."

108 *eleven billion dollars:* "Deere & Co.," *MarketWatch,* accessed June 25, 2020, https://www.marketwatch.com/investing/stock/de/financials.

   that same year: "2020 Farm Sector Income Forecast," USDA Eco-nomic Research Service, last updated February 5, 2020, https://www .ers.usda.gov/topics/farm-economy/farm-sector-income-finances/ farm-sector-income-forecast/.

7. Dust and Depression

109 *"essence of Leninism":* Serhii Plokhy, "Stalin and Roosevelt," *Dip-lomatic History* 42, no. 4 (September 2018), 525–27, https://doi.org/ 10.1093/dh/dhy050.

110 *peasants were required:* Andrea Graziosi, *Stalinism, Collectiv-ization and the Great Famine* (Cambridge, MA: Ukrainian Studies Fund, 2009).

111 *"esteemed grain growers":* Thomas P. Bernstein, "Stalinism, Fam-ine, and Chinese Peasants: Grain Procurements During the Great Leap Forward," *Theory and Society* 13, no. 3 (May 1984).

   four key elements: Graziosi, *Stalinism, Collectivization and the Great Famine.*

112 *analysis of famines:* Amartya Sen, *Poverty and Famines: An Es-say on Entitlement and Deprivation* (Oxford: Clarendon Press, 1981).

shipped to the cities: James Kai-sing Kung and Justin Yifu Lin, "The Causes of China's Great Leap Famine, 1959–1961," *Economic Development and Cultural Change* 52, no. 1 (October 2003).

digging up a potato: Frank Dikötter, *Mao's Great Famine: The History of China's Most Devastating Catastrophe, 1958–1962* (New York: Bloomsbury, 2011).

Mao cut grain acreage: Kung and Lin, "Causes of China's Great Leap Famine."

113 *thirteen and a half million new acres:* John Opie, Char Miller, and Kenna Lang Arche, *Ogallala: Water for a Dry Land* (Lincoln: University of Nebraska Press, 2003), 88.

"until thou be destroyed": R. Douglas Hurt, *The Dust Bowl: An Agricultural and Social History* (Chicago: Nelson Hall, 1981).

114 *trains were slowed:* Maureen Ogle, *In Meat We Trust: An Unexpected History of Carnivore America* (Boston: Houghton Mifflin Harcourt, 2013).

almost forty percent of the entire land area of southwest Kansas: Hurt, *The Dust Bowl.*

115 *living in chicken coops: The Dust Bowl*, directed by Ken Burns, aired 2012 on PBS.

116 *three hundred million tons of dust:* Montgomery, *Dirt.*

President Roosevelt's desk: The Dust Bowl, Burns.

"sullen and rebellious": Dan Morgan, *Merchants of Grain* (New York: Penguin, 1980), 73.

"a 'Farmers Holiday'": Janet Poppendieck, *Breadlines Knee-Deep in Wheat: Food Assistance in the Great Depression* (Berkeley: University of California Press, 2014).

117 *roadblocks on highways:* Bill Ganzel, "Radical Farm Protests," Wessels Living History Farm, https://livinghistoryfarm.org/farminginthe30s/money_11.html.

"revolution in the countryside": Agricultural Adjustment Relief Plan: Hearings on H.R. 13991 Before the Senate Comm. on Agriculture and Forestry, 72nd Cong., 2nd session, p. 12, 1933.

"indomitable American farmers": Franklin D. Roosevelt, *Fireside Chats of Franklin Delano Roosevelt: Radio Addresses to the American People About the Depression, the New Deal, and the Second World War*, 1933–1944 (St. Petersburg, FL: Red and Black Publishers, 2008).

118 *"extraordinary population increase":* Cochrane, *Curse of American Agricultural Abundance.*

122 *equal and opposite directions:* Bruce Reynolds, *Black Farmers in*

America, 1865–2000, RBS Research Report 194 (Washington, DC: U.S. Department of Agriculture, 2002), https://www.rd.usda.gov/sites/default/files/RR194.pdf.

123 *mechanical cotton picker:* Wayne Grove and Craig Heinicke, "Better Opportunities or Worse? The Demise of Cotton Harvest Labor, 1949–1964," *Economic History* 63, no. 3 (September 2003).

real estate was concentrated: Mark Arax, *The Dreamt Land: Chasing Water and Dust Across California* (New York: Knopf, 2019).

125 *irrigated land in California grew:* Alan L. Olmstead and Paul W. Rhode, "The Evolution of California Agriculture 1850–2000," in *California Agriculture: Dimensions and Issues,* ed. Jerome B. Siebert (Berkeley: University of California Press, 2003), http://citeseerx.ist.psu.edu/viewdoc/download?doi=10.1.1.389.2184&rep=rep1&type=pdf.

126 *"The ill wind":* Ernesto Galarza, *Merchants of Labor: The Mexican Bracero Story* (Santa Barbara, CA: McNally & Loftin, 1964).

"army of cheap labor": Walter Goldschmidt, quoted in Galarza, *Merchants of Labor.*

"the double effect": Galarza, *Merchants of Labor.*

127 *"'shock troops'":* Galarza, *Merchants of Labor.*

"rent-a-slave": José Angel Gutiérrez, *The Eagle Has Eyes: The FBI Surveillance of César Estrada Chávez of the United Farm Workers Union of America 1965–1975* (East Lansing: Michigan State University Press, 2019).

8. Food and the Brand

131 *three percent of the meatpacking industry as a whole:* William Cronon, *Nature's Metropolis: Chicago and the Great West* (New York: W. W. Norton & Co., 1991).

controlled by just a few firms: Cronon, *Nature's Metropolis,* 244.

second-largest industry in the country: "Abstract of the Twelfth Census of the United States, 1900," Table 154 (Washington, DC: Government Printing Office, 1902), https://www2.census.gov/library/publications/decennial/1900/abstract/abstract-1902-p1.pdf.

132 *company biplanes:* David Gerard, "White Castle," *The Oxford Companion to American Food and Drink,* ed. Andrew Smith (Oxford University Press, 2007), 622.

White Palace: Gerard, "White Castle."

proto–Betty Crocker: Francis A. Kwansa and H. G. Parsa, *Quick*

Service Restaurants, Franchising, and Multi-Unit Chain Management (London: Routledge, 2014), 131.

nothing but hamburgers: Jack El-Hai, "An Unusual Hamburger Experiment, from the University's Dietary Research Annals," *MinnPost*, March 14, 2008.

133   *"leap toward immortality":* Clifton Fadiman, *Any Number Can Play* (Cleveland: World Publishing, 1957).

canned milk production increased: T. R Pirtle, "Factory Butter, Cheese, and Condensed Milk Production During the War," *Hoard's Dairyman* 57 (June 6, 1919), 1000.

"fifty-two concerns": Harvey Levenstein, *Revolution at the Table: The Transformation of the American Diet* (Berkeley: University of California Press, 2003).

"non-milk using peoples": Elmer McCollum, *The Newer Knowledge of Nutrition: The Use of Food for the Preservation of Vitality and Health* (New York: Macmillan, 1918).

134   *"educated" to drink four glasses:* Bruce Kraig, *Food Cultures of the United States: Recipes, Customs, and Issues* (Santa Barbara: Greenwood, 2020), 113.

135   *five or six cows:* Bruce Kraig, *A Rich and Fertile Land: A History of Food in America* (London and Islington: Reaktion, 2017).

ended cheese-making artisans: Kraig, *A Rich and Fertile Land.*

136   *the "Poison Squad":* Deborah Blum, *The Poison Squad* (New York: Penguin, 2018).

137   *make ketchup appetizing:* Andrew F. Smith, *Pure Ketchup: A History of America's National Condiment, with Recipes* (Columbia: University of South Carolina Press, 1996).

138   *"Benzoate of soda":* John Hoenig, *Garden Variety: The American Tomato from Corporate to Heirloom* (New York: Columbia University Press, 2018).

139   *"Brand is everything":* Dan Pallotta, "A Logo Is Not a Brand," *Harvard Business Review,* June 15, 2011.

141   *Campbell's multiplied its marketing budget:* Anna Zeide, *Canned: The Rise and Fall of Consumer Confidence in the American Food Industry* (Berkeley: University of California Press, 2018), 130.

142   *"Who could ask for anything better":* Devjani Sen, "From Betty Crocker to the Geikko Gekko: An Information Processing Analysis of the Role of the Spokes-Character in Visual Advertising" (PhD diss., Carleton University, Ottawa, Ontario).

144   *more people left farms:* Associated Press, "Farm Population Low-

est Since 1850's," *New York Times*, July 20, 1988, https://www
.nytimes.com/1988/07/20/us/farm-population-lowest-since-1850-s
.html.

145 *a taste of canned food:* Kraig, *A Rich and Fertile Land.*

147 *650 stores:* Paul B. Ellickson, "The Evolution of the Supermarket
Industry: From A&P to Walmart," in *Handbook on the Economics of
Retail and Distribution* (Cheltenham, UK: Edward Elgar, 2016), 368–
91, http://paulellickson.com/SMEvolution.pdf, 4.

By 1930 it had sixteen thousand: "How the A&P Changed the Way
We Shop," *Fresh Air*, NPR, August 23, 2011, https://www.npr.org/
2011/08/23/139761274/how-the-a-p-changed-the-way-we-shop.

a seismic shift: Raj Patel, *Stuffed and Starved: The Hidden Battle for
the World Food System* (New York: Melville House, 2012).

9. Vitamania and "the Farm Problem"

149 *died from pellagra:* Karen Kruse Thomas, *Deluxe Jim Crow: Civil
Rights and American Health Policy, 1935–1954* (Athens: University of
Georgia Press, 2011).

151 *the "dietetic trinity":* Justus Freiherr von Liebig, *Researches on the
Chemistry of Food, and the Motion of the Juices in the Animal Body*,
ed. William Gregory and Eben N. Horsford (Lowell, MA: Daniel
Bixby, 1848), via University of Missouri Libraries Special Collections and Rare Books, https://library.missouri.edu/exhibits/food/
liebig.html.

room calorimeter: W. O. Atwater, C. D. Woods, and F. G. Bene-
dict, "Report of Preliminary Investigations on the Metabolism of
Nitrogen and Carbon in the Human Organism, with a Respiration
Calorimeter of Special Construction," United States Department of
Agriculture Office of Experiment Stations, Bulletin No. 44, 1897.

152 *the vitamin market:* Scott Mowbray, *The Food Fight: Truth, Myth,
and the Food-Health Connection* (Toronto: Random House of Canada,
1992).

153 *white loaves were "chaste":* Aaron Bobrow-Strain, *White Bread: A
Social History of the Store-Bought Loaf* (Boston: Beacon Press, 2012).

155 *twenty-five percent of calories:* Bobrow-Strain, *White Bread.*

"by skillful advertising": Elmer McCollum, *The American Home
Diet: The Answer to the Ever-Present Question, What Shall We Have for
Dinner?* (Detroit: Frederick C. Matthews, 1920).

McCollum was later bought off: Harvey Levenstein, *Fear of Food:*

A History of Why We Worry About What We Eat (Chicago: University of Chicago Press, 2012), 89.

"the pernicious teachings": F. J. Schlink, *Eat, Drink, and Be Wary* (Washington, DC: Consumers' Research, 1935).

Physical exams of men: Whet Moser, "How Hostess's Project to Twinkieize Bread Crippled the Company," *Chicago*, November 16, 2012.

156 *"symbol of bondage":* Helen Zoe Veit, *Modern Food, Moral Food: Self-Control, Science, and the Rise of Modern American Eating in the Early Twentieth Century* (Chapel Hill: University of North Carolina Press, 2013).

157 *a meeting in Lake Placid:* Emma Seifrit Weigley, "It Might Have Been Euthenics: The Lake Placid Conferences and the Home Economics Movement," *American Quarterly* 26, no. 1 (Spring 1974).

"train women in consumption": Harvey Levenstein, *Revolution at the Table: The Transformation of the American Diet* (Berkeley: University of California Press, 2003).

158 *for the Cooperative Extension:* "Elsie Carper Collection on Extension Service, Home Economics, and 4-H, " USDA National Agricultural Library Special Collections, June 25, 2020, https://specialcollections.nal.usda.gov/guide-collections/elsie-carper-collection-extension-service-home-economics-and-4-h.

causes of World War II: Lizzie Collingham, *The Taste of War: World War II and the Battle for Food* (New York: Penguin, 2012).

159 *died from starvation:* Collingham, *The Taste of War.*

More Japanese soldiers died from hunger: Timothy Snyder, "On Their Stomachs," *New York Times*, May 4, 2012.

160 *abundance of the empire:* Lizzie Collingham, "Birthday Onions: What Can We Learn from Wartime Rationing?," *Times Literary Supplement*, April 17, 2020.

The wartime famine: Collingham, *The Taste of War.*

161 *biggest wheat harvest in history:* Harvey Levenstein, *Paradox of Plenty: A Social History of Eating in Modern America* (New York: Oxford University Press, 1993).

"Total food production": Levenstein, *Paradox of Plenty.*

"decreased by six million": Stephanie Ann Carpenter, "'Regular Farm Girl': The Women's Land Army in World War II," *Agricultural History* 71, no. 2 (1997), 164.

162 *"It is absurd":* Wendell Berry, *The Unsettling of America: Culture & Agriculture* (San Francisco: Sierra Club Books, 1977), 37.

hundreds of products: "Products from NCAUR," USDA Agricultural Research Service, May 3, 2018, https://www.ars.usda.gov/midwest-area/peoria-il/national-center-for-agricultural-utilization-research/docs/products/.

164 *government held in storage:* Douglas Bowers, Wayne D. Rasmussen, and Gladys L. Baker, "History of Agricultural Price-Support and Adjustment Programs, 1933–84," USDA Economic Research Service, December 3, 1984.

income of rural people: Jim Hightower, *Hard Tomatoes, Hard Times: A Report of the Agribusiness Accountability Project on the Failure of America's Land Grant College Complex* (Washington, DC: Agribusiness Accountability Project, 1972).

165 *"Agriculture's chief need":* Committee for Economic Development, *An Adaptive Program for Agriculture: A Statement on National Policy by the Research and Policy Committee* (New York: Committee for Economic Development, 1962).

Hormel, Coke, and others: Wenonah Hauter, *Foodopoly: The Battle Over the Future of Food and Farming in America* (New York: New Press, 2012).

Charles Brannan: Bowers, Rasmussen, and Baker, "History of Agricultural Price-Support."

166 *exports multiplied by a factor of ten:* "The Wheat Situation," USDA Agricultural Marketing Service, December 1953, https://downloads.usda.library.cornell.edu/usda-esmis/files/cz30ps64c/xd07gv99z/5138jh375/WHS-10-15-1953.pdf.

167 *unprecedented sales and profits:* Dan Morgan, *Merchants of Grain* (New York: Penguin, 1980).

"any US-aligned government": Raj Patel, *Stuffed and Starved: The Hidden Battle for the World Food System* (New York: Melville House, 2012).

10. Soy, Chicken, and Cholesterol

169 *grain to be fed to animals:* Stephanie Mercier, "Corn: Background for 1990 Farm Legislation," Commodity Economics Division, USDA Economic Research Service, September 1989, https://www.ers.usda.gov/webdocs/publications/41785/50427_ages8947.pdf?v=8786.3.

popular mostly among enslaved people: Andrew Lawler, "How the Chicken Built America," *New York Times*, November 25, 2014, https://www.nytimes.com/2014/11/26/opinion/how-the-chicken -built-america.html.

170 *They're all women:* Lu Ann Jones, *Mama Learned Us to Work: Farm Women in the New South* (Chapel Hill: University of North Carolina Press, 2002).

171 *just about every available chicken:* Steve Striffler, *Chicken: The Dangerous Transformation of America's Favorite Food* (New Haven, CT: Yale University Press, 2005).

modern chicken industry: Striffler, *Chicken.*

"chickens produced annually": Pew Commission on Industrial Farm Animal Production, "Putting Meat on the Table: Industrial Farm Animal Production in America," Pew Charitable Trusts and Johns Hopkins Bloomberg School of Public Health, 2008.

Drugs paved the way: Maryn McKenna, *Big Chicken: The Incredible Story of How Antibiotics Created Modern Agriculture and Changed the Way the World Eats* (Washington, DC: National Geographic, 2017).

era of cheap chicken: Christopher Leonard, *The Meat Racket: The Secret Takeover of America's Food Business* (New York: Simon & Schuster, 2014).

172 *ten times as many chickens:* Pew Environment Group, "Big Chicken: Pollution and Industrial Poultry Production in America," Pew Charitable Trusts, 2011.

Value-added products: "How Broilers Are Marketed," National Chicken Council, https://www.nationalchickencouncil.org/about -the-industry/statistics/how-broilers-are-marketed/.

particulars of McDonald's story: Eric Schlosser, *Fast Food Nation: The Dark Side of the All-American Meal* (New York: Houghton Mifflin, 2001); John F. Love, *McDonald's: Behind the Arches* (New York: Bantam, 1995).

173 *"big, big volumes":* Love, *Behind the Arches.*

174 *"enterprise into the ghetto":* Chin Jou, *Supersizing Urban America: How Inner Cities Got Fast Food with Government Help* (Chicago: University of Chicago Press, 2017).

twenty-five million dollars in all: Jou, *Supersizing Urban America.*

175 *"the lion's share":* Jou, *Supersizing Urban America.*

calorie consumption from fast food quadrupled: Jou, *Supersizing Urban America.*

fat, fiber, fruits, and vegetables: Jou, *Supersizing Urban America.*

177 *"Available calories" — all production:* "Food Availability (Per Capita)

Data System," USDA Economic Research Service, January 9, 2020, https://www.ers.usda.gov/data-products/food-availability-per -capita-data-system/food-availability-per-capita-data-system/ #Food%20Availability.

179 *1923 USDA publication:* Marion Nestle, *Food Politics: How the Food Industry Influences Nutrition and Health* (Berkeley: University of California Press, 2002).

180 *the most obvious factor:* Sharad P. Paul, *The Genetics of Health: Understand Your Genes for Better Health* (New York: Simon and Schuster, 2017).

182 *"coronary disease was non-existent":* Ivan Oransky, "Obituary: Ancel Keys," *The Lancet* 364 (December 2004), 2174.

11. Force-Feeding Junk

184 *American Heart Association concluded:* David Kritchevsky, "History of Recommendations to the Public About Dietary Fat," *Journal of Nutrition* 128, no. 2 (February 1998).

the fat content and total calories: I. H. Page, F. H. Stare, A. C. Corcoran, and H. Pollack, "Atherosclerosis and the Fat Content of the Diet," *Journal of the American Medical Association* 164 (1957), 2048–51.

type of fat: James E. Dalen and Stephen Devries, "Diets to Prevent Coronary Heart Disease 1957–2013: What Have We Learned?" *American Journal of Medicine* 127, no. 5 (May 2014).

185 *"injure the nutrition of the American people":* Council on Foods and Nutrition of the American Medical Association, "Some Nutritional Aspects of Sugar, Candy and Sweetened Carbonated Beverages," *Journal of the American Medical Association,* November 7, 1942.

"How much sugar do you need? None!": Gary Taubes, *The Case Against Sugar* (New York: Knopf, 2016).

novel wet milling process: Tom Philpott, "The Secret History of Why Soda Companies Switched from Sugar to High-Fructose Corn Syrup," *Mother Jones,* July 26, 2019, https://www.motherjones.com/ food/2019/07/the-secret-history-of-why-soda-companies-switched -from-sugar-to-high-fructose-corn-syrup/.

Corn ethanol, a form: Tom Philpott, "How Cash and Corporate Pressure Pushed Ethanol to the Fore," *Grist,* December 7, 2006.

ADM's executive team: Kurt Eichenwald, "Three Sentenced in Archer Daniels Midland Case," *New York Times,* July 10, 1999.

186 *very same price supports:* James Bovard, "Cato Institute Policy Analysis No. 241: Archer Daniels Midland: A Case Study in Corporate Welfare," Cato Institute, September 26, 1995, https://www.cato .org/sites/cato.org/files/pubs/pdf/pa241.pdf.

HFCS as a cheap alternative: Philpott, "The Secret History."

187 *published in 1972:* John Yudkin, *Pure, White and Deadly: The Problem of Sugar* (London: Davis-Poynter, 1972).

"mountain of nonsense": Ian Leslie, "The Sugar Conspiracy," *The Guardian,* April 7, 2016, https://www.theguardian.com/society/ 2016/apr/07/the-sugar-conspiracy-robert-lustig-john-yudkin.

Sugar Research Foundation: Cristin E. Kearns, Laura A. Schmidt, and Stanton A. Glantz, "Sugar Industry and Coronary Heart Disease Research: A Historical Analysis of Internal Industry Documents," *JAMA Internal Medicine* 176, no. 11 (2016), 1680–85.

188 *"no practical importance":* Robert B. McGandy, D. M. Hegsted, and F. J. Stare, "Dietary Fats, Carbohydrates and Atherosclerotic Vascular Disease," *New England Journal of Medicine,* July 27, 1967.

190 *the refined carbohydrates:* David L. Katz, *The Truth About Food: Why Pandas Eat Bamboo and People Get Bamboozled* (New York: Dystel & Goderich, 2018).

addictive as possible: David Kessler, *The End of Overeating* (Emmaus, PA: Rodale, 2009); Michael Moss, *Salt Sugar Fat: How the Food Giants Hooked Us* (New York: Random House, 2013).

191 *seven hundred calories per person:* "Food Availability (Per Capita) Data System," USDA Economic Research Service, https://www.ers .usda.gov/data-products/food-availability-per-capita-data-system/.

Sixty percent of the calories: Eurídice Martínez Steele, Larissa Galastri Baraldi, Maria Laura da Costa Louzada, Jean-Claude Moubarac, Dariush Mozaffarian, and Carlos Augusto Monteiro, "Ultra-Processed Foods and Added Sugars in the US Diet: Evidence from a Nationally Representative Cross-Sectional Study," *BMJ Open* 6, no. 3 (2016).

193 *Coke's cavity-causing characteristics:* Marion Nestle, *Soda Politics: Taking on Big Soda (and Winning)* (New York: Oxford University Press, 2015).

reward-confirming neurotransmitter: Nicole M. Avena, Pedro Rada, and Bartley G. Hoebel, "Evidence for Sugar Addiction: Behavioral and Neurochemical Effects of Intermittent, Excessive Sugar Intake," *Neuroscience Biobehavior Review,* May 2007.

"almost nothing for it": Robert Lustig, "The Sugar Addiction Ta-

boo," *The Atlantic*, January 2, 2014, https://www.theatlantic.com/health/archive/2014/01/the-sugar-addiction-taboo/282699/.

marker of addiction: Robert Lustig, *Fat Chance: Beating the Odds Against Sugar, Processed Food, Obesity, and Disease* (New York: Avery, 2013).

195 *breast milk cannot be reproduced:* Kristin Lawless, *Formerly Known as Food: How the Industrial Food System Is Changing Our Minds, Bodies, and Culture* (New York: St. Martin's, 2018).

third most abundant substance: Lawless, *Formerly Known as Food.*

programming our metabolic operations: Steven A. Frese et al., "Persistence of Supplemented *Bifidobacterium longum* subsp. *infantis* EVC001 in Breastfed Infants," *American Society for Microbiology*, December 2017.

numerous autoimmune diseases: Bethany Henrick et al., "Restoring *Bifidobacterium infantis* EVC001 to the Infant Gut Microbiome Significantly Reduces Intestinal Inflammation," *Current Developments in Nutrition*, June 2019.

196 *"single most effective intervention":* Save the Children, *Don't Push It: Why the Formula Milk Industry Must Clean Up Its Act* (London: Save the Children Fund, 2018), https://resourcecentre.savethechildren.net/node/13218/pdf/dont-push-it.pdf.

"famous baby specialists": Carnation ad, 1950s, Vintage Ad Browser, http://www.vintageadbrowser.com/food-ads-1950s/27.

"Marxists marching under": Jonathan Ratner, "Influence Peddling, Nestle Style," Multinational Monitor, February 1981, https://www.multinationalmonitor.org/hyper/issues/1981/02/ratner.html.

197 *United States was the only country:* Nestle, *Food Politics.*

"are picky eaters": Lawless, *Formerly Known as Food.*

198 *testified before Congress:* Levenstein, *Paradox of Plenty.*

199 *"big and strong like me":* Tracy Westen, "Government Regulation of Food Marketing to Children: The Federal Trade Commission and the Kid-Vid Controversy," *Loyola of Los Angeles Law Review* 79 (2006).

crippled the FTC: Molly Niesen, "Crisis of Consumerism: Advertising, Activism, and the Battle over the U.S. Federal Trade Commission, 1969–1980" (PhD diss., University of Illinois at Urbana-Champaign, 2013).

200 *"legislative prefrontal lobotomy":* Michael Pertschuk, *Revolt Against Regulation* (Berkeley: University of California Press, 1982), 90, cited in Niesen, "Crisis of Consumerism."

12. The So-Called Green Revolution

203 *"I call it the Green Revolution":* William S. Gaud, "The Green
Revolution: Accomplishments and Apprehensions," speech given
before the Society of International Development, Washington,
DC,1968,http://www.agbioworld.org/biotech-info/topics/borlaug/
borlaug-green.html.

food production in the developing world: Stephen Parker, "Agricultural Progress in the Third World and Its Effect on U.S. Farm Exports," U.S. Congressional Budget Office, 1989.

importer of wheat to an exporter: Parker, "Agricultural Progress
in the Third World."

rice production in Indonesia: G. S. Khush, "Green Revolution:
Challenges Ahead," presented at the "In the Wake of the Double
Helix: From the Green Revolution to the Gene Revolution" interna-
tional congress, Bologna, Italy, May 31, 2003.

Latin American corn production: Gordon Conway, *The Doubly
Green Revolution: Food for All in the Twenty-first Century* (Ithaca, NY:
Cornell University Press, 1997).

new hybrid varieties: Peter Rosset, Joseph Collins, and Frances
Moore Lappé, "Lessons from the Green Revolution: Do We Need
New Technology to End Hunger?," *Tikkun* 15, no. 2 (March–April
2000), 52–56.

doubled food supply in Asia: M. Lipton, "Plant Breeding and Poverty: Can Transgenic Seeds Replicate the 'Green Revolution' as a
Source of Gains for the Poor?," *Journal of Development Studies* 43, no.
1 (2007), 31–62.

people going hungry decreased: N. E. Borlaug and C. R. Dowswell,
"Feeding a World of 10 Billion People: A 21st Century Challenge,"
presented at the "In the Wake of the Double Helix: From the Green
Revolution to the Gene Revolution" international congress, Bologna, Italy, May 31, 2003.

show global yields: Prabhu L. Pingali, "Green Revolution: Toward 2.0," *Proceedings of the National Academy of Sciences,* July 2012.

"millions of these unfortunates": Norman Borlaug, "The Green
Revolution, Peace, and Humanity," Nobel lecture, December 11,
1970, Nobel Foundation.

204 *"Green Revolution in India Wilts":* Geeta Anand, "Green Revolution in India Wilts as Subsidies Backfire," *Wall Street Journal,*

February 22, 2010, wsj.com/articles/SB100014240527487036159 04575052921612723844.

"India's Farming 'Revolution'": Daniel Zwerdling, "India's Farming 'Revolution' Heading for Collapse," *All Things Considered,* NPR, April 13, 2009, https://www.npr.org/templates/story/story.php ?storyId=102893816.

"The Toxic Consequences": Daniel Pepper, "The Toxic Consequences of the Green Revolution," *U.S. News & World Report,* July 7, 2008.

"actually marked a slowdown": Glenn Davis Stone, "Commentary: New Histories of the Indian Green Revolution," *Geographic Journal* 185, no. 2 (June 2019), 243–50.

Tobacco, jute, cotton: W. C. Paddock, "How Green Is the Green Revolution?," *BioScience* 20, no. 16 (1970), 897–902.

205 *massive price subsidies:* Raj Patel, "The Long Green Revolution," *Journal of Peasant Studies* 40, no. 1 (2013), 1–63.

"90 percent for water": Gordon Conway, *One Billion Hungry: Can We Feed the World?* (Ithaca, NY: Cornell University Press, 2013).

investment in private wells: Kapil Subramanian, "Revisiting the Green Revolution: Irrigation and Food Production in 20th Century India" (PhD diss., King's College London, 2015).

internal agricultural revolution: M. Rezaul Islam, "Hunger Reduction in China: An Analysis of Contextual Factors," *Asian Social Work and Policy Review* 10, no. 3 (October 2016), 295–310, https://doi .org/10.1111/aswp.12098.

World Bank statistics: World Development Indicators 2016, World Bank, 2016, http://documents.worldbank.org/curated/en/ 805371467990952829/World-development-indicators-2016.

206 *nine percent increase:* Ellen Messer and Peter Uvin, eds., *The Hunger Report 1995* (London: Routledge, 1996).

result of pesticide poisoning: Wasim Aktar, Dwaipayan Sengupta, and Ashim Chowdhury, "Impact of Pesticides Use in Agriculture: Their Benefits and Hazards," *Interdisciplinary Toxicology* 2, no. 1 (March 2009), 1–12, https://doi.org/10.2478/v10102-009-0001 -7.

207 *Great Grain Robbery:* Martha McNeil Hamilton, *The Great American Grain Robbery and Other Stories* (Washington, DC: Agribusiness Accountability Project, 1972).

208 *a third of the American wheat harvest:* Dan Morgan, *Merchants of Grain* (New York: Penguin, 1980).

causing grain supplies to plunge: Morgan, *Merchants of Grain.*

lied to Congress: Morgan, *Merchants of Grain.*

Cargill's earnings: Morgan, *Merchants of Grain.*

Secretary of Agriculture Earl Butz: Tom Philpott, "A Reflection on the Lasting Legacy of 1970s USDA Secretary Earl Butz," *Grist,* February 8, 2008.

211 *"to produce one ton":* Alyshia Gálvez, *Eating NAFTA: Trade, Food Policies, and the Destruction of Mexico* (Berkeley: University of California Press, 2018).

"trains with benches": Karen Lehman and Dr. Steve Suppan, "Food Security and Agricultural Trade Under NAFTA," Institute for Agriculture & Trade Policy, July 10, 1997, https://www.iatp.org/documents/food-security-and-agricultural-trade-under-nafta.

they've doubled again: Lesley Ahmed, "U.S. Corn Exports to Mexico and the North American Free Trade Agreement," Office of Industries, U.S. International Trade Commission, May 2018, https://www.usitc.gov/publications/332/working_papers/ahmed.htm.

212 *generally horrific living:* Richard Marosi, "In Mexico's Fields, Children Toil to Harvest Crops That Make It to American Tables," *Los Angeles Times,* December 14, 2014, https://www.latimes.com/world/mexico-americas/la-product-of-mexico-faces-20141214-storylink.html.

214 *more than a billion pounds:* "DDT Regulatory History: A Brief Survey (to 1975)," U.S. Environmental Protection Agency, September 14, 2016, https://archive.epa.gov/epa/aboutepa/ddt-regulatory-history-brief-survey-1975.html.

215 *Monsanto came early:* Daniel Charles, *Lords of the Harvest: Biotech, Big Money, and the Future of Food* (Cambridge, MA: Perseus, 2001).

216 *Recombinant bovine growth hormone:* Christine Escobar, "The Tale of rBGH, Milk, Monsanto and the Organic Backlash," *Huffington Post,* April 2, 2009.

Monsanto tried and failed: Jeffrey Smith, "Monsanto Forced Fox TV to Censor Coverage of Dangerous Milk Drug," *Huffington Post,* May 25, 2011.

217 *"Monsanto alone accounted":* Jennifer Clapp, *Food* (Cambridge, UK: Polity, 2016).

use of glyphosate: Patricia Cohen, "Roundup Weedkiller Is Blamed for Cancers, but Farmers Say It's Not Going Away," *New*

York Times, September 20, 2019, https://www.nytimes.com/2019/09/20/business/bayer-roundup.html.

and funding studies: Leemon B. McHenry, "The Monsanto Papers: Poisoning the Scientific Well," *International Journal of Risk & Safety in Medicine* 29, no. 3–4 (2018), 193–205, doi: 10.3233/JRS-180028.

yield bigger harvests: Jorge Fernandez-Cornejo, Seth Wechsler, Mike Livingston, and Lorraine Mitchell, "Genetically Engineered Crops in the United States," USDA Economic Research Service, ERR-162, February 2014.

218 *"ever in civil litigation":* Patricia Cohen, "Roundup Maker to Pay $10 Billion to Settle Cancer Suits," *New York Times*, June 24, 2020, https://www.nytimes.com/2020/06/24/business/roundup-settlement-lawsuits.html.

largely responsible for the massive die-off: Christian H. Krupke, Greg J. Hunt, Brian D. Eitzer, Gladys Andino, and Krispn Given, "Multiple Routes of Pesticide Exposure for Honey Bees Living Near Agricultural Fields," *PLoS ONE* 7, no. 1 (January 3, 2012).

13. The Resistance

221 *"inexhaustible in its gifts":* John Bellamy Foster and Brett Clark, "The Robbery of Nature: Capitalism and the Metabolic Rift," *Monthly Review*, July 1, 2018, https://monthlyreview.org/2018/07/01/the-robbery-of-nature/.

222 *"Four Laws of Ecology":* Barry Commoner, *The Closing Circle: Nature, Man, and Technology* (New York: Random House, 1971).

223 *Four Laws of Capitalism:* John Bellamy Foster, *The Vulnerable Planet: A Short Economic History of the Environment* (New York: Monthly Review Press, 1999).

"an adequate accounting": Foster, *The Vulnerable Planet*.

224 *"Before he was ten":* Christina Vella, *George Washington Carver: A Life* (Baton Rouge: Louisiana State University Press, 2015).

225 *"he learned more":* E. Fairlie Watson, "The Lessons of the East," *Organic Gardening Magazine* 13, no. 8 (September 1948).

"Law of Return": Sir Albert Howard, *An Agricultural Testament* (Oxford: Oxford University Press, 1940).

226 *seminal 1943 book:* Lady Eve Balfour, *The Living Soil* (London: Faber and Faber, 1943).

227 *"the ghastly deaths":* Rachel Carson and Dorothy Freeman, *Always, Rachel: The Letters of Rachel Carson and Dorothy Freeman, 1952–1964: The Story of a Remarkable Friendship,* ed. Martha Freeman (Boston: Beacon Press, 1994).

exposing the toxic: Rachel Carson, *Silent Spring* (Boston: Houghton Mifflin, 1962).

"probably a Communist": Ted Genoways, "Corn Wars," *New Republic,* August 16, 2015, https://newrepublic.com/article/122441/corn-wars.

228 *According to biographer:* Linda Lear, *Rachel Carson: Witness for Nature* (Boston: Mariner, 2009).

Frances Moore Lappé: Frances Moore Lappé, *Diet for a Small Planet* (New York: Ballantine, 1971).

229 *Black-owned acreage:* Bruce Reynolds, *Black Farmers in America, 1865–2000,* RBS Research Report 194 (Washington, DC: U.S. Department of Agriculture, 2002), https://www.rd.usda.gov/sites/default/files/RR194.pdf.

Black people farm: "United States Farms with American Indian or Alaska Native Producers," 2017 Census of Agriculture, USDA National Agricultural Statistics Service, https://www.nass.usda.gov/Publications/AgCensus/2017/Online_Resources/Race,_Ethnicity_and_Gender_Profiles/cpd99000.pdf.

"Slavery, sharecropping, and tenant farming": Monica M. White, "Freedom's Seeds: Reflections of Food, Race, and Community Development," *Journal of Agriculture, Food Systems, and Community Development* (2017), advance online publication, http://dx.doi.org/10.5304/jafscd.2017.073.011.

"find communal success": White, "Freedom's Seeds."

well-deserved claim: Monica M. White, *Freedom Farmers: Agricultural Resistance and the Black Freedom Movement* (Chapel Hill: University of North Carolina Press, 2018).

Fannie Lou Hamer: White, *Freedom Farmers.*

230 *"Land is the key":* White, *Freedom Farmers.*

"what we could": Helen Nearing and Scott Nearing, *Living the Good Life: How to Live Sanely and Simply in a Troubled World* (New York: Schocken, 1970).

31 *Pigford's own story:* David Zucchino, "Farmer Who Sued USDA —and Won—Now Grappling with IRS," *Seattle Times,* March 31, ?.

In *"willful obstruction":* Abril Castro and Zoe Willingham, "Progressive Governance Can Turn the Tide for Black Farmers," Center for American Progress, April 3, 2019, https://www.americanprogress.org/issues/economy/reports/2019/04/03/467892/progressive-governance-can-turn-tide-black-farmers/.

232 *Public Law 320:* Gordon W. Gunderson, *The National School Lunch Program: Background and Development* (Hauppauge, NY: Nova Science Publishers, 2003).

233 *"an inadequate dole":* "Hunger in America," *CBS Reports,* CBS, aired May 21, 1968.

234 *free breakfast program:* Joshua Bloom and Waldo E. Martin Jr., *Black Against Empire: The History and Politics of the Black Panther Party* (Berkeley: University of California Press, 2013).

235 *"super-rich, fat-loaded":* Gerald M. Oppenheimer and I. Daniel Benrubi, "McGovern's Senate Select Committee on Nutrition and Human Needs Versus the Meat Industry on the Diet-Heart Question (1976–1977)," *American Journal of Public Health* 104, no. 1 (2014), 59–69, https://doi.org/10.2105/AJPH.2013.301464.

"our food industry": *Diet Related to Killer Diseases: Hearings Before the Select Committee on Nutrition and Human Needs of the United States Senate, Ninety-Fourth Congress* (Washington, DC: Government Printing Office, 1976).

236 *"reduce meat" language:* Marion Nestle, *Food Politics: How the Food Industry Influences Nutrition and Health* (Berkeley: University of California Press, 2002).

"The revised goals": Marion Nestle, *Soda Politics: Taking on Big Soda (and Winning)* (Oxford: Oxford University Press, 2015), 55.

"Total elimination of soft drinks": *Dietary Goals for the United States: Prepared by the Staff of the Select Committee on Nutrition and Human Needs, United States Senate,* 2nd ed. (Washington, DC: Government Printing Office, 1977), cited in Nestle, *Soda Politics,* 55.

237 *"SnackWell's phenomenon":* Nestle, *Food Politics.*

241 *"merely an approach":* Brian K. Obach, *Organic Struggle: The Movement for Sustainable Agriculture in the United States* (Cambridge, MA: MIT Press, 2015).

242 *existing organic processors:* Phillip H. Howard, "Consolidation in the North American Organic Food Processing Sector, 1997 to 2007," *International Journal of Sociology and Agriculture and Food* 16, no. 1 (2009), 13–30.

14. Where We're At

244 *"a broken world":* Bill McKibben, "A Very Hot Year," *New York Review of Books*, March 12, 2020, https://www.nybooks.com/articles/2020/03/12/climate-change-very-hot-year/.

more emissions than: IATP, GRAIN, and Heinrich Böll Stiftung, "Big Meat and Dairy's Supersize Climate Footprint," Institute for Agriculture & Trade Policy, November 7, 2017, https://www.iatp.org/supersized-climate-footprint.

size of Germany: IATP, GRAIN, and Stiftung, "Big Meat."

all of Ireland: Kevin O'Sullivan, "Ireland Has Third Highest Emissions of Greenhouse Gas in EU," *Irish Times*, August 26, 2019, https://www.irishtimes.com/news/environment/ireland-has-third-highest-emissions-of-greenhouse-gas-in-eu-1.3998041.

as little as ten percent: "Sources of Greenhouse Gas Emissions," U.S. Environmental Protection Agency, April 11, 2020.

more than fifty: Robert Goodland and Jeff Anhang, "Livestock and Climate Change," Worldwatch, November/December 2009, https://awellfedworld.org/wp-content/uploads/Livestock-Climate-Change-Anhang-Goodland.pdf.

245 *seventy billion livestock worldwide:* Alex Thornton, "This Is How Many Animals We Eat Each Year," World Economic Forum, February 8, 2019.

ice-free land: Leanne N. Phelps and Jed O. Kaplan, "Land Use for Animal Production in Global Change Studies: Defining and Characterizing a Framework," *Global Change Biology* 23, no. 11 (November 2017).

total global emissions: P. J. Gerber, H. Steinfeld, B. Henderson, A. Mottet, C. Opio, J. Dijkman, A. Falcucci, and G. Tempio, *Tackling Climate Change Through Livestock: A Global Assessment of Emissions and Mitigation Opportunities* (Rome: Food and Agriculture Organization of the United Nations, 2013), http://www.fao.org/3/a-i3437e.pdf.

double the contribution: Aleksandra Arcipowska, Emily Mangan, You Lyu, and Richard Waite, "5 Questions About Agricultural Emissions, Answered," World Resources Institute, July 29, 2019, ~tp://www.wri.org/blog/2019/07/5-questions-about-agricultural ~sions-answered.

as much as seventy percent: R. Lal, W. Negassa, and K. Lorenz, "Carbon Sequestration in Soil," *Current Opinion in Environmental Sustainability* 15 (2015), 79–86.

deforestation for growing animal feed: David Gibbs, Nancy Harris, and Frances Seymour, "By the Numbers: The Value of Tropical Forests in the Climate Change Equation," World Resources Institute, October 4, 2018, https://www.wri.org/blog/2018/10/numbers-value-tropical-forests-climate-change-equation.

disappearing Amazon rainforest: Ignacio Amigo, "When Will the Amazon Hit a Tipping Point?," *Nature,* February 25, 2020, https://www.nature.com/articles/d41586-020-00508-4.

at least thirty percent: Jenny Gustavsson et al., *Global Food Losses and Food Waste: Extent, Causes and Prevention* (Rome: Food and Agriculture Organization of the United Nations, 2011), http://www.fao.org/3/a-i2697e.pdf.

in Iowa alone: "Crop and Land Use: Statewide Data," Iowa State University Extension and Outreach, accessed July 2020, https://www.extension.iastate.edu/soils/crop-and-land-use-statewide-data.

markets are disrupted: Adam Jeffery and Emma Newburger, "Wasted Milk, Euthanized Livestock: Photos Show How Coronavirus Has Devastated US Agriculture," CNBC, May 2, 2020.

246 *Trucking and shipping food:* Sigal Samuel, "How to Reduce Your Food's Carbon Footprint, in 2 Charts," *Vox,* February 20, 2020.

rice cultivation produces: Aine Quinn and Jeremy Hodges, "Your Bowl of Rice Is Hurting the Climate Too," *Bloomberg,* June 3, 2019, https://www.bloomberg.com/news/articles/2019-06-03/your-bowl-of-rice-is-hurting-the-climate-too.

eight of the ten warmest years: "Top 10 Warmest Years on Record," Climate Central, January 15, 2020.

highest annual rainfall: "Assessing the U.S. Climate in June 2019," National Oceanic and Atmospheric Administration, National Centers for Environmental Information, July 9, 2019.

possibility of water shortages: "Water Scarcity," UN Water, September 2018.

five billion by 2050: David Wallace-Wells, *The Uninhabitable Earth: Life After Warming* (New York: Tim Duggan, 2019).

The Ogallala Aquifer: Jeremy Frankel, "Crisis on the High Plains: The Loss of America's Largest Aquifer," *University of Denver Water Law Review,* May 17, 2018, http://duwaterlawreview.com/

crisis-on-the-high-plains-the-loss-of-americas-largest-aquifer-the
-ogallala/.

247 *chronic water issues:* Nathanael Johnson, "It's Time for California
to Let Some of Its Thirsty Farmland Go," *Grist,* February 21, 2019,
https://grist.org/article/its-time-for-california-to-let-some-of
-its-thirsty-farmland-go/.

"potentially nutrient poor": Louis Ziska, interview with author,
July 6, 2020.

triple by midcentury: "Goal 2: Zero Hunger," Sustainable Development Goals, United Nations, https://www.un.org/sustainablede
velopment/hunger/.

too hot for farmers: Bill McKibben, *Falter: Has the Human Game
Begun to Play Itself Out?* (New York: Henry Holt, 2019).

harvests will fail: Julian Cribb, *Food or War* (Cambridge: Cambridge University Press, 2019).

"worse, much worse": Wallace-Wells, *The Uninhabitable Earth.*

"stuffed and starved": Raj Patel, *Stuffed and Starved: The Hidden
Battle for the World Food System* (New York: Melville House, 2012).

calories for every person: Marion Nestle and Malden Nesheim,
Why Calories Count: From Science to Politics (Berkeley: University of
California Press, 2012).

248 *linked to being overweight:* J. Min, Y. Zhao L. and Slivka Y. Wang,
"Double Burden of Diseases Worldwide: Coexistence of Undernu-
trition and Overnutrition-Related Non-Communicable Chronic
Diseases," *Obesity Reviews* 19, no. 1 (2018).

quadrupled since 1980: "Diabetes: Key Facts," World Health Organization, accessed May 15, 2020, https://www.who.int/news-room/
fact-sheets/detail/diabetes.

chronic kidney disease: Vivekanand Jha and Gopesh K. Modi, "Getting to Know the Enemy Better—the Global Burden of Chronic
Disease," *Kidney International* 94 (2018).

global sugar consumption: BDJ Team 4, "A Global Outlook on
Sugar," article no. 17045 (2017), https://doi.org/10.1038/bdjteam
.2017.45.

obesity have nearly tripled: NCD Risk Factor Collaboration, "Trends
in Adult Body-Mass Index in 200 Countries from 1975 to 2014: A
Pooled Analysis of 1698 Population-Based Measurement Studies
with 19.2 Million Participants," *The Lancet* 387, no. 10026 (April 2,
2016), 1377–96, https://doi.org/10.1016/S0140-6736(16)30054-X.

Mediterranean diet: Caitlin Dewey, "Mediterranean Children

Stopped Eating the Mediterranean Diet, and Now They Have the Highest Obesity Rates in Europe," *Washington Post*, May 30, 2018, https://www.washingtonpost.com/news/wonk/wp/2018/05/30/mediterranean-children-stopped-eating-the-mediterranean-diet-and-they-now-have-the-highest-obesity-rates-in-europe/.

increased their international sales: Dionne Searcey and Matt Michtel, "Obesity Was Rising as Ghana Embraced Fast Food. Then Came KFC," *New York Times*, October 2, 2017.

international fast-food market: "World Bank National Accounts Data, and OECD National Accounts Data Files," World Bank, https://data.worldbank.org/indicator/NY.GDP.MKTP.CD.

expected to double: Zion Market Research, "Global Industry Trends in Fast Food Market Size & Share Will Surpass USD 690.80 Billion by 2022," GlobeNewswire, http://www.globenewswire.com/news-release/2019/07/12/1882007/0/en/Global-Industry-Trends-in-Fast-Food-Market-Size-Share-Will-Surpass-USD-690-80-Billion-by-2022.html.

248 *seventy percent of all deaths:* Wullianallur Raghupathi and Viju Raghupathi, "An Empirical Study of Chronic Diseases in the United States: A Visual Analytics Approach," *International Journal of Environmental Research and Public Health* 15, no. 3 (March 2018).

249 *optimum human diet:* Mark Bittman and David Katz, MD, *How to Eat: All Your Food and Diet Questions Answered* (Boston: Houghton Mifflin Harcourt, 2020).

251 *food advertising budget:* "Food Marketing," UConn Rudd Center for Food Policy & Obesity, http://www.uconnruddcenter.org/food-marketing.

"disease prevention and health promotion": Rudd Center, "Food Marketing."

ultra-processed foods: Eurídice Martínez Steele et al., "Ultra-Processed Foods and Added Sugars in the US Diet: Evidence from a Nationally Representative Cross-Sectional Study," *BMJ Open* 6, no. 3 (March 9, 2016), doi: 10.1136/bmjopen-2015-009892.

suffer most acutely: Julie Guthman, *Weighing In: Obesity, Food Justice, and the Limits of Capitalism* (Berkeley: University of California Press, 2011).

economic insecurity and overeating: Nicholas Rohde, K. K. Tang, and Lars Osberg, "The Self-Reinforcing Dynamics of Economic Insecurity and Obesity," *Applied Economics* 49, no. 17 (September 27, 2016), 1668–78, https://doi.org/10.1080/00036846.2016.1223826.

seventy-seven percent higher: "New CDC Report: More than 100 Million Americans Have Diabetes or Prediabetes," press release, CDC, July 18, 2017, https://www.cdc.gov/media/releases/2017/p0718-diabetes-report.html.

fast-food restaurants: Patrick W. McLaughlin, "Growth in Quick-Service Restaurants Outpaced Full-Service Restaurants in Most U.S. Counties," USDA Economic Research Service, November 5, 2018.

for every supermarket: "Number of Supermarket Stores in the United States from 2011 to 2018, by Format," Statista, April 2019, https://www.statista.com/statistics/240892/number-of-us-supermarket-stores-by-format/.

doesn't improve things: Guthman, *Weighing In.*

252 *actually reaches the target species:* David Pimentel and Michael Burgess, "Small Amounts of Pesticides Reaching Target Insects," *Environment, Development and Sustainability* 14, no. 1–2 (September 2011).

eighty-five percent of all foods: Carey Gillam, "Hold the Plum Pudding: US Food Sampling Shows Troubling Pesticide Residues," *Environmental Health News,* December 21, 2017.

a scary cycle: Wasim Aktar, Dwaipayan Sengupta, and Ashim Chowdhury, "Impact of Pesticides Use in Agriculture: Their Benefits and Hazards," *Interdisciplinary Toxicology* 2, no. 1 (March 2009), 1–12, https://doi.org/10.2478/v10102-009-0001-7.

it proposed a variety: Johnathan Hettinger, "New Bayer-Engineered Seed Raises Questions Among Experts on the Future of Weed Control," Midwest Center for Investigative Reporting, July 3, 2020.

caused mass deaths: Michael DiBartolomeis, Susan Kegley, Pierre Mineau, Rosemarie Radford, and Kendra Klein, "An Assessment of Acute Insecticide Toxicity Loading (AITL) of Chemical Pesticides Used on Agricultural Land in the United States," *PLoS ONE* 14, no. 8 (August 6, 2019), https://doi.org/10.1371/journal.pone.0220029.

seventy-five percent population decline: Caspar A. Hallmann et al., "More than 75 Percent Decline over 27 Years in Total Flying Insect Biomass in Protected Areas," *PLoS ONE,* October 18, 2017, https://doi.org/10.1371/journal.pone.0185809.

253 *people die from these poisons:* "An Estimated 12.6 Million Deaths Each Year Are Attributable to Unhealthy Environments," World Health Organization, March 15, 2016.

endocrine-disrupting chemicals: Kristin Lawless, *Formerly Known as Food: How the Industrial Food System Is Changing Our Minds, Bodies, and Culture* (New York: St. Martin's, 2018); Guthman, *Weighing In.*

bird biomass on this planet: Yinon M. Bar-On, Rob Phillips, and Ron Milo, "The Biomass Distribution on Earth," *Proceedings of the National Academy of Sciences* 115, no. 25 (June 19, 2018).

254 *industry is concentrated:* Charlie Mitchell and Austin Frerick, "Restoring Independence and Fairness to Agriculture Under a Green New Deal," Data for Progress, October 2019, http://filesforprogress .org/memos/agriculture-antitrust.pdf.

fifty-three Iowas: Chris Jones, "50 Shades of Brown," *Chris Jones, IIHR Research Engineer* (blog), University of Iowa, https://www.iihr .uiowa.edu/cjones/50-shades-of-brown/.

255 *within smelling distance of a CAFO:* Leah Douglas, "Finally, Somebody Heard What the People Were Saying Was Happening to Them," *Mother Jones,* May 1, 2018.

256 *five thousand of them unaccounted for:* Donnelle Eller, "Iowa Uses Satellites to Uncover 5,000 Previously Undetected Animal Confinements," *Des Moines Register,* September 19, 2017.

struck a deal with livestock producers: Leah Douglas, "The Breathtaking Lack of Oversight for Air Emissions from Animal Farms," *The Nation,* December 20, 2019, https://www.thenation.com/ article/archive/air-emissions-environment/.

in alarming quantities: Carrie Hribar, *Understanding Concentrated Animal Feed Operations and Their Impact on Communities* (Bowling Green, OH: National Association of Local Boards of Health, 2010), https://www.cdc.gov/nceh/ehs/docs/Understanding_CAFOs _NALBOH.pdf.

257 *fertile ground for transmission:* Rob Wallace, *Big Farms Make Big Flu: Dispatches on Influenza, Agribusiness, and the Nature of Science* (New York: New York University Press, 2016).

tuna and swordfish: "Overfishing," *National Geographic,* April 27, 2010, https://www.nationalgeographic.com/environment/oceans/ critical-issues-overfishing/.

259 *Current aquaculture techniques:* Brian Halwell, *Farming Fish for the Future,* Worldwatch Institute Report 176 (Washington, DC: Worldwatch Institute, 2008).

eighty percent of those drugs: Felipe C. Cabello, Henry P. Godfrey, Alexandra Tomova, Larisa Ivanova, Humberto Dölz, Ana Millanao, and Alejandro H. Buschmann, "Antimicrobial Use in Aquaculture Re-Examined: Its Relevance to Antimicrobial Resistance and to Animal and Human Health," *Environmental Microbiology,* April 10, 2013.

260 *bought up by non-operators:* Katy Keiffer, "Who Really Owns American Farmland?" *The Counter*, July 31, 2017.
holdings equivalent to the size of Ohio: Keiffer, "Who Really Owns?"
foreign investors: GRAIN, "The Global Farmland Grab in 2016: How Big, How Bad?," June 14, 2016, https://grain.org/en/article/5492-the-global-farmland-grab-in-2016-how-big-how-bad.

261 *food system jobs:* Saru Jayaraman and Kathryn De Master, *Bite Back: People Taking on Corporate Food and Winning* (Berkeley: University of California Press, 2020).

262 *deadliest industry for children:* Margaret Wurth, "More US Child Workers Die in Agriculture Than in Any Other Industry," Human Rights Watch, December 4, 2018.

263 *eighty percent of the farmworker population:* Jayaraman and De Master, *Bite Back.*
one and a half times the rest of: Jayaraman and De Master, *Bite Back.*
four percent of its total sales: Krissy Clark, "The Secret Life of a Food Stamp Might Become a Little Less Secret," *Slate*, August 5, 2014.

264 *"monoculture of the mind":* Vandana Shiva, "Monocultures of the Mind," *Trumpeter* 10, no. 4 (1993).

15. The Way Forward

266 *agroecology is more:* "The International Peasant's Voice," La Via Campesina, https://viacampesina.org/en/international-peasants-voice/.
Gliessman argues that: Steve Gliessman, "Transforming Food Systems with Agroecology," *Agroecology and Sustainable Food Systems* 40, no. 3 (2016).

267 *"an agricultural act":* Wendell Berry, "The Pleasures of Eating," from *What Are People For?* (New York: North Point Press, 1990).

269 *fast-food workers risked their jobs:* Steven Greenhouse, "With Day of Protests, Fast-Food Workers Seek More Pay," *New York Times*, November 29, 2012, https://www.nytimes.com/2012/11/30/nyregion/fast-food-workers-in-new-york-city-rally-for-higher-wages.html.
gains made by the Fight for $15: "Why We Strike," Fight for $15, https://fightfor15.org/why-we-strike/.

270 *country's winter tomatoes:* "Tomato 101," Florida Tomatoes, https://www.floridatomatoes.org/tomato-101/.

a four-year battle: "About CIW," Coalition of Immokalee Workers, accessed July 5, 2020.

By signing the code, employers: "2017 Annual Report," Fair Foods Standards Council, 2017, http://ciw-online.org/wp-content/uploads/Fair-Food-Program-2017-Annual-Report.pdf.

272 *"we're growing community":* Stephen Satterfield, "Behind the Rise and Fall of Growing Power," *Civil Eats,* March 13, 2018, https://civileats.com/2018/03/13/behind-the-rise-and-fall-of-growing-power/.

"but to thrive": Monica M. White, *Freedom Farmers: Agricultural Resistance and the Black Freedom Movement* (Chapel Hill: University of North Carolina Press, 2018).

273 *Farm to School programs:* Federal Reserve Bank of St. Louis, *Harvesting Opportunity: The Power of Regional Food System Investments to Transform Communities* (St. Louis: Federal Reserve Bank of St. Louis and the Board of Governors of the Federal Reserve System, 2017), 24.

number of CSAs: Federal Reserve Bank of St. Louis, *Harvesting Opportunity,* 31.

fruits and vegetables: Fair Food Network, "Double Up Food Bucks," accessed July 5, 2020, https://fairfoodnetwork.org/projects/double-up-food-bucks/.

fifty million dollars annually: "A Closer Look at the 2018 Farm Bill: Gus Schumacher Nutrition Incentive Program," National Sustainable Agriculture Coalition, January 24, 2019, https://sustainableagriculture.net/blog/closer-look-2018-farm-bill-fini/.

275 *Quebec residents buy:* Tirtha Dhar and Kathy Baylis, "Fast Food Consumption and the Ban on Advertising Targeting Children: The Quebec Experience," *Journal of Marketing Research* 48, no. 5 (October 2011), https://doi.org/10.2307/23033520.

world's strongest combination: Paige Sutherland, "Chile's New Food Labeling Laws Have Created Creepy, Faceless Chocolate Santas," *Vice,* https://www.vice.com/en_us/article/439b3n/chiles-new-food-labeling-laws-have-created-creepy-faceless-chocolate-santas.

8,500 junk-food advertisements: Sutherland, "Chile's New Food Labeling Laws."

changed their buying habits: Sutherland, "Chile's New Food Labeling Laws."

nearly twenty-five percent: Lindsey Smith Taillie, Marcela Reyes,

M. Arantxa Colchero, Barry Popkin, and Camila Corvalán, "An Evaluation of Chile's Law of Food Labeling and Advertising on Sugar-Sweetened Beverage Purchases from 2015 to 2017: A Before-and-After Study," *PLOS Medicine* 17, no. 2 (February 11, 2020), https://doi.org/10.1371/journal.pmed.1003015.

clean water universally available: Stephen Daniells, "Mexico's Sugar Tax Effective for Reducing Soda Purchases: New Data," FoodNavigator, January 3, 2019, https://www.foodnavigator-latam.com/Article/2019/01/03/Mexico-s-sugar-tax-effective-for-reducing-soda-purchases-New-data.

276 *However, soda taxes:* "U.S. Soda Taxes Work, Studies Suggest—But Maybe Not as Well as Hoped," *All Things Considered*, NPR, https://www.npr.org/transcripts/696709717.

"little to no nutritional value": Associated Press, "Junk Food Tax Goes into Effect on Navajo Nation," *AZ Central*, April 1, 2015.

in Belo Horizonte: Much of this section is from conversations with American and Canadian visitors to B.H., as well as Jahi Chappell, *Beginning to End Hunger: Food and the Environment in Belo Horizonte, Brazil, and Beyond* (Berkeley: University of California Press, 2018).

278 *four million family farms:* Anna Sophie Gross, "As Brazilian Agribusiness Booms, Family Farms Feed the Nation," *Mongabay*, January 17, 2019, https://news.mongabay.com/2019/01/as-brazilian-agribusiness-booms-family-farms-feed-the-nation/.

ZBNF focuses on: Himachal Pradesh Department of Agriculture, No. Agr-B-F-(1)1/2018, government notification, May 29, 2018, http://www.hillagric.ac.in/aboutus/registrar/pdf/2018/GA/30.05.2018/GA-30.05.2018-24882-98-29.05.2018.pdf.

Two fundamental principles: Himachal Pradesh Department of Agriculture, government notification.

279 *training in agroecology:* Steve Brescia, ed., *Fertile Ground: Scaling Agroecology from the Ground Up* (Oakland: Food First Books, 2017).

glyphosate is restricted or forbidden: "Where Is Glyphosate Banned?," Baum, Hedlund, Aristei, and Goldman, February 2020, https://www.baumhedlundlaw.com/toxic-tort-law/monsanto-roundup-lawsuit/where-is-glyphosate-banned/.

280 *"Let's produce differently":* Rachel Ajates Gonzalez, Jessica Thomas, and Marina Chang, "Translating Agroecology into Policy: The Case of France and the United Kingdom," *Sustainability* 10, no. 8 (2018), 2930, https://doi.org/10.3390/su10082930.

281 *was Shepherd's Grain:* "The Los Angeles Good Food Purchasing

Program: Changing Local Food Systems, One School, Supplier, and Farmer at a Time," Policy Link, https://www.policylink.org/sites/default/files/LA_GFFP_FINAL_0.pdf.

local fruit and vegetable purchases: Alexis Stephens, "Tracking the Ripple Effects of LA's Good Food Purchasing Program," Center for Good Food Purchasing, accessed July 5, 2020, https://goodfoodpurchasing.org/tracking-the-ripple-effects-of-las-good-food-purchasing-program/.

282 *a "kitchen classroom":* Interview with Alice Waters, 2018; "About" and "2018 Annual Report," Edible Schoolyard Project, https://edibleschoolyard.org/about.

283 *City of Copenhagen:* "Copenhagen's Organic Food Revolution," City of Copenhagen, May 23, 2016, https://international.kk.dk/nyheder/copenhagens-organic-food-revolution.

Minneapolis Public Schools: Jennifer E. Gaddis, *The Labor of Lunch: Why We Need Real Food and Real Jobs in American Public Schools* (Berkeley: University of California Press, 2019).

284 *Health Care Without Harm:* Health Care Without Harm, "2019 Healthcare Food Trends," *Medium,* November 13, 2019.

a "prairie strip": "What Are Prairie Strips?," Iowa State University, https://www.nrem.iastate.edu/research/STRIPS/content/what-are-prairie-strips.

285 *Enough Kernza is now being grown:* "Kernza Grain," Land Institute, accessed July 5, 2020, https://landinstitute.org/our-work/perennial-crops/kernza/.

286 *Full Belly's caliber: Farms and Land in Farms 2018 Summary* (Washington, DC: USDA National Agricultural Statistics Service, 2019), https://www.nass.usda.gov/Publications/Todays_Reports/reports/fnlo0419.pdf.

287 *Milk with Dignity agreement:* Migrant Justice, "Milk with Dignity Turns Two—and Launches a New Campaign!," accessed July 6, 2020, https://migrantjustice.net/milk-with-dignity-turns-two-and-launches-a-new-campaign.

Conclusion: We Are All Eaters

291 *peasant food system:* ETC Group, *Who Will Feed Us? The Peasant Food Web vs. The Industrial Food Chain,* 3rd ed. (Val David, Canada: ETC Group, 2017), https://www.etcgroup.org/sites/www.etcgroup.org/files/files/etc-whowillfeedus-english-webshare.pdf.

294 The Shock Doctrine: Naomi Klein, *The Shock Doctrine* (Toronto: Random House of Canada, 2007).

As does Rebecca Solnit: Especially in *Hope in the Dark* (Chicago: Haymarket, 2016).

295 *health and well-being:* Ariel Shapiro, "70% of Americans Want Officials to Prioritize Public Health Over Restarting Economy," *Forbes*, April 23, 2020.

"like an emergency": Naomi Klein, *On Fire: The Burning Case for a Green New Deal* (New York: Simon & Schuster, 2019), 39.

296 *"The black revolution":* Martin Luther King, Jr., *A Testament of Hope: The Essential Writings and Speeches of Martin Luther King, Jr.*, ed. James Melvin Washington (New York: Harper & Row, 1986).

the divine right of kings: Ursula K. Le Guin, speech at the National Book Awards ceremony, 2014, quoted in Rachel Arons, "'We Will Need Writers Who Can Remember Freedom': Ursula Le Guin and Last Night's N.B.A.s," *The New Yorker*, November 20, 2014, https://www.newyorker.com/books/page-turner/national-book-awards-ursula-le-guin.

298 This Changes Everything: Naomi Klein, *This Changes Everything: Capitalism vs. the Climate* (New York: Simon & Schuster, 2015).

299 *"the world can be much better":* Max Roser, "The World Is Much Better; the World Is Awful; the World Can Be Much Better," Our World in Data, October 31, 2018, https://ourworldindata.org/much-better-awful-can-be-better.

Selected Readings

Of the many sources I consulted to write *Animal, Vegetable, Junk*, these are the ones I either found most helpful or meaningful or felt would be most interesting to those who want to read more on a given aspect. It's also a favorites list of sorts.

Mark Arax, *The Dreamt Land: Chasing Water and Dust Across California* (New York: Knopf, 2019).

Edward E. Baptist, *The Half Has Never Been Told: Slavery and the Making of American Capitalism* (New York: Basic Books, 2014).

Wendell Berry, *The Unsettling of America: Culture & Agriculture* (San Francisco: Sierra Club Books, 1977).

Fernand Braudel, *Memory and the Mediterranean*, trans. Siân Reynolds (New York: Vintage, 2001).

Rachel Carson, *Silent Spring* (Boston: Houghton Mifflin, 1962).

Jahi Chappell, *Beginning to End Hunger: Food and the Environment in Belo Horizonte, Brazil, and Beyond* (Berkeley: University of California Press, 2018).

Carlo M. Cipolla, *Before the Industrial Revolution: European Society and Economy, 1000–1700*, 3rd ed. (New York: Norton, 1994).

Jennifer Clapp, *Food* (Cambridge, UK: Polity, 2016).

Willard Cochrane, *The Curse of American Agricultural Abundance: A Sustainable Solution* (Lincoln: University of Nebraska Press, 2003).

Lizzie Collingham, *The Taste of War: World War II and the Battle for Food* (New York: Penguin, 2012).

Julian Cribb, *Food or War* (Cambridge: Cambridge University Press, 2019).

William Cronon, *Nature's Metropolis: Chicago and the Great West* (New York: W. W. Norton & Co., 1991).

Mike Davis, *Late Victorian Holocausts: El Niño Famines and the Making of the Third World* (New York: Verso, 2002).

Deborah Fitzgerald, *Every Farm a Factory: The Industrial Ideal in American Agriculture* (New Haven, CT: Yale University Press, 2003).

John Bellamy Foster, *The Vulnerable Planet: A Short Economic History of the Environment* (New York: Monthly Review Press, 1999).

Ernesto Galarza, *Merchants of Labor: The Mexican Bracero Story* (Santa Barbara, CA: McNally & Loftin, 1964).

Alyshia Gálvez, *Eating NAFTA: Trade, Food Policies, and the Destruction of Mexico* (Berkeley: University of California Press, 2018).

D. B. Grigg, *Agricultural Systems of the World: An Evolutionary Approach* (Cambridge: Cambridge University Press, 1974).

Julie Guthman, *Weighing In: Obesity, Food Justice, and the Limits of Capitalism* (Berkeley: University of California Press, 2011).

John Ikerd, *Crisis and Opportunity: Sustainability in American Agriculture* (Lincoln: University of Nebraska Press, 2008).

Saru Jayaraman and Kathryn De Master, *Bite Back: People Taking on Corporate Food and Winning* (Berkeley: University of California Press, 2020).

Chin Jou, *Supersizing Urban America: How Inner Cities Got Fast Food with Government Help* (Chicago: University of Chicago Press, 2017).

David L. Katz, *The Truth About Food: Why Pandas Eat Bamboo and People Get Bamboozled* (New York: Dystel & Goderich, 2018).

David Kessler, *The End of Overeating* (Emmaus, PA: Rodale, 2009).

Naomi Klein, *This Changes Everything: Capitalism vs. the Climate* (New York: Simon and Schuster, 2015).

Bruce Kraig, *A Rich and Fertile Land: A History of Food in America* (London and Islington: Reaktion, 2017).

Frances Moore Lappé, *Diet for a Small Planet* (New York: Ballantine, 1971).

Kristin Lawless, *Formerly Known as Food: How the Industrial Food System Is Changing Our Minds, Bodies, and Culture* (New York: St. Martin's, 2018).

Christopher Leonard, *The Meat Racket: The Secret Takeover of America's Food Business* (New York: Simon & Schuster, 2014).

Harvey Levenstein, *Revolution at the Table: The Transformation of the American Diet* (Berkeley: University of California Press, 2003).

Charles C. Mann, *1493: Uncovering the New World Columbus Created* (New York: Knopf, 2011).

Maryn McKenna, *Big Chicken: The Incredible Story of How Antibiotics Created Modern Agriculture and Changed the Way the World Eats* (Washington, DC: National Geographic, 2017).

David R. Montgomery, *Dirt: The Erosion of Civilizations* (Berkeley: University of California Press, 2007).

Dan Morgan, *Merchants of Grain: The Power and Profits of the Five Giant Companies at the Center of the World's Food Supply* (New York: Penguin, 1980).

Michael Moss, *Salt Sugar Fat: How the Food Giants Hooked Us* (New York: Random House, 2013).

Marion Nestle, *Food Politics: How the Food Industry Influences Nutrition and Health* (Berkeley: University of California Press, 2002).

———, *Soda Politics: Taking on Big Soda (and Winning)* (Oxford: Oxford University Press, 2015).

Maureen Ogle, *In Meat We Trust: An Unexpected History of Carnivore America* (Boston: Houghton Mifflin Harcourt, 2013).

Raj Patel, *Stuffed and Starved: The Hidden Battle for the World Food System* (New York: Melville House, 2012).

Raj Patel and Jason W. Moore, *A History of the World in Seven Cheap Things: A Guide to Capitalism, Nature, and the Future of the Planet* (Berkeley: University of California Press, 2017).

Amartya Sen, *Poverty and Famines: An Essay on Entitlement and Deprivation* (Oxford: Clarendon Press, 1981).

Steve Striffler, *Chicken: The Dangerous Transformation of America's Favorite Food* (New Haven, CT: Yale University Press, 2005).

David Wallace-Wells, *The Uninhabitable Earth: Life After Warming* (New York: Tim Duggan, 2019).

Monica M. White, *Freedom Farmers: Agricultural Resistance and the Black Freedom Movement* (Chapel Hill: University of North Carolina Press, 2018).

Timothy A. Wise, *Eating Tomorrow: Agribusiness, Family Farmers, and the Battle for the Future of Food* (New York: New Press, 2019).

Ellen Meiksins Wood, *The Origin of Capitalism* (New York: Monthly Review Press, 1999).

Index